UNDERSTANDING NATURAL DEDUCTION

UNDERSTANDING NATURAL DEDUCTION

A Formalist Approach to Introductory Logic

JOHN KOZY, JR.

East Carolina University

Dickenson Publishing Company, Inc.
Encino, California, and Belmont, California

ISBN-0-8221-0128-9
Library of Congress Catalog Card Number: 73-88122

Printed in the United States of America
Printing (last digit): 9 8 7 6 5 4 3 2 1

CONTENTS

CONTENTS

PREFACE

This text is meant to be used by professors who are neither specialists in logic nor mathematicians but who nevertheless want to present their students of elementary logic with a simple yet rigorous and modern course. Because of this intention, there is perhaps less flexibility built into this text than there is in many others. Nevertheless the text contains a considerable amount of flexibility: there is an overly abundant core course and three appendices, any or all of which may be used to supplement it.

The overly abundant core course is to be found in the text's four chapters. The introduction and the three appendices are supererogatory. But even within the core course, some alternatives are possible:

Alternative 1 (truth-table approach to invalidity): Chapter 1; Chapter 2, sections 8 through 16; Chapter 3, sections 18 through 22; Chapter 4, section 24, section 25 paragraphs 1 through 11; section 26 and section 27.

Alternative 2 (semantic tableaux approach to invalidity): Chapter 1; Chapter 2, sections 8 through 16; Chapter 3, section 18 through 22; Chapter 4, section 24, section 25 paragraphs 1 through 4 and 12 through 29; section 26 and section 27.

Regardless of which of these alternatives is chosen, most instructors will want to include sections 17, 23, and 28 which consist of applications of logic to English as a model. An instructor who wants his students to learn more about symbolic logic can assign Appendix 1, while an instructor who wants his students to learn more about traditional logic than is found in Chapter 3 can then assign Appendix 2. Appendix 3 was added to the book at the suggestion of some reviewers for use by those instructors who may not want to devote an entire course to formal logic. But another reason for adding it is that treating informal logic in an appendix to a book on formal logic is an excellent way of defining *informal* as the negation of *formal*, since by the time the appendix is used, the student will already know what formal logic is. So the material in the third appendix is presented as a contrast to the formal logic presented in the core course. The short introduction to the text is merely meant to lead students to the idea that *logic* now means the science of reasoning.

The chapters and appendices are arranged as they are to avoid giving the book the character of a mere assemblage: Every succeeding chapter and appendix is related to a preceding chapter, and everything about the same topic is put in the same place. For instance, Chapters 1, 2, and 3 contain no discussions of invalidity. Discussions of invalidity appear only in Chapter 4, and all the well-known techniques for showing invalidity are discussed together: analysis, counterexample, truth-tables, and semantic tableaux. So this book is not a mere pile of discrete chapters; it is an organized whole in which even informal logic is defined in relation to formal logic.

Throughout all of the text, I tried to achieve two goals: to teach students what logic is and to teach them to think logically. Because I wanted to stress the abstract nature of thought, I present—side by side—both Polish and Principia notations (although a student only needs to learn one). And because I wanted to exhibit the characteristics of a logical system, I give a stricter presentation of logic than is usually found in elementary and even many intermediate books. Yet this book is not very difficult, although many readers may initially judge it to be less elementary than it is. A book could not be much more elementary and still be academically respectable.

The distinctive features of this book are to be found in its organization, its use of dual notations, its detailed explanations, its simple style, its formalist approach that emphasizes logic rather than its relation to language, its step-by-step examples, and its use of exercises as integral parts of the text.

There are many people whom I would like to thank: First there are my colleagues at East Carolina and their students on whom the book was classroom-tested. They provided many helpful suggestions. Other helpful suggestions were supplied by the book's reviewers: Monroe C. Beardsley,

Temple University; Tom L. Beauchamp, Georgetown University; Howard Pospesel, University of Miami; R. C. Sleigh, Jr., University of Massachusetts; Paul Wheatcroft, Grossmont College; and Peter W. Woodruff, University of California, Irvine. My secretary, Mrs. Agnes W. Jones, is to be thanked for her careful typing of the manuscript, and finally Miss Georgene Matson and Ms. Beverly Burkett are to be thanked for compiling the index. For their patient help, I am grateful to all of these people.

John Kozy, Jr.

UNDERSTANDING NATURAL DEDUCTION

INTRODUCTION: A short history of what logic has been about

That everything is what it is and not another thing is a famous logical maxim, but logic is as true love—it has, from time to time, meant different things to different people. In 1662 Antoine Arnauld published a book that became famous as *The Port-Royal Logic* in which he wrote that

> Logic is the art of directing reason to a knowledge of things for the instruction of both ourselves and others. This art consists in man's reflection on the mind's four principal operations—conceiving, judging, reasoning, and ordering . . . [which] are all done quite naturally.

Since, according to Arnauld, these operations are all done naturally, when you learn logic, you do not learn how to conceive, judge, reason, or order; you merely learn to do these things well. Arnauld, by his words, means that logic is the art of conceiving, judging, reasoning, and ordering that a man awakens by introspecting in order to scrutinize these four principal operations of the mind. Logic is likened to a sleeping patient who, breathing with difficulty while asleep, is awakened merely by the physician's stares and who then can breathe easily because he can "give new attention to" his breathing.

1

The word *logic* whenever it is used today, however, rarely means reflection on all four of the mental operations which Arnauld mentions—even when it means reflection on anything at all. Philosophers sometimes use the word to refer to discussions of how concepts and judgments are formed (for instance, Kant's "Transcendental Logic") and at other times to discussions on how concepts should be ordered (for instance, Hegel's *Science of Logic*). But both of these philosophical uses of *logic* are understood only by philosophers. Most people think of logic as W. Stanley Jevons did in 1870 when he wrote his famous *Elementary Lessons in Logic*: "Logic may be most briefly defined as the Science of Reasoning."

But in fact, logic has not always been called logic. Aristotle (B.C. 384–322), who can be thought of as the first logician, never used the word *logician* in the sense in which it is used today. A logician to him was merely a person who spoke well, that is, could deliver good speeches. When Aristotle's logical writings were collected together, the Aristotelians who collected them called the collection "The Organon," which means the tool that is to be used to acquire knowledge. In the seventeenth and eighteenth centuries, Francis Bacon (1561–1628), Johann Heinrich Lambert (1728–1777), and William Whewell (1794–1866) tried to revive the use of this term *organon*, but they failed. Opposed to Aristotle, on the other hand, were the Stoic philosophers who called logic *dialectic,* which is the art of debate by question and answer, and many logicians during the Middle Ages continued to use this word: Martianus Capella (ca. 430), Cassiodorus (ca. 500), and Peter Abelard (1078–1142) used it. Not until the middle of the thirteenth century did logic come to be called logic, for that is when the *Summa Totius Logicae Aristotelis* (for which St. Thomas Aquinas [1225–1274] has often been given credit) appeared, and Petrus Hispanus (ca. 1250) and William of Ockham (1300?–1349?) continued this practice. These people were the first to apply the word *logic* to what Aristotle was concerned with in his *Organon*. But in the sixteenth century, *dialectic* again became the popular term: Melanchthon (1497–1560), Petrus Ramus (1515–1572), and Petrus Fonseca (1528–1599) used it. In the seventeenth century, *logic* was the word that again predominated: Cristoph Scheibler (1589–1653), Joachim Jungius (1587–1657), Johannes Clauberg (1622–1655), Arnould Geulincx (1625–1699), Antoine Arnauld, Jakob Thomasius (1622–1684), Mariotte (?–1684), John Wallis (1616–1703), and Ehrenfried Walther von Tschirnhausen (1631–1708) all wrote books that have the word *logic* in their titles. But during this time, some German philosophers favored still another word. In the eighteenth century, Christian Wolff (1679–1754), Christian Thomasius (1655–1754), and Herman Samuel Reimarus (1694–1768) recommended the use of the phrase "the art or doctrine of reason." This art or doctrine of reason or *Vernunftlehre* is what has now become known as logic.

So over the years, the word *logic* has meant a number of different things: the art of delivering good speeches; the art of debate by question and answer; the tool that is to be used to acquire knowledge; the art of conceiving, judging, reasoning, and ordering; and most recently, the science of reasoning.

Logic is not just about reasoning however, for a logical person does not merely reason, he reasons well. As Wilhelm Windelband wrote in his *Theories of Logic* (1912),

> Pure or Formal Logic . . . or Logic in the narrower sense of the word, is generally defined as the doctrine of the . . . *forms of right thinking,* with those which are deliberately selected . . . as conductive to the attainment of truth. It must not be supposed to teach how people actually think, but how they *should* think if they want to think rightly.

Thus to reason correctly should be the goal of all those who study logic. Logic is a noble art which should not be debased to mere reasoning, a silver coin which should not be confused with one of German silver.

Chapter ONE FOUNDATIONS

SECTION 1. Reasoning

1.1   Those who read this book are to think of *logic as the study of the methods and principles that distinguish good from bad reasoning.* The key word in this definition is *reasoning.* As it is used in this definition, *reasoning* is a gerund. It belongs to the concept that is laid out in the following array:

noun:	[a or the] reason
adjective:	reasonable
adverb:	reasonably
finite verb:	[he, she, or it] reasons, [they] reason
infinitive:	to reason
gerund:	reasoning
past participle:	reasoned

1.2   The basic meaning of this concept, as it is to be understood by those reading this book, is this: *reasoning is the activity of giving reasons.* So, to reason is to give reasons; something that is reasoned has been given reasons; and being reasonable or thinking reasonably is to take reasons for your beliefs or thoughts into account.

1.3　But what is a reason? Suppose someone believes or thinks something is true or wishes to put it across to others. If he says what he thinks, believes, or wishes to put across, you can ask him why he believes or thinks it. What he says in answer to the question "Why do you believe that is true?" is a reason. Of course, when you ask the question "Why?" you are not always asking for a reason in the sense in which *reason* is used in this book. If someone says "I"m going to bed" and you ask him "Why?", the answer "Because I'm tired" is not a reason in the sense in which the word is being used in this book, for "I'm going to bed" is merely a declaration rather than something that is believed to be true by the person who says it. The person who says "I'm going to bed" is merely declaring his intention to do something.

SECTION 2. Arguments

2.1　When someone tells us what he believes—that is, affirms it—and then gives us his reasons for believing it, his reasons, if they are good, are said to support his belief. The pattern that this metaphor of support is drawn from is this:

$$\frac{\text{affirmation}}{}$$
reason
reason
.
.
.
reason

(The three dots mean that any number of reasons can be listed.) The reasons, when good, support the affirmation as an architectural column supports its architrave. But logicians like to turn this pattern upside down:

reason
reason
.
.
.
$$\frac{\text{reason}}{\text{affirmation}}$$

Logicians like to say that affirmations follow from good reasons, and if you work out the idea of "following from," the logical place for an affirmation is last. Logicians also like to use special words to point out what sentence is being affirmed and which sentences are the reasons that the affirmation follows from. The words are *conclusion,* which means the close or end, and *premise,* which means that which is put before. So the logical pattern can be written like this:

premises

---

conclusion

An *argument* is a series of declarative sentences that fits into this pattern. (Notice that the word *argument,* as it is used in this book, does not mean a fight or an altercation.) Of course, when a person argues in everyday life, he does not always order his sentences in either of these ways. Affirmations quite often come between reasons, but the logical place for an affirmation is last.

2.2   A logician is a person who wants to find ways of telling when a conclusion follows from its premises, that is, when the reasons given in support of the conclusion are good reasons. Obviously, arguments of many different kinds can be put together. The following, for example, are all good arguments:

I see the sunshine.

Therefore [I believe that] the sun is shining.

Livy says that Caesar visited Britain.

So [I believe that] Caesar visited Britain.

Nietzsche was unmarried.
Unmarried men are bachelors.

So Nietzsche was a bachelor.

Either Plato or Aristotle was the teacher of Dionysius the younger.
His teacher was not Aristotle.

Thus Plato must have taught Dionysius.

Men are animals.
Animals are mortal.

Therefore men are mortal.

$2 + 3 = 5.$
$4 + 1 = 5.$
Things equal to the same thing are equal to one another.

Consequently, $2 + 3 = 4 + 1.$

2.2.1 Exercise

Which of the following are arguments?

(1) Socrates was the son of Sophroniscus, a sculptor, and of Phaenarete, a midwife. He was a citizen of Athens and belonged to the deme Alopece. Some think that he helped Euripides write his plays; hence Mnesimachus writes: "This new play of Euripides is the *Phrygians,* and Socrates provides the wood for frying."

(2) Because he was formidable in public speaking, the thirty forbade Socrates to teach the art of words.

(3) When Alcibiades offered Socrates a large site on which to build a house, Socrates said this:

> If I wanted a pair of shoes and you offered me a whole hide to make them from, to take it would be ridiculous. So to take a large site on which to build a small house is equally ridiculous.

(4) Socrates showed equal ability in both persuading and dissuading men; thus after conversing with Theaetetus about knowledge, he sent him away fired with divine impulse, and when Euthyphro had indicted his father for manslaughter, Socrates, after some conversation with him upon piety, diverted him from his purpose.

(5) We ought not to object, Socrates used to say, to be subjects for the comic poets, for if they satirize our faults, they will do us good, and if not, they do not touch us.

SECTION 3. Argument-forms

3.1 Now look at the following arguments:

(a) If Socrates was the teacher of Plato, then Plato lived in Athens.
Socrates was the teacher of Plato.

So Plato lived in Athens.

(b) If Thales measured the height of the pyramids, then Thales visited Egypt.
Thales measured the height of the pyramids.

So Thales visited Egypt.

(c) Either Thales was a sage or Diogenes was a sage.
Diogenes was not a sage.

So Thales was a sage.

(d) Either Antisthenes was a Cynic or Solon was a Cynic.
Solon was not a Cynic.

So Antisthenes was a Cynic.

By inspecting them, you will see that (a) is like (b), and (c) is like (d). This likeness is important. Logicians name it by saying that (a) and (b) have the same form, while (c) and (d) share another form. What are the two forms? One way of showing them is this:

(a-b)   If x then y.   (c-d)   Either x or y.

      x _____   Not y. _____

      So y.   So x.

Forms of arguments are called argument-forms. They are, in a figurative sense, mere shapes, patterns, or outlines of arguments. Now although the conclusion of a good argument must be true, it must also be reasoned well. But whether an argument is reasoned well depends on how the premises are connected to the conclusion. Logicians have found that for a large class of arguments, these connections can be seen best by studying the forms of arguments. This large class of arguments is the basic matter of this book; it will teach you to use the most basic forms that good reasoning depends upon.

3.2   Because this book deals with argument-forms, it is a book about *formal logic*. So formal logic deals with the methods and principles of good reasoning, not good arguing. Since this book deals with argument-forms (that is, merely the shapes, patterns, or outlines of arguments), we will not be interested in what arguments say; consequently, we will not be interested in whether what they say is true.

SECTION 4. Statement-forms

4.1   If you review the arguments that have been given as examples, you will see that their premises and conclusions are all declarative sentences. Some logicians call such sentences *statements*. (Others call them—or their meanings—*propositions*.) Statements, of course, are usually either true or false. If you say that Socrates was executed, you have said something true; and if you say that Socrates was not executed you have said something false. Because statements are usually true or false, we call truth and falsehood a statement's *truth-values*. Of course, statements can be said to have other truth-values. You may not be able to tell if a specific statement is true even though you know that what it says is possible. Such statements can be said to have possibility as a truth-value. In this book, however, only statements that are either true or false will occupy our attention. Because of this, the logic dealt with in this book is often called *two-valued logic.* So a statement has two possible truth-values; its truth-values are the values it may have. We do not need to know if a statement is actually true or false to know its truth-values.

4.2 Obviously, statements also have forms. Such forms are called statement-forms. In the two argument-forms cited in section 3, there are four different statement-forms, namely, *x* (which stands for a simple declarative sentence), *not x, if x then y,* and *either x or y.* The letters *x* and *y* merely mark places where simple declarative sentences go. As you can see, statements and statement-forms are related: you get a statement-form from a statement by replacing some information in the statement by markers. So some statement-forms are made of markers and words that connect the markers together. For example, look at the following two statements again:

(a) Either Thales was a sage or Diogenes was a sage.
(b) Either Antisthenes was a Cynic or Solon was a Cynic.

The form of these statements is shown in both of the following ways:

Either _____ or _____.   Either *x* or *y*.

In the first of these, the marker is _____ and the connectors are the words *either* and *or.* In the second, the letters *x* and *y* are the markers. Although the two statements cited above have the same form, the information that the markers replace in each is different. For instance, *x* stands for "Thales was a sage" in statement (a) and "Antisthenes was a Cynic" in statement (b). So you see, statement-forms can be simple or compound and affirmative or negative: *x* is an example of a simple statement-form, *not x* is an example of a negative statement-form, and the others are examples of compound statement-forms.

4.3 Now if we adopt the pattern for arguments that lists premises first and the conclusion last, we can (for our purposes) define an *argument* as a sequence of statements the last of which is a conclusion and the rest of which are premises. Since we get an argument-form from an argument by putting markers in place of information, we can (for our purposes) define an *argument-form* as a sequence of statement-forms the last of which is a conclusion and the rest of which are premises.

5.1   In any ordinary language, many words and phrases can be attached to simple statements in order to change them into statements that mean something else. For instance, look at the statement "Socrates was executed." By attaching various words and phrases to it, we can change it drastically. By attaching the phrase *it is false that* to the statement, we can say

It is false that Socrates was executed.

By attaching the phrase *nobody seriously believes that* to the statement, we can say

Nobody seriously believes that Socrates was executed.

By attaching the word *maybe* to the statement, we can say

Maybe Socrates was executed.

By attaching the phrase *it is likely that* to the statement, we can say

It is likely that Socrates was executed.

And by attaching the phrase *I am certain that* to the statement, we can say

I am certain that Socrates was executed.

In these sentences, the expressions *it is false that, nobody seriously believes that, maybe, it is likely that,* and *I am certain that* alter the statement "Socrates was executed" into other statements; yet the statement that these expressions are attached to remains untouched; the attachments are merely joined to it. By attaching these alterants to a statement, you merely embed the statement in a longer statement, which usually has a different meaning than the embedded statement. These specific alterants are joined to one statement. Other alterants, however, join two statements together and thus change them into other, compound, statements. The word *and* is such an alterant. Other alterants like *and* that we will focus our attention on in this book are *or, if . . . then . . .* , and *if and only if.* Those alterants that join two statements together are often called *connectives.* The word *connectives,* thus, is used by logicians to refer to a specific group of connectors.

5.2   Although many linguistic acts (a grammarian might use the word *transformations*) alter statements, only five such acts will now be discussed.

These five are (1) *negation* which is usually indicated by the word *not,* phrases like *it is false that,* and prefixes; (2) *conjunction* which is usually indicated by the word *and* but other words like *but, while,* and *likewise* also indicate it; (3) *alternation* (some logicians prefer to call this linguistic act *disjunction*) which is usually indicated by the word *or*; (4) *material implication* which is usually indicated by the pair of words *if . . . then . . .* , but is also indicated by the phrase *only if* and the word *if* alone; and (5) *material equivalence* which is usually indicated by the phrase *if and only if.* These five alterants, when they are used by logicians as connectives, are usually called truth-functors; the kind of logic that is based on these truth-functors is often called *truth-functional logic.* The truth-functor called negation, although it does not connect sentences, is often called a connective too. Because it is attached to single statements, it is said to be monadic. The other four are said to be dyadic, because they each connect two statements. *Monadic* is an adjective made from the Greek word *monos* which means sole, single, or alone, and *dyadic* is another adjective made from the Greek word *duo* which means two.

5.3   Although these truth-functors are named for the specific linguistic acts of negating, conjoining, alternating, implying, and equivalenting, they are abstractions and can be defined abstractly, that is, without relating them to any particular words, objects, or real things. To do this, however, we must have an abstract way of designating each; so logicians have put together abstract languages. These languages are made up of (1) *symbols* (sometimes called *primitive symbols*) that are not defined concretely, (2) *formation-rules* that tell you how to put these symbols together in various ways, and (3) *transformation-rules* that tell you how to go from one symbolic expression (sometimes called a *string*), which may be thought of as either a word or a sentence, to another symbolic expression or string. Two different abstract languages that have the same meaning are popular. Both are given in this book, but you only need to learn one. You may, however, find switching from one to the other fun and instructive. So that you can learn just one, the pages on which symbols are written are divided. On the left, Polish notation is written. It is called Polish notation because it was put together by a Polish logician named Jan Lukasiewicz. On the right, Principia notation is written. It is called Principia notation because it is the language used in a famous book by Bertrand Russell and Alfred North Whitehead named *Principia Mathematicia.* As a student, you need to read only the appropriate part of such pages.

11

5.4 Polish notation is made up of the five capital letters N, K, A, C, and E. They stand for negation, conjunction, alternation, material implication, and material equivalence, respectively. These symbols are always written in front of the statement or statements they are attached to. Negation, since it is monadic, is always written in front of one statement. The others, since they are dyadic, are always written in front of two statements.

5.4 Principia notation is made up of the five symbols $\sim$, $\cdot$, $\vee$, $\supset$, and $\equiv$. They stand for negation, conjunction, alternation, material implication, and material equivalence, respectively. Negation, since it is monadic, is always written in front of one statement. The others, since they are dyadic, are always written between two statements. We have to punctuate this notation with pairs of parentheses; otherwise, it becomes ambiguous.

5.5 If we are going to define the truth-functors abstractly, we must also have a way of designating statements abstractly. We can do this by generalizing on the idea of a marker. For instance, if lower-case letters such as p and q are statement-markers, that is, symbols that mark the position of statements,

$$Np \qquad\qquad \| \qquad\qquad \sim p$$

is the negation of p,

$$Kpq \qquad\qquad \| \qquad\qquad (p \cdot q)$$

is the conjunction of p and q,

$$Apq \qquad\qquad \| \qquad\qquad (p \vee q)$$

is the alternation of p and q,

$$Cpq \qquad\qquad \| \qquad\qquad (p \supset q)$$

is the material implication of p and q, and

$$Epq \qquad\qquad \| \qquad\qquad (p \equiv q)$$

is the material equivalence of p and q. Strings like these five are completely abstract statement-forms: not only the information, which we previously replaced by markers, but also the alterants, which sometimes act as connectors, have been replaced by symbols.

5.6 To define these truth-functors abstractly, a device known as a *truth-table* is used. It is an array that shows the truth-values of a statement. For instance, let the letter *p* serve as a marker for any simple statement (such markers for simple statements are called *statement-variables*), let the letter *t* stand for the truth-value *true,* and let the letter *f* stand for the truth-value *false.* That any statement has these two truth-values can now be shown like this:

$$\frac{p}{\begin{matrix} t \\ f \end{matrix}}$$

This is the simplest truth-table. Logicians use this truth-table as the basis for definitions of the truth-functors, since the new statements that you get from attaching the truth-functors to statements also have truth-values.

5.7 When you understand why this truth-table is built as it is, you can forget that lower-case letters like *p* are statement-markers, that *t* stands for truth, and that *f* stands for falsehood. The truth-table then becomes a completely abstract array that says that any statement-variable has two truth-values: *t* and *f*. (At this point, many logicians like to replace the letters *t* and *f* with neutral symbols. A popular pair of such neutral symbols is 1 and 0.)

5.8 Now let's define negation. Look at the following truth-table:

p	Np		p	~p
t	f		t	f
f	t		f	t

This table is to be read as follows: when *p* has *t* as its truth-value, the negation of *p* has *f* as its truth-value; and when *p* has *f* as its truth-value, the negation of *p* has *t* as its truth-value. This truth-functor is called negation because the negation of a statement denies it, and the word *negate* comes from the Latin root *negare* which means to say no or deny. A simpler way of writing the same truth-table follows; this simpler table is to be read exactly like the one above:

Np		~p
f t		f t
t f		t f

The simplicity of this table results from our having to write the letter *p* only once. Then we put the truth-values of *p* under the letter *p* and the truth-values of the negation of *p* under the symbol for negation. Truth-tables of this latter kind are used in this book.

5.9   Next look at conjunction. Since it is dyadic, we must use two variables to define it. Let the letters *p* and *q* be the variables. By using them, we put the following truth-table together:

Kpq				*(p · q)*		
t t t				*t t t*		
f t f				*t f f*		
f f t				*f f t*		
f f f				*f f f*		

The letters *t* and *f* under the letter *p* are *p*'s truth-values; the letters *t* and *f* under the letter *q* are *q*'s truth-values; and the truth-values of the conjunction of *p* and *q* are listed in the column of truth-values under the symbol for conjunction. Again, the table is to be read as follows:

When the truth-value of *p* is *t*, and the truth-value of *q* is *t*, then the truth-value of the conjunction of *p* and *q* is *t;* when the truth-value of *p* is *t*, and the truth-value of *q* is *f*, then the truth-value of the conjunction of *p* and *q* is *f*; when the truth-value of *p* is *f*, and the truth-value of *q* is *t*, then the truth-value of the conjunction of *p* and *q* is *f*; and when the truth-value of *p* is *f*, and the truth-value of *q* is *f*; then the truth-value of the conjunction *p* and *q* is *f*.

This truth-functor is called conjunction, because the statement you get by joining together, that is conjoining, two statements is true only when both statements joined together, that is, both conjuncts, are true together.

5.10   Notice that the table that defines conjunction has four lines of values while the table that defines negation has only two. The reason for this difference is that negation is attached to only one statement-variable while conjunction connects two, that is, negation is monadic while conjunction is dyadic. Since one statement-variable has only two truth-values, namely, *t* and *f*, tables defining monadic truth-functors have only two lines of values. When two different statement-variables are combined by a truth-functor, however, the number of possible ways of combining the truth-values is four, for we must combine *t* with *t*, *t* with *f*, *f* with *t*, and *f* with *f*. So tables that define dyadic truth-functors have four lines of values. If we had a truth-functor that combined three different statement-variables, its truth-table would have eight lines. Anyone familiar with algebra will now see a pattern. The number of lines a truth-table has is two raised to the power that is equal to the number of different statement-variables in the table. Mathematically, this is written

2^n, where n equals the number of different statement-variables in the table.

So a truth-table with one statement-variable has $2^1 = 2$ lines, a table with two different statement-variables has $2^2 = 4$ lines, a table with three different statement-variables has $2^3 = 8$ lines, and a table with four different statement-variables has $2^4 = 16$ lines, etc. The following array shows a method of combining the values of any number of different statement-variables. The numbers across the top indicate the number of different statement-variables in a table:

6	5	4	3	2	1
t	t	t	t	t	t
t	t	t	t	t	f
t	t	t	t	f	t
t	t	t	t	f	f
t	t	t	f	t	t
t	t	t	f	t	f
t	t	t	f	f	t
t	t	t	f	f	f
t	t	f	t	t	t
t	t	f	t	t	f
t	t	f	t	f	t
t	t	f	t	f	f
t	t	f	f	t	t
t	t	f	f	t	f
t	t	f	f	f	t
t	t	f	f	f	f
f					
f					
f					
f					
f					
f					
f					
f					

SECTION 5. Truth-functors

	6	5	4	3	2	1
		f				
		f				
		f				
		f				
		f				
		f				
		f				

Each time a different statement-variable is added to a table, you double the number of lines in the table by repeating the previous table below it and then adding on the left a new column made of half *t*'s and half *f*'s.

5.11 Now look at alternation. Its truth-table is this:

Apq			*(p ∨ q)*		
t t t			*t*	*t*	*t*
t t f			*t*	*t*	*f*
t f t			*f*	*t*	*t*
f f f			*f*	*f*	*f*

This truth-functor is called alternation because it lays out the circumstances for alternatives: the truth-value of an alternation is *t* whenever the truth-value of either of its alternatives is *t*. Some logicians prefer to call alternation disjunction and alternatives disjuncts.

5.12 Material implication is also defined with a truth-table:

Cpq			*(p ⊃ q)*		
t t t			*t*	*t*	*t*
f t f			*t*	*f*	*f*
t f t			*f*	*t*	*t*
t f f			*f*	*t*	*f*

The first statement in such compounds is always called the *antecedent*, and the second, the *consequent*. In this compound, *p* is the antecedent and *q* is the consequent. The compound itself is called a *conditional statement*. This truth-functor is called *material* implication because it does not show what conditions are at work when one statement implies another; instead, it merely defines a relationship between the truth-values of two statement-variables or forms. Ordinary implication, of course, is a relationship between two statements. For example, you might say that the statement, "Socrates died after drinking hemlock," implies the statement, "Socrates died from poison." But since we are dealing only with statement-forms (which contain no information), to ask if one statement-variable implies another is out of the question. Ordinary implication is out of the question when all you have to work with are statement-variables. So we settle for the next best thing—perhaps it's even better—material implication.

5.13   Finally, the truth-table that defines material equivalence is this:

Epq			$(p \equiv q)$		
t	t	t	t	t	t
f	t	f	t	f	f
f	f	t	f	f	t
t	f	f	f	t	f

This truth-functor is called material equivalence because the statement you get by connecting two others with the truth-functor has the truth-value t whenever the truth-values of the statements that are joined together have the same, that is, equivalent, truth-values.

5.14   The truth-tables that define the five truth-functors must be memorized by anyone who studies logic seriously, because statement-variables and the symbols for these truth-functors are the primitive symbols of our abstract languages. The pairs of parentheses that serve as punctuation marks in Principia notation are also primitive symbols.

SECTION 6. Well-formedness

6.1   Given any number of simple statement-variables p, q, r, s, etc., quite complex formulas, that is, strings, can be built up by using truth-functors. Unless these complex formulas are built right, however, they will not make any sense, that is, they will be ill-formed, not well-formed. To make sense, these formulas must stay within definite restraints: statement-variables by themselves always make sense; any formula that makes sense still makes sense when it is negated; any two formulas each of which makes sense still makes sense when they are joined together by any of the dyadic truth-functors; and nothing else makes sense. These restraints are usually stated abstractly: (The Greek letters α and β that are used in stating these restraints are variables that stand for any symbolic expression, well-formed or not.)

(1)   Statement-variables standing alone are well-formed.

(2)   If α is well-formed, then the negation of α is well-formed.

(3) If α and β are each well-formed, then
    (a) the conjunction of α and β is well-formed,
    (b) the alternation of α and β is well-formed,
    (c) the material implication of α and β is well-formed, and
    (d) the material equivalence of α and β is well-formed.
(4) Nothing else is well-formed.

These four conditions define the phrase *well-formed formula*. When a definition is written like this one, it is called a *recursive definition*. The phrase *well-formed formula* is often abbreviated by the letters *wff*. This abbreviation is an acronym and is often pronounced *woof*.

It is easy now to see the importance of the parentheses that are used for punctuation in Principia notation. If instead of writing $(p \cdot q)$ for the conjunction of p and q we just wrote

$$p \cdot q$$

any formula that this conjunction were a part of would be ambiguous. For example, let's suppose that it is part of a larger alternation, the other part of which is the variable r. This latter alternation might look like this:

$$p \cdot q \lor r$$

Without parentheses, however, we cannot tell if the p and q go together or if the q and r go together; the formula can mean either of these:

$$((p \cdot q) \lor r)$$
$$(p \cdot (q \lor r))$$

Without parentheses, the notation is ambiguous.

6.2 From these formation-rules, a test for well-formedness can be made up. The test is carried out by drawing lines under well-formed formulas. Look at the following example:

$KNpq$ ‖ $(\sim p \cdot q)$

FOUNDATIONS

First draw a line under each statement-variable:

KN<u>p</u><u>q</u>   ‖   (~<u>p</u> · <u>q</u>)

Next draw a line under any negated statement-variable, that is, the variable and the negation sign that goes with the variable:

KN<u>pq</u>   ‖   (<u>~p</u> · <u>q</u>)

Now draw a line under any two well-formed formulas that are joined together by a dyadic truth-functor, that is, draw a line under the well-formed formulas and the dyadic truth-functor that connects them. (In Principia notation, draw a line under the appropriate parentheses too.):

<u>KN<u>pq</u></u>   ‖   <u>(<u>~p</u> · <u>q</u>)</u>

If the formula is now entirely underlined (as this one is), it is well-formed; if it is not entirely underlined, begin the test over again by first underlining any negated well-formed formulas, that is, the formulas and the negation signs that go with the formulas, and then any well-formed formulas that are joined together by dyadic truth-functors, that is, the formulas and the dyadic truth-functors that connect them. Repeat this test until the entire formula is underlined. If you can never underline the entire formula by following the test's directions, the formula in question is ill-formed. For example, look at this formula:

Kpqr   ‖   ((p · q) r)

First underline the statement-variables:

K<u>pqr</u>   ‖   ((<u>p</u> · <u>q</u>) <u>r</u>)

Since no statement-variables are negated, underline the variables that are linked by dyadic truth-functors, that is, underline the variables and the truth-functors that link the variables (and the appropriate parentheses in Principia notation):

<u>K<u>pq</u>r</u>   ‖   ((<u>p</u> · <u>q</u>) <u>r</u>)

The result is two well-formed formulas without a dyadic truth-functor connecting them; so there is no way to draw a line under the entire formula and still follow the test's directions. The formula is ill-formed.

6.3 You should now be able to see why a recursive definition is called recursive. The test for well-formedness is based on the four conditions listed in the definition. First you underline formulas that meet the first condition. Then you underline the formulas that meet the second condition. Next you underline the formulas that meet the third condition. Then you go back and underline formulas that now meet the second condition. Next you underline formulas that now meet the third condition. Then you go back again and underline formulas that now meet the second condition, etc. Because you keep going back over and over again to look for formulas that meet the conditions, the conditions are said to recur over and over again. Because they recur, the definition is called recursive.

6.3.1 Exercise

Which of the following formulas are well-formed?

(1) $CApqr$	$((p \vee q) \supset r)$
(2) $CpqAr$	$((p \supset q) \; (r \vee))$
(3) $KpAqN$	$(p \cdot (q \vee \sim))$
(4) Npq	$(p \sim q)$
(5) $NEpq$	$\sim(p \equiv q)$

6.4 Besides putting formulas together to get other formulas, there is another, and perhaps more important, way of getting them. They can be gotten from argument-forms. For instance, in section 3, the following argument-form was used as an illustration:

$$\text{Either } x \text{ or } y$$
$$\underline{\text{Not } x}$$
$$\text{So } y.$$

This same argument-form can be written out as a complex statement-form: If either x or y and not x, then y. Although these are alternate ways of writing the same argument-form, the second is useful to our studies because it lays out the argument-form as a statement-form by making use of truth-functors. This shows that any argument-form can be changed into a formula by using truth-functors. The procedure for doing this is easy and never varies. As an example, let's look at the following argument-form:

$$p$$
$$\underline{q}$$
$$r$$

To turn this into a formula, you first conjoin the premises:

$$Kpq \qquad \| \qquad (p \cdot q)$$

Then this conjunction is made the antecedent of a conditional statement:

$$CKpq \qquad \| \qquad (p \cdot q) \supset$$

This, of course, is ill-formed, but then you make the conclusion of the argument-form the consequent of this conditional statement:

$$CKpqr \qquad \| \qquad ((p \cdot q) \supset r)$$

This procedure is called conditionalizing an argument form. If an argument-form has more than two premises, a compound conjunction must be formed. For instance, look at the following argument-form that has three premises, some of which are themselves compound statement-forms:

Cpq	‖	$(p \supset q)$
$KNqNr$		$(\sim q \cdot \sim r)$
$CNrp$		$(\sim r \supset p)$
s		s

First you conjoin the first two premises:

$$KCpqKNqNr \qquad \| \qquad ((p \supset q) \cdot (\sim q \cdot \sim r))$$

Next you conjoin this conjunction to the third premise:

$$KKCpqKNqNrCNrp \qquad \| \qquad (((p \supset q) \cdot (\sim q \cdot \sim r)) \cdot (\sim r \supset p))$$

Then you make this conjunction the antecedent of a conditional statement:

$$CKKCpqKNqNrCNrp \qquad \| \qquad (((p \supset q) \cdot (\sim q \cdot \sim r)) \cdot (\sim r \supset p)) \supset$$

Finally, you make the conclusion of the argument-form the consequent of this conditional statement:

$$CKKCpqKNqNrCNrps \qquad \| \qquad ((((p \supset q) \cdot (\sim q \cdot \sim r)) \cdot (\sim r \supset p)) \supset s)$$

Any argument-form can be turned into a formula by using this procedure.

6.4.1 Exercise

Turn the following argument-forms into complex formulas by means of the procedure presented in 6.4. That is, conditionalize these argument-forms.

(1)

$$p$$
$$q$$
$$r$$
$$\overline{\quad}$$
$$s$$

(2) p $\|$ p

Kqr $(q \cdot r)$

Apr $(p \vee r)$

Cqr $(q \supset r)$

$\overline{Erp}$ $\overline{(r \equiv p)}$

(3) Kpq $(p \cdot q)$

$CAprs$ $((p \vee r) \supset s)$

$\overline{Kps}$ $\overline{(p \cdot s)}$

6.4.2 Exercise

Turn the following complex formulas into argument-forms by reversing the procedure presented in 6.4:

(1) $CKKpqCNNprArs$ $\|$ $(((p \cdot q) \cdot (\sim\sim p \supset r)) \supset (r \vee s))$

(2) $CKKCpqCqrCrsCps$ $((((p \supset q) \cdot (q \supset r)) \cdot$
$$(r \supset s)) \supset (p \supset s))$$

(3) $CKKCpqKNqNrCNrps$ $((((p \supset q) \cdot (\sim q \cdot \sim r)) \cdot$
$$(\sim r \supset p)) \supset s)$$

SECTION 7. Truth-tables

7.1   Once you have a well-formed formula (regardless of its length), you can build its truth-table. For instance, you know what the truth-values for the conjunction of p and q are. So you can figure out the truth-values for the negation of the conjunction of p and q by reading these values from the table that defines negation: if a statement has the value t, its negation has the value f and vice versa:

$NKpq$		$\sim(p \cdot q)$	
ft		f	t
tf		t	f
tf		t	f
tf		t	f

In the same way, larger formulas can be conjoined and the truth-values of the conjunction can be figured out. If, for example, we take the alternation of p and q as one formula and the material implication of p and q as another formula, we can conjoin these two formulas:

$KApqCpq$			$((p \lor q) \cdot (p \supset q))$	
t	t		t	t
t	f		t	f
t	t		t	t
f	t		f	t

Now you can read the truth-values of this conjunction from the table that defines conjunction. The table tells us that the truth-value of a conjunction is t whenever the two formulas it joins together have t as their truth-value; otherwise, the value of a conjunction is f. So the values of this conjunction are these:

$KApqCpq$		$((p \lor q) \cdot (p \supset q))$
t		t
f		f
t		t
f		f

Truth-tables can be built in the same way for formulas of any length and that use any of the truth-functors. Notice, however, that you must always figure out the values of the compound formulas that are parts of larger formulas before the values of the larger formulas can be figured out. When you make truth-tables, the values of the smaller formulas must always be figured out first.

7.2   These alterants are called truth-functors because the truth-values of any well-formed formula can be figured out by referring to the truth-tables that define the truth-functors. The truth-values of the new formulas that you get by attaching these truth-functors to formulas are a function, that is, the result of, the abstract meanings of these alterants: in other words, the truth-value of a compound statement is a function of the truth-values of its parts.

7.3   Look at another example:

$$CKCpqCrqCpr \qquad \| \qquad (((p \supset q) \cdot (r \supset q)) \supset (p \supset r))$$

By using the tables given in section 5, you can make a truth-table for this formula by using the following procedure: First, the appropriate values are assigned to p, q, and r in accordance with the table for three different statement-variables:

CKCpqCrqCpr	$(((p \supset q) \cdot (r \supset q)) \supset (p \supset r))$
tt tt tt	t t t t t t
tt ft tf	t t f t t f
tf tf tt	t f t f t t
tf ff tf	t f f f t f
ft tt ft	f t t t f t
ft ft ff	f t f t f f
ff tf ft	f f t f f t
ff ff ff	f f f f f f

(Notice that p has the same column of values everywhere p is written. The same is true of q and r. You always put the same column of values under the same statement-variable no matter how often it appears in a formula.) Next you look at the table that defines material implication, for the three inner material implications are the smallest compound formulas. You will recall that a material implication has the value f only when its antecedent has the value t and its consequent has the value f. With this knowledge, you can fill in three more columns of values:

CKCpqCrqCpr	$(((p \supset q) \cdot (r \supset q)) \supset (p \supset r))$
tttttttt	t t t t t t t t t
ttttftftf	t t t f t t t f f
ftfftfttt	t f f t f f t t t
ftftffftf	t f f f t f t f f
tftttttft	f t t t t t f t t
tfttfttff	f t t f t t f t f
tfftfttft	f t f t f f f t t
tfftftff	f t f f t f f t f

Now you look at the table that defines conjunction, since the conjunction is the smallest part of the formula that is left. A conjunction, you will remember, has the value t only when both of its conjuncts have the value t. With this knowledge, you can fill in another column:

CKCpqCrqCpr	$(((p \supset q) \cdot (r \supset q)) \supset (p \supset r))$
tt t	t t t
tt t	t t t
ff f	f f f
ff t	f f t
tt t	t t t
tt t	t t t
ft f	t f f
tt t	t t t

Finally, you again turn to the definition of material implication and fill in the final column:

CKCpqCrqCpr			$(((p \supset q) \cdot (r \supset q)) \supset (p \supset r))$		
t t	t		t	t	t
f t	f		t	f	f
t f	t		f	t	t
t f	f		f	t	f
t t	t		t	t	t
t t	t		t	t	t
t f	t		f	t	t
t t	t		t	t	t

The truth-values for the entire formula are those in the column figured out last. The symbol over this column of values is often called the formula's main truth-functor. In Polish notation, the main truth-functor is always the very first one; in Principia notation, however, the main truth-functor is somewhere inside the formula unless the whole formula is negated.

7.3.1 Exercise

Make truth-tables for the following formulas:

(1)	CpApp	$(p \supset (p \lor p))$
(2)	NCpCqp	$\sim(p \supset (q \supset p))$
(3)	KpAqr	$(p \cdot (q \lor r))$
(4)	CpEqArs	$(p \supset (q \equiv (r \lor s)))$
(5)	EKApqCrsNt	$(((p \lor q) \cdot (r \supset s)) \equiv \sim t)$

7.4   In terms of the different sets of values that formulas may have, only three kinds of truth-tables are possible. Some formulas will have the value t on each line of the column of values under the main truth-functor. For example,

ApNp	$(p \lor \sim p)$
t	t
t	t

Others will have the value f on each line of the column of values under the main truth-functor. For example,

KpNp	$(p \cdot \sim p)$
f	f
f	f

And others will have the value t on some line or lines of the column of values under the main truth-functor and the value f on the others. All of the truth-tables previously shown are like this. Formulas that have sets of truth-values of these three kinds are called tautologies, logical absurdities (sometimes called self-contradictions), and contingencies, respectively. In other words, a formula that always has the value t is called a *tautology*; a formula that always has the value f is called a *logical absurdity*; and a formula that sometimes has the value t and sometimes has the value f is called a *contingency*. A tautological formula whose main truth-functor is material equivalence, however, plays an important role in logic. Because of this special role, such a formula is called a *logical equivalence*. An example of one follows:

$ENNpp$		$(\sim \sim p \equiv p)$
t	‖	t
t	‖	t

7.4.1 Exercise

Which of the formulas in 7.3.1 are tautological, logically absurd, and contingent? Are any logical equivalences?

7.4.2

The following terms have been introduced in this chapter. You should know the meaning of each one.

logic	reasoning
reason	argument
conclusion	premise
form	argument-form
statement-form	formal logic
truth-value	negation
conjunction	alternation
material implication	material equivalence
truth-functor	truth-table
monadic	dyadic
well-formed formula	ill-formed formula
conditional statement	antecedent
consequent	tautology
logical absurdity	contingency
logical equivalence	statement
two-valued logic	connective
primitive symbol	formation-rule

transformation-rule
statement-variable
alternative
disjunction
main truth-functor
string

abstract language
conjunct
truth-functional logic
disjunct
recursive definition

Chapter TWO **PROPOSITIONAL LOGIC**

8.1 The goal of those who study logic seriously is to learn to think in a way that does not let them stray from the truth. The idea is this: if you think in this way and if the facts you begin your thinking with are true, your conclusions will be true too. Because a tautology is never false—since its truth-value is always *t*—all tautologies lay out ways of reasoning that keep falsehood out. So all tautological formulas are laws of logic.

8.2 Certain laws of logic, however, are more useful than others. Those that are most useful are written as tautological, conditional statements and logical equivalences, because formulas of these kinds lay out ways of going from one string to another. Because these formulas lay out ways of going from one string to another, such formulas can serve as the transformation-rules of our abstract languages. (You should remember that an abstract language is made up of three kinds of things: symbols, formation-rules, and transformation-rules. In chapter 1, you learned the symbols and the formation-rules of the abstract languages we are dealing with.) In this chapter, you will learn the main transformation-rules of our languages and how to use these rules to go from one formula to another.

8.3   Tautological, conditional statements can serve as transformation-rules because if the formula that makes up the antecedent has the truth-value t, then the formula that makes up the consequent also has the truth-value t. So each tautological, conditional statement can serve as one transformation-rule. For instance,

$$CpApq \qquad \| \qquad (p \supset (p \vee q))$$

is a tautological, conditional statement; so whenever p has the value t, the alternation of p and q has the same value. This means that if you start with p and if you know that its truth-value is t, then you can conclude that the alternation of p and q also has t as its truth-value. The reasoning in this last sentence, however, can be written out as an argument-form:

$$\frac{p}{Apq} \qquad \qquad \| \qquad \qquad \frac{p}{(p \vee q)}$$

The statement-variable p is the premise of this argument-form, and its conclusion is the alternation of p and q. In words, this tautological, conditional statement (transformation-rule) tells us that we can go from the formula

$$p \qquad \| \qquad p$$

to the formula

$$Apq \qquad \| \qquad (p \vee q)$$

This transformation-rule tells us how to go from one formula to another.

8.4   Logical equivalences work in the same way, because the two formulas joined together by the main truth-functor always have the same truth-value. So if one formula has the value t, the other does too. Since the two formulas always have the same truth-value, you can, however, not only go from the one on the left to the one on the right, but you can go from the one on the right to the one on the left too. So each logical equivalence gives us two transformation-rules. For instance,

$$EpNNp \qquad \| \qquad (p \equiv \sim \sim p)$$

is a logical equivalence. When p has t as its truth-value, t is also the truth-value of the double negation of p (the name of the formula on the right);

29

and when the double negation of p has t as its truth-value, t is also the truth-value of p. So from this logical equivalence, you can write out two argument-forms:

$$\frac{p}{NNp} \text{ and } \frac{NNp}{p} \qquad\qquad \Big\| \qquad\qquad \frac{p}{\sim\sim p} \text{ and } \frac{\sim\sim p}{p}$$

In words, this logical equivalence tells us that we can go from the formula

$$p \qquad\qquad \Big\| \qquad\qquad p$$

to the formula

$$NNp \qquad\qquad \Big\| \qquad\qquad \sim\sim p$$

and that we can go from the formula

$$NNp \qquad\qquad \Big\| \qquad\qquad \sim\sim p$$

to the formula

$$p \qquad\qquad \Big\| \qquad\qquad p$$

8.5   Although tautological, conditional statements and logical equivalences are the most useful laws of logic, the use of any tautology in reasoning is safe. So any tautology is a law of logic. But some basic laws of logic are too complicated to be written out as simple tautologies. You will have to learn only three of these. In more advanced logic books, these laws are proven in complicated ways; in this book, you will merely be shown why these laws always work, but you should have no trouble understanding them when you read the explanations in the next section.

8.6   The point of this section, then, is simple: All tautological, conditional statements and logical equivalences are laws of logic from which the trans-formation-rules of the abstract languages we are dealing with are gotten.

SECTION 9. The basic transformation-rules

9.1   Ten laws of logic are very important; you will begin by learning these. They give us twelve basic transformation-rules. Five of these rules are gotten from tautological, conditional statements, four are gotten from two logical equivalences, and three are gotten from more complicated laws of the kind mentioned in subsection 8.5. So although there are only ten basic laws, twelve transformation-rules are gotten from them. To make things easier, some of these transformation-rules are set out in alternate ways. The alternatives, however, are nothing more than different ways of writing the same thing.

9.2   The twelve basic transformation-rules and the names of the ten basic laws that these rules are gotten from follow:

THE LAW OF CONJUNCTION (conj.)

1. $\dfrac{\begin{array}{c}p\\q\end{array}}{Kpq}$ or $\dfrac{\begin{array}{c}p\\q\end{array}}{Kqp}$ ‖ $\dfrac{\begin{array}{c}p\\q\end{array}}{(p \cdot q)}$ or $\dfrac{\begin{array}{c}p\\q\end{array}}{(q \cdot p)}$

THE LAW OF SIMPLIFICATION (simp.)

2. $\dfrac{Kpq}{p}$ or $\dfrac{Kpq}{q}$ ‖ $\dfrac{(p \cdot q)}{p}$ or $\dfrac{(p \cdot q)}{q}$

THE LAW OF ASSUMPTION (assump.)

3.
$$\dfrac{\left[\begin{array}{c}p\\ \cdot \\ \cdot \\ \cdot \\ q\end{array}\right.}{Cpq} \qquad \Big\| \qquad \dfrac{\left[\begin{array}{c}p\\ \cdot \\ \cdot \\ \cdot \\ q\end{array}\right.}{(p \supset q)}$$

THE LAW OF MODUS PONENS (m.p.)

4. $\dfrac{\begin{array}{c}Cpq\\p\end{array}}{q}$ ‖ $\dfrac{\begin{array}{c}(p \supset q)\\p\end{array}}{q}$

THE LAW OF ADDITION (add.)

5. $\dfrac{p}{Apq}$ or $\dfrac{p}{Aqp}$ ‖ $\dfrac{p}{(p \vee q)}$ or $\dfrac{p}{(q \vee p)}$

THE LAW OF CASES (cases)

6.

31

SECTION 9. The basic transformation-rules

THE NEGATIVE LAW OF ABSURDITY (neg. abs.)

7.

$$\begin{array}{c} \ulcorner\, p \\ \cdot \\ \cdot \\ \cdot \\ KqNq \\ \hline Np \end{array} \quad \text{or} \quad \begin{array}{c} \ulcorner\, p \\ \cdot \\ \cdot \\ \cdot \\ q \\ \hline Nq \\ \hline Np \end{array} \quad \Bigg|\Bigg| \quad \begin{array}{c} \ulcorner\, p \\ \cdot \\ \cdot \\ \cdot \\ (q \cdot \sim q) \\ \hline \sim p \end{array} \quad \text{or} \quad \begin{array}{c} \ulcorner\, p \\ \cdot \\ \cdot \\ \cdot \\ q \\ \hline \sim q \\ \hline \sim p \end{array}$$

THE POSITIVE LAW OF ABSURDITY (pos. abs.)

8.

$$\frac{KNpp}{q} \quad \text{or} \quad \frac{\dfrac{Np}{p}}{q} \quad \Bigg|\Bigg| \quad \frac{(\sim p \cdot p)}{q} \quad \text{or} \quad \frac{\dfrac{\sim p}{p}}{q}$$

THE LAW OF MATERIAL EQUIVALENCE (m.e.)

9.

$$\frac{KCpqCqp}{Epq} \quad \text{or} \quad \frac{\dfrac{Cpq}{Cqp}}{Epq} \quad \Bigg|\Bigg| \quad \frac{((p \supset q) \cdot (q \supset p))}{(p \equiv q)} \quad \text{or} \quad \frac{\dfrac{(p \supset q)}{(q \supset p)}}{(p \equiv q)}$$

10.

$$\frac{Epq}{KCpqCqp} \quad \Bigg|\Bigg| \quad \frac{(p \equiv q)}{((p \supset q) \cdot (q \supset p))}$$

THE LAW OF DOUBLE NEGATION (d.n.)

11.

$$\frac{p}{NNp} \quad \Bigg|\Bigg| \quad \frac{p}{\sim \sim p}$$

12.

$$\frac{NNp}{p} \quad \Bigg|\Bigg| \quad \frac{\sim \sim p}{p}$$

It is customary to refer to these rules by the names of the laws that the rules are gotten from. So we will call rules 11 and 12 double negation, rule 4 modus ponens, etc. If you are going to master this chapter, you must memorize these transformation-rules.

9.3   The transformation-rules numbered 1, 2, 4, 5, and 8 (conj., simp., m.p., add., and pos. abs.) are gotten from tautological, conditional statements. One of these statements was used as an example in section 8. By conditionalizing these argument forms you can build the conditional statements that the other transformation-rules in this group are gotten from. You can build a truth-table for each one of these statements to show that it is tautological. The transformation-rules numbered 9, 10, 11, and 12 (m.e. and d.n.) are gotten from two logical equivalences. One of these also was used as an example in section 8. By studying that example, you can see how to put the other logical equivalence together and then test it by making a truth-table. All nine of these transformation-rules are to be understood in exactly the same way: each tells you that you can transform the formula or formulas that are written above the line into the formula that is written below the line. For instance, the rule of conjunction tells you that if you have two different formulas written separately, you can conjoin them. The rule of simplification tells you that if you have a conjunction of two formulas, you can write either one of them by itself. The rule of modus ponens says that if you have a conditional statement as one formula and a formula written by itself that matches the antecedent, then you can write down by itself the formula that matches the consequent. Given these examples, you should be able to understand the other transformation-rules mentioned in this subsection, for all of these are to be understood in exactly the same way. Each tells you that you can go from the formula or formulas that are written above the line to the formula that is written below the line.

9.3.1 Exercise

Make formulas that correspond to the following transformation-rules, then make truth-tables for these formulas:
(1) conjunction
(2) simplification
(3) modus ponens
(4) positive absurdity
(5) material equivalence
(6) double negation

9.3.2 Exercise

In section 8, the law of addition and the law of double negation are used as examples. Make truth-tables for the two formulas that correspond to these transformation-rules.

9.4   The transformation-rules numbered 3, 6, and 7 (assump., cases, and neg. abs.) are more complicated. Strictly speaking, they are not argument-forms but rather argument-schemas. They cannot be made into argument-forms or formulas (so they cannot be tautologies) because of the new sign that looks like this:

$$\begin{bmatrix} \cdot \\ \cdot \\ \cdot \end{bmatrix}$$

This sign means that the formula that the sign starts in front of is being assumed. The three dots mean that any number of formulas can be written inside this sign. The formulas that are written inside this sign usually cannot be gotten without the use of the assumed formula, so they are said to lie within its scope. By being drawn in front of all of the formulas within the scope of an assumption, this assumption-sign marks the extent of the assumption's scope. Every formula inside this sign except the first one is gotten by using some transformation-rule on some formulas that are already written down. For instance, suppose we assume the formula

(1) $\ulcorner Kpq$ $\quad \| \quad \ulcorner (p \cdot q)$ assumed

We can, by using the rule of simplification, write

(2) $\mid q$ $\quad \| \quad \mid q$ from line 1 by simp.

as the next line. Then by using the rule of addition, we can write the formula

(3) $\mid Apq$ $\quad \| \quad \mid (p \lor q)$ from line 2 by add.

Then we can write

(4) $\mid NNApq$ $\quad \| \quad \mid \sim \sim (p \lor q)$ from line 3 by d. n.

We can keep on doing this as long as each succeeding formula is gotten from one or more formulas that have already been written down by using some transformation-rule. But let's stop with line 4. The sequence of formulas now looks like this:

(1) $\ulcorner Kpq$ $\qquad \ulcorner (p \cdot q)$ assumed
(2) q $\qquad q$ from line 1 by simp.
(3) Apq $\qquad (p \lor q)$ from line 2 by add.
(4) $NNApq$ $\qquad \sim \sim (p \lor q)$ from line 3 by d.n.

When, as in the rule of assumption, a formula immediately follows the underlined formula and is itself not another assumption, that formula is said to discharge the assumption. So the material implication of p and q stands for a formula that discharges the assumption that p stands for in the rule of assumption. Similarly, the last statement-variable r stands for a formula that discharges the two assumptions made in the rule of cases, and the negation of p stands for a formula that discharges the assumption that p stands for in the negative rule of absurdity. Every assumption must eventually be discharged if you are to correctly use the rules that use assumptions. The formulas that are written inside the assumption sign usually cannot be written outside of the sign, for they usually depend on the assumption, that is, they do not have the value t unless the assumption has that value.

9.5   These twelve transformation-rules are completely general. That is, the statement-variables p, q, and r stand for any well-formed formula whatsoever. So different and even larger well-formed formulas can be substituted for these statement-variables. When different or larger formulas are substituted for these statement-variables, however, the substitute must be put in every place that the variable being substituted for is written. For instance, look at modus ponens again:

$$\frac{\begin{array}{c} Cpq \\ p \end{array}}{q} \qquad\qquad \Big\| \qquad\qquad \frac{\begin{array}{c} (p \supset q) \\ p \end{array}}{q}$$

If you substitute q for p and p for q, you get this:

$$\frac{\begin{array}{c} Cqp \\ q \end{array}}{p} \qquad\qquad \Big\| \qquad\qquad \frac{\begin{array}{c} (q \supset p) \\ q \end{array}}{p}$$

And of course, you can substitute larger formulas. For example, suppose you substitute

$$Epq \qquad\qquad \| \qquad\qquad (p \equiv q)$$

for

$$p \qquad\qquad \| \qquad\qquad p$$

and

$$Kqr \qquad\qquad \| \qquad\qquad (q \cdot r)$$

SECTION 9. The basic transformation-rules

for

$$q \qquad \| \qquad q$$

Then modus ponens looks like this:

$$\begin{array}{c} CEpqKqr \\ Epq \\ \hline Kqr \end{array} \qquad \Big\| \qquad \begin{array}{c} ((p \equiv q) \supset (q \cdot r)) \\ (p \equiv q) \\ \hline (q \cdot r) \end{array}$$

For the sake of clarity, the last two examples of modus ponens are called *substitution-instances* of modus ponens, because they are gotten by substituting different well-formed formulas for the variables used in writing the rule. Obviously, there is no limit to the number of substitution-instances that can be written for any of these transformation-rules. However, the following argument-form is not a substitution-instance of modus ponens:

$$\begin{array}{c} CEpqKqr \\ p \\ \hline Kqr \end{array} \qquad \Big\| \qquad \begin{array}{c} ((p \equiv q) \supset (q \cdot r)) \\ p \\ \hline (q \cdot r) \end{array}$$

The variable p has not been substituted for each place it is written in the rule.

9.5.1 Exercise

(1) Take the rules of conjunction, simplification, modus ponens, addition, positive absurdity, and material equivalence. In place of p, substitute q, and in place of q, substitute p.

(2) In the rule of double negation, substitute

$$ApCqr \qquad \| \qquad (p \vee (q \supset r))$$

for p.

(3) In the rules of conjunction and modus ponens, substitute

$$Kpq \qquad \| \qquad (p \cdot q)$$

for p and

$$Apq \qquad \| \qquad (p \vee q)$$

for q.

(4) In the rules of simplification and material equivalence, substitute r for p and

$$CNpr \qquad \| \qquad (\sim p \supset r)$$

for *q*.

(5) In the rules of addition and positive absurdity, substitute

$$Epq \qquad \| \qquad (p \equiv q)$$

for *p* and

$$Nr \qquad \| \qquad \sim r$$

for *q*.

9.5.2 Exercise

Make up a substitution instance for each of the following rules:

(1) conjunction
(2) simplification
(3) modus ponens
(4) addition
(5) positive absurdity
(6) material equivalence
(7) double negation

9.6 Why do these transformation-rules always work? Let's take another look at some of the rules. The idea behind logic, remember, is this: if you can learn to think in ways that do not let you stray from the truth, and if the facts you begin your thinking with are true, then your conclusion will be true too. These transformation-rules lay out ways of reasoning that do not let you stray from the truth. For instance, let's look at modus ponens again:

$$\begin{array}{c} Cpq \\ p \\ \hline q \end{array} \qquad \| \qquad \begin{array}{c} (p \supset q) \\ p \\ \hline q \end{array}$$

Now recall the truth-table that defines material implication. It looks like this:

$$\begin{array}{c} Cpq \\ \hline t\ t\ t \\ f\ t\ f \\ t\ f\ t \\ t\ f\ f \end{array} \qquad \| \qquad \begin{array}{c} (p \supset q) \\ \hline t\ t\ t \\ t\ f\ f \\ f\ t\ t \\ f\ t\ f \end{array}$$

So suppose we know that the formula

$$Cpq \qquad\qquad \| \qquad\qquad (p \supset q)$$

has the value *t*. Then we know that the second line of values in the truth-table does not apply, for in that line the formula has the value *f*. That leaves us with these values:

Cpq		$(p \supset q)$
t t t	$\|$	*t t t*
t f t		*f t t*
t f f		*f t f*

Now let's suppose we know that *p* also has *t* as its truth-value. Then we know that the last two lines of the table do not apply either, for in those lines *p* has the value *f*. So the only values left are

Cpq		$(p \supset q)$
t t t	$\|$	*t t t*

This shows that *q* must have the value *t*. So if

$$Cpq \qquad\qquad \| \qquad\qquad (p \supset q)$$

and

$$p \qquad\qquad \| \qquad\qquad p$$

are given, you can write down

$$q \qquad\qquad \| \qquad\qquad q$$

In other words, if

$$Cpq \qquad\qquad \| \qquad\qquad (p \supset q)$$

and

$$p \qquad\qquad \| \qquad\qquad p$$

both have the value *t,* then *q* has the value *t* too. Modus ponens can never lead your reasoning astray.

9.6.1 Exercise

In similar ways, show that conjunction, simplification, material equivalence, and the positive rule of absurdity (a tricky one) can never lead your reasoning astray.

9.7   Now let's look at the rule of assumption. Its first line is always an assumption. Since there is no reason to assume something that you already know has the value t, only formulas whose truth-values are unknown are usually assumed. So whenever you assume a formula, you are asking what can be gotten if that formula is true. Let's look at the example in 9.4:

1.	⌐Kpq ‖ ⌐$(p \cdot q)$	assumed
2.	q ‖ q	from line 1 by simp.
3.	Apq ‖ $(p \lor q)$	from line 2 by add.
4.	$NNApq$ ‖ $\sim \sim (p \lor q)$	from line 3 by d.n.

What this sequence shows is this: if the formula on line 1 has the value t, then the formula on line 2 also has the value t, the formula on line 3 also has the value t, and the formula on line 4 also has the value t. But what if the formula on line 1 has the value f? Then the other formulas may or may not have the value t. There is no way of knowing. We can, nevertheless, still write a fifth line that does have the value t, namely,

   5. $CKpqNNApq$ ‖ $((p \cdot q) \supset \sim \sim (p \lor q))$ from lines 1-4 by assumption

Why? Because of the truth-table that defines material implication. We know that if

   Kpq ‖ $(p \cdot q)$

has the value t, then

   $NNApq$ ‖ $\sim \sim (p \lor q)$

also has the value t. Under these conditions, the formula on line 5 also has the value t. If

   Kpq ‖ $(p \cdot q)$

on the other hand has the value f, the formula on line 5 still has the value t, for a conditional statement's value is t whenever the antecedent has f as its value. So in either case, the formula on line 5 must have the value t. Even if we do not know the truth-value of the formula on line 1, we know that the formula on line 5 must have the value t. Because we know that the formula on line 5 must have the value t, we can write the formula outside of the scope of the assumption made on line 1. In fact, the formula on line 5 discharges that assumption.

9.8 Now it is easy to see why the rule of cases always works. It begins with a formula that we assume has the value *t*, since the formula is given. The formula, however, is an alternation. If an alternation has the value *t*, we know that *t* is the value of one or both of the alternatives. Now suppose you can get some formula that the letter *r* stands for by assuming the first alternative and that you can get the same formula again by assuming the other alternative. Since you can get the formula that *r* stands for from both alternatives, and since you know that at least one of the alternatives has the value *t*, the formula that *r* stands for must also have the value *t*. So the formula that *r* stands for can be written outside of the scope of any assumption. Of course, the letter *r* stands for a formula that can be gotten by using some rule, and the letters *p* and *q* stand for other formulas that the formula that *r* stands for can be gotten from. (There is no way to get *r* from *p* and again from *q*.) For instance, look at the following example of a use of the rule of cases:

1.	*AKpqKpr*	$((p \cdot q) \lor (p \cdot r))$	given
2.	⌐*Kpq*	⌐$(p \cdot q)$	assumed
3.	⌊ *p*	⌊ *p*	from line 2 by simp.
4.	⌐*Kpr*	⌐$(p \cdot r)$	assumed
5.	⌊ *p*	⌊ *p*	from line 4 by simp.
6.	*p*	*p*	from lines 3, 5 by cases

In this example,

$$Kpq \quad \| \quad (p \cdot q)$$

is the substitute for *p*,

$$Kpr \quad \| \quad (p \cdot r)$$

is the substitute for *q*, and *p* is the substitute for *r*. In this example, *p* can be gotten from both alternatives, so it must have the value *t*. The variable *p* that is written on line 6 discharges the assumptions made on lines 2 and 4.

9.9 Finally, look at the negative rule of absurdity. It says that if you assume a formula and get a logical absurdity from it, the negation of the assumption must have the value *t*. We know that this is so because of the truth-tables for material implication and negation. Suppose we have this:

We already know that we can write

$$CpKqNq \qquad \| \qquad (p \supset (q \cdot \sim q))$$

by the rule of assumption. Now a logical absurdity always has f as its value. But if the consequent of a conditional statement has the value f, and if the conditional statement itself has the value t, then we know from the truth-table that defines material implication that the antecedent must have the value f. In this example, however, the antecedent is the formula being assumed. If it has the value f, its negation has the value t. So we can write down the negation of the assumption, and since we know that its value is t, the negation of the assumption does not have to be written inside the scope of the assumption. Now let's look at an actual example:

1.	$\ulcorner KKCpqNqp$	$\ulcorner (((p \supset q) \cdot \sim q) \cdot p)$	given
2.	p	p	from line 1 by simp.
3.	$KCpqNq$	$((p \supset q) \cdot \sim q)$	from line 1 by simp.
4.	Cpq	$(p \supset q)$	from line 3 by simp.
5.	q	q	from lines 2, 4 by m.p.
6.	Nq	$\sim q$	from line 3 by simp.
7.	$NKCpqNqp$	$\sim(((p \supset q) \cdot \sim q) \cdot p)$	from lines 2-6 by neg. abs.

In this example,

$$KKCpqNqp \qquad \| \qquad (((p \supset q) \cdot \sim q) \cdot p)$$

is the substitute for p. The formula on line 7, of course, discharges the assumption made on line 1.

9.10   In naming the basic ten laws and the twelve basic transformation-rules, for the most part the traditional names for them have been used. Because of what these transformation-rules do, however, they are sometimes called introduction and elimination-rules. For example, conjunction lets you introduce the symbol for conjunction. So the rule can be called conjunction-introduction. Simplification, on the other hand, lets you eliminate the symbol for conjunction and can therefore be called conjunction-elimination. If you look at the list of basic transformation-rules again, you will notice that there is one that let's you put in every truth-functor and one that lets you take out every truth-functor, and in addition, one that lets you put in double negation and one that lets you take it out. So the following twelve names can also be used to identify the twelve basic transformation-rules:

1. conjunction-introduction
2. conjunction-elimination
3. material-implication introduction
4. material-implication elimination
5. alternation-introduction
6. alternation-elimination
7. negation-introduction
8. negation-elimination
9. material-equivalence introduction
10. material-equivalence elimination
11. double-negation introduction
12. double-negation elimination

The traditional names for these transformation-rules, however, are also descriptive. The names listed above describe what each rule does; the traditional names describe how the rules work. For instance, conjunction conjoins, simplification simplifies, assumption assumes, addition adds, etc. Modus ponens, however, requires some explanation, for these are Latin words. They merely mean the mode that affirms. In other words, the second premise affirms the antecedent of the first premise, so the consequent of the first premise can then also be affirmed. By looking at the other rules now, you should be able to see how their names are also descriptive. In order to distinguish rule 9 from 10 and rule 11 from 12, rule 9 is sometimes called the converse law of material equivalence, and rule 11 is sometimes called the converse rule of double negation. The rule of assumption is often also called the rule of conditional proof, and the negative rule of absurdity has two other names that are often used—the rule of indirect proof and reduction to absurdity.

9.11 The two laws that are logical equivalences have a feature that distinguishes them from the other eight. The other eight, which give us transformation-rules that cannot be turned upside down, can only be used on whole formulas. The rules that are gotten from logical equivalences, however, can be used on parts of formulas. For instance, to simplify a formula, the whole formula must be a conjunction. You cannot simplify a formula that is part of a formula that is itself not a conjunction. The formula

$$Kpq \qquad\qquad \| \qquad\qquad (p \cdot q)$$

can be simplified; the formula

$$ApKqr \qquad\qquad \| \qquad\qquad (p \vee (q \cdot r))$$

cannot. The law of double negation, which is a logical equivalence, gives us two transformation-rules that can be used on any part of a formula, however. The formula

$$Kpq \qquad \| \qquad (p \cdot q)$$

can be changed into

$$KNNpq \qquad \| \qquad (\sim\sim p \cdot q)$$

as well as

$$NNKpq \qquad \| \qquad \sim\sim(p \cdot q)$$

Similarly, the formula

$$ApKqr \qquad \| \qquad (p \vee (q \cdot r))$$

can be changed into

$$ApKNNqr \qquad \| \qquad (p \vee (\sim\sim q \cdot r))$$

and since logical equivalences gives us two transformation-rules, one of which is the reverse of the other, the formula

$$CNNqr \qquad \| \qquad (\sim\sim q \supset r)$$

can be changed into

$$Cqr \qquad \| \qquad (q \supset r)$$

All transformation-rules gotten from logical equivalences can be used on parts of formulas. Because of this feature, these transformation-rules are sometimes called *replacement-rules*. Replacement, therefore, is not like substitution. A formula being replaced need not be replaced everywhere it is written, but a formula being substituted for must be substituted for everywhere it is written.

9.11.1 Exercise

(1) Take the rule of conjunction. Replace the p in the conclusion by

$$NNp \qquad \| \qquad \sim\sim p$$

(2) Take the rule of conjunction again. Replace only the q in the premise by

$$NNq \qquad \| \qquad \sim\sim q$$

(3) Take the positive rule of absurdity. Replace only the first p in the premise by

$$NNp \qquad \| \qquad \sim\sim p$$

(4) There are two transformation-rules of double negation. The first, as you may recall, is sometimes called the converse rule of double negation. In the transformation-rule for the rule of double negation (not for the converse rule of double negation), replace the premise

$$NNp \qquad \| \qquad \sim\sim p$$

by p.

(5) Take the following argument form:

$$
\begin{array}{l}
CApqr \\
CArqCpKCstCts \\
Kpt \\
\hline
Est
\end{array}
\qquad \left\|
\begin{array}{l}
((p \vee q) \supset r) \\
((r \vee q) \supset (p \supset ((s \supset t) \cdot (t \supset s)))) \\
(p \cdot t) \\
\hline
(s \equiv t)
\end{array}
\right.
$$

Replace the

$$KCstCts \qquad \| \qquad ((s \supset t) \cdot (t \supset s))$$

in the second premise by

$$Est \qquad \| \qquad (s \equiv t)$$

9.11.2 Exercise

Take the following argument-form again:

$$
\begin{array}{l}
CApqr \\
CArqCpKCstCts \\
Kpt \\
\hline
Est
\end{array}
\qquad \left\|
\begin{array}{l}
((p \vee q) \supset r) \\
((r \vee q) \supset (p \supset ((s \supset t) \cdot (t \supset s)))) \\
(p \cdot t) \\
\hline
(s \equiv t)
\end{array}
\right.
$$

Are the following statements true or false?
(1) The antecedent of the first premise can be replaced by r.
(2) The consequent of the first premise can be replaced by

$$Arp \qquad \| \qquad (r \vee p)$$

(3) The first p in the second premise can be replaced by

$$NNp \qquad \| \qquad \sim\sim p$$

(4) The third premise can be replaced by p.

(5) The conclusion can be replaced by something else.

(6) The conclusion can be replaced by

$$Cst \qquad \| \qquad (s \supset t)$$

(7) The conclusion can be replaced by

$$KCstCts \qquad \| \qquad ((s \supset t) \cdot (t \supset s))$$

(8) The s in the conclusion can be replaced by

$$NNs \qquad \| \qquad {\sim}{\sim}s$$

(9) You can substitute u for t everywhere t is written in the argument-form.

(10) You can replace both t's in the second premise by

$$NNt \qquad \| \qquad {\sim}{\sim}t$$

SECTION 10. Formalism

10.1   In chapter 1, a number of ideas about logic were brought out: We said that logic is the study of the methods and principles that distinguish good from bad reasoning. We also said that what distinguishes good from bad reasoning is how premises are connected to conclusions rather than what information the reasoning is about. Because of this, we said that logicians study argument-forms. So logic, as we are using the word, is formal logic. Now that you know what a transformation-rule is and how transformation-rules are gotten from laws of logic, we can show what logicians mean when they say that premises are connected to conclusions: the conclusion of an argument-form is connected to its premises if they can be transformed into the conclusion by using one or more of the transformation-rules. So if you want to find out if an argument-form is a good one, you can try to transform the premises into the conclusion by using one or more of the transformation-rules. If it is impossible to get the conclusion from its premises by using the transformation-rules, the argument-form in question is not a good one. If it is possible, the argument-form is a good one, for then the transformations show that the premises are connected to the conclusions by laws of logic. Laws of logic connect the premises of good argument-forms to their conclusions.

10.2   Because the premises of an argument that is reasoned well can be transformed into its conclusion, readers of this book are for the time being to think of logic as the game of transforming formulas into other formulas by using the transformation-rules. This view of logic is called formalism. After you master the transformation-rules and how they let you go from one or more formulas to another, you will be taught to use your knowledge on arguments that are written out in English. For the time being, however, you will learn only how to go from one or more formulas to other formulas. You will learn how to do this by studying examples. Each example in this section illustrates the use of one or more of the twelve basic transformation-rules.

10.3 Example 1.

The rule of assumption lets us assume any formula. To illustrate the use of this rule, assume the statement-variable p:

1. $\ulcorner p$ $\|$ $\ulcorner p$ assumed

What you want to do now is see what other formulas you can get from this one by using the transformation-rules. So the thing to do is go through the rules one by one to see which ones can be used. Look at the rule of conjunction. To use it you must already have two separate formulas. But in this illustration, you only have one; so conjunction is out. What about simplification? To use it, the formula you start with must be a conjunction. So this rule is out too. (Since this example is meant to illustrate the use of the rule of assumption, we will skip over it.) Now check the rule of modus ponens. It too requires two separate formulas, so you cannot use this rule either. But now look at addition. It begins with one formula of any kind; so you can write the first transformation:

1. $\ulcorner p$ $\|$ $\ulcorner p$ assumed
2. $\lfloor Apq$ $\| \lfloor (p \lor q)$ from line 1 by add.

Now you can discharge the assumption if you want to and get this:

3. $\underline{\lfloor}$ $CpApq$ $\| \underline{\lfloor} (p \supset (p \lor q))$ from line 1-2 by assump.

10.4 Example 1 continued.

Let's leave this transformation for the time being and illustrate the alternate way of using addition if you start from the same assumed premise:

1. $\ulcorner p$ $\|$ $\ulcorner p$ assumed
2. $\lfloor Aqp$ $\| \lfloor (q \lor p)$ from line 1 by add.
3. $CpAqp$ $\| (p \supset (q \lor p))$ from line 1-2 by assump.

This transformation is almost exactly like the other one; only the order of some of the statement-variables is different. In some rules, the order of the variables is not important; in other rules, however, it is very important. So when you use the transformation-rules, you must use them exactly as they are written; you cannot go changing things around unless you have a transformation-rule that lets you change things around.

10.5 Example 1 continued.

Now let's continue our review of the rules. The next one is the rule of cases. It begins with a formula that is an alternation; so you can't use this rule on p. Nor can you use the negative rule of absurdity, for although its schema begins wth the assumption of a formula, that formula must either by itself or in combination with other formulas be logically absurd. But a statement-variable that stands by itself is never logically absurd. You cannot use the positive rule of absurdity either, for it begins with a logically absurd formula (or two formulas that are logically absurd when they are conjoined). You must also rule out the two transformation-rules called material equivalence, for the formulas they start with are more complex than the statement-variable p. But you can use the (converse) rule of double negation, that is, rule 11:

$$
\begin{array}{lll}
1. & \ulcorner p & \text{assumed} \\
2. & \;\; NNp & \text{from line 1 by d.n.} \\
3. & CpNNp & \text{from lines 1-2 by assump.}
\end{array}
\qquad
\begin{array}{ll}
\ulcorner p & \text{assumed} \\
\;\; \sim\; \sim p & \text{from line 1 by d.n.} \\
(p \supset\; \sim\; \sim p) & \text{from lines 1-2 by assump.}
\end{array}
$$

10.6 Example 1 continued.

These illustrations lay out before your eyes the simplest transformations you can make from the assumption of a statement-variable. Of course, we need not have stopped where we did. For instance, look at the first illustration again. You can develop it further in two different ways: you can develop line 2 or you can develop line 3. You can, for instance, write

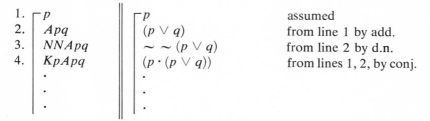

and end by discharging the assumption whenever you like. Or you can do this:

1. $\ulcorner p$		$\ulcorner p$	assumed
2. $\llcorner Apq$		$\llcorner (p \lor q)$	from line 1 by add.
3. $CpApq$		$(p \supset (p \lor q))$	from lines 1-2 by assump.
4. $NNCpApq$		$\sim \sim (p \supset (p \lor q))$	from line 3 by d.n.
5. $ApNNCpApq$		$(p \lor \sim \sim (p \supset (p \lor q)))$	from line 4 by add.

and again end wherever you like. The other illustrations used in this example can be developed in the same way, and obviously there is no limit to the number of formulas you can get if you are willing to use the same rules over and over again.

10.7 Transformations like these are sometimes called *inferences*, sometimes *deductions*. Since the last line of such a sequence of transformations is in effect a conclusion (not only of the argument-form but literally the end of the sequence), the sequence is often called a *proof* or *demonstration* of that line. Notice too that alongside of each line in the sequence, we write the name of the rule that allows us to write that line and the numbers of the other lines used in the transformation. These justifications, since they show exactly how we got the formula, enable us to check the correctness of the transformations.

10.8 Example 2.

An assumption can be made inside the scope of another assumption. This ability is very useful. For instance, suppose you first assume

| 1. $\ulcorner Kpq$ | | $\ulcorner (p \cdot q)$ | assumed |

and then

| 2. $\mid \ulcorner r$ | | $\mid \ulcorner r$ | assumed |

You can now carry out the following transformations:

3. $\mid\mid p$		$\mid\mid p$	from line 1 by simp.
4. $\mid\llcorner Aps$		$\mid\llcorner (p \lor s)$	from line 3 by add.
5. $\llcorner CrAps$		$\llcorner (r \supset (p \lor s))$	from lines 2-4 by assump.
6. $CKpqCrAps$		$((p \cdot q) \supset (r \supset (p \lor s)))$	from lines 1-5 by assump.

Again, we do not have to stop the transformations where we did. We could have extended this sequence in many ways. But since the purpose of this example is to illustrate the use of making an assumption inside the scope of another, the sequence above is long enough.

In this example the use of both the negative and positive rules of absurdity will be illustrated. Of course, these rules do not have to be used together; as a matter of fact, it is very unusual to do so. Nevertheless, let's use them together to see how they work. Suppose the statement-variable p is given. (When we say that a formula is *given*, this means that it usually has the value t. Remember, when something is *assumed*, its truth-value is usually unknown.) So we begin with this:

1. p $\qquad\qquad \|\qquad p$ $\qquad\qquad\qquad$ given

Now suppose that for some reason we are led to assume the negation of p:

2. $\ulcorner Np$ $\qquad\qquad \|\qquad \ulcorner \sim p$ $\qquad\qquad\qquad$ assumed

As line 3, you can write

3. $|\ q$ $\qquad\qquad \|\qquad |\ q$ $\qquad\qquad\qquad$ from lines 1, 2 by
$\qquad\qquad\qquad\qquad\qquad\qquad\qquad\qquad\qquad\qquad\qquad\qquad$ pos. abs.

Notice that when the positive rule of absurdity was presented, the negated premise was written first, while in this illustration, the negated premise is second. The order has been reversed to show that when a transformation-rule has more than one premise, the order of the premises makes no difference. Since the letter q in the presentation of the positive rule of absurdity stands for any well-formed formula, and since the letter q does not appear in the premises of that transformation-rule, you can write this:

4. $|\ N q$ $\qquad\qquad \|\qquad |\ \sim q$ $\qquad\qquad\qquad$ from lines 1, 2 by
$\qquad\qquad\qquad\qquad\qquad\qquad\qquad\qquad\qquad\qquad\qquad\qquad$ pos. abs.

But now, lines 2, 3, and 4 illustrate the negative rule of absurdity. So you can discharge the assumption made on line 2 and write this:

5. $\underline{NNp}$ $\qquad\qquad \|\qquad \underline{\sim \sim p}$ $\qquad\qquad\qquad$ from lines 2-4 by
$\qquad\qquad\qquad\qquad\qquad\qquad\qquad\qquad\qquad\qquad\qquad\qquad$ neg. abs.

From this, however, you can get

6. p $\qquad\qquad \|\qquad p$ $\qquad\qquad\qquad$ from line 5 by d.n.

Now, of course, line 6 is the same as line 1. And this is exactly what you should have expected, for if p is given, the negation of p should have the value f. This is exactly what lines 2 through 6 prove. Again, this sequence of transformations can be extended as far as you like by applying the rules to line 6, but for the purposes of this illustration, the sequence is already long enough.

10.10 Example 4.

Now let's illustrate the rule of cases by starting from the following formula:

1. $ANNpKCqpq$ $\quad \| \quad (\sim \sim p \lor ((q \supset p) \cdot q))$ given

You must first assume the first alternative in this alternation, so line 2 is this:

2. $\ulcorner NNp$ $\quad \| \quad \ulcorner \sim \sim p$ $\qquad$ assumed

The most obvious formula you can get from this is

3. $\lfloor p$ $\quad \| \quad \lfloor p$ $\qquad$ from line 2 by d.n.

Let's stop with this and close the scope of the assumption. Now, if the rule of cases is to work, you must assume the second alternative and get p out of it also. Let's try

4. $\ulcorner KCqpq$ $\quad \| \quad \ulcorner ((q \supset p) \cdot q)$ $\qquad$ assumed

From this you can simplify two more lines:

5. $\vert\ Cqp$ $\qquad \| \ \vert\ (q \supset p)$ $\qquad$ from line 4 by simp.
6. $\vert\ q$ $\qquad\quad \| \ \vert\ q$ $\qquad\qquad$ from line 4 by simp.

Lines 5 and 6, now, fit the form of modus ponens, so you can write

7. $\lfloor p$ $\quad \| \quad \lfloor p$ $\qquad$ from lines 5, 6 by m.p.

Since you have gotten p again, you can close the scope of the assumption made in line 4. And because p has been gotten from both alternatives, you can write it by itself as the next line.

8. $\quad p$ $\qquad \| \quad p$ $\qquad$ from lines 3, 7 by cases

Again, this sequence can be extended as far as you like.

10.11 Example 5.

All of the examples so far have been built around assumptions. But of course, sequences of transformations do not have to use assumptions. The only difference between sequences that use assumptions and those that do not is the lines that discharge assumptions. If you do not make an assumption, you cannot discharge it. For instance, look at the following illustration.

1. Cpq	$(p \supset q)$	given
2. Cqp	$(q \supset p)$	given
3. Epq	$(p \equiv q)$	from lines 1, 2 by m.e.
4. $NNEpq$	$\sim\sim (p \equiv q)$	from line 3 by d.n.
5. $NNKCpqCqp$	$\sim\sim ((p \supset q) \cdot$ $(q \supset p))$	from line 4 by m.e.
6. $NNKCpqNNCqp$	$\sim\sim ((p \supset q) \cdot$ $\sim\sim (q \supset p))$	from line 5 by d.n.

Notice that in this sequence of transformations, line 5 is gotten from line 4 by using the rule of material equivalence as a replacement-rule, since it is used on only the part of the formula that comes after the double negation. Line 6 is gotten from line 5 in a similar way, only there the rule of double negation is being used as a replacement-rule. This distinction between transformation-rules and replacement-rules is very important. You must remember that the only transformation-rules that can be applied to parts of formulas are those which are also transformation-rules when they are turned upside down. If you forget this, you are apt to do some transformations incorrectly.

10.12   In the five preceding examples, the use of all twelve of the basic rules has been illustrated. Remember that these illustrations can be extended and varied infinitely. The only restriction on any of them is that each line must be gotten from one or more of the others by using some transformation-rule or else be given or assumed. In working with such sequences of transformations, always be sure to mark any assumptions with the assumption sign and discharge all assumptions before you finish the sequence.

10.12.1 Exercise

This is an exercise in creative thinking. Use as much imagination as you can in working these problems. What you should do is develop as many formulas from the given formulas as you can by trying to use all of the basic transformation-rules:

(1) Kpq	$(p \cdot q)$
(2) Apq	$(p \lor q)$
(3) p	p
Np	$\sim p$
(4) NNp	$\sim\sim p$
Cpq	$(p \supset q)$
Cqp	$(q \supset p)$
(5) $ApKpq$	$(p \lor (p \cdot q))$
(6) $CpKqNq$	$(p \supset (q \cdot \sim q))$

SECTION 11. Simple arguments

11.1 Now that you have seen how the basic rules are used, the next task is to see how a specific conclusion is gotten from a given set of premises. Again you will be taught to do this by a series of examples. Each example presents an argument-form with the conclusion that is to be proved. The way of proving it is explained, and a demonstration (sometimes called a derivation) is then set out. The difference between what is put forth in this section and what was put forth in the last section is very slight: in this section, you will know beforehand what formula is to end the sequence of transformations, that is, what formula is to be proved. The task before you is to learn how to choose the transformation-rules that will allow you to transform the given premises into the desired conclusion. So you should especially study the paragraphs marked 'strategy'.

11.2 Example 1.

Problem

1. Kpq	$(p \cdot q)$	given
2. $CAprs$	$((p \lor r) \supset s)$	given
$\underline{Kps}$	$\underline{(p \cdot s)}$	to be proved

Strategy First notice that the conclusion is a conjunction of p and s. If you look at the premises, you will notice that p and s are not conjoined. This means that if you are to get the conclusion, you must first prove p and s separately, for if you can prove them separately, the rule of conjunction will allow you to write the conclusion. So you look for p in the premises. You will notice that it is a conjunct in the first premise; so you can get p from that premise by simplification. Now the problem is to find a way of getting s. The first thing to notice about s is that it is the consequent of the second premise, and you know that modus ponens allows you to write the consequent of a premise if you have or can get the antecedent. In this case, the antecedent is the alternation of *p* and *r*. So now the problem is to find a way of getting that. If you know the rules, however, you know that the alternation of *p* and *r* can be gotten from *p* (which you already have) by addition. This is all you need, so you can easily write out the proof.

Demonstration

1. Kpq		$(p \cdot q)$	given
2. $CAprs$		$((p \lor r) \supset s)$	given
Kps		$(p \cdot s)$	to be proved
3. p		p	from 1 by simp.
4. Apr		$(p \lor r)$	from 3 by add.
5. s		s	from 4, 2 by m.p.
6. Kps		$(p \cdot s)$	from 3, 5 by conj.

The make-up of this demonstration can be displayed on a kind of diagram that has come to be known as a tree. The numbers in the diagram that follows correspond to lines in the demonstration. By reading the diagram from top to bottom, the arrows and arrow-points, often called branches, that are drawn between the numbers, show where lines which come later in the demonstration are gotten from. For instance, look at the following diagram of the demonstration:

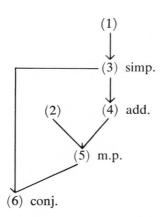

The first line in the demonstration yields line 3. The third line yields line 4. Lines 4 and 2 yield line 5. And lines 5 and 3 yield line 6.

SECTION 11. Simple arguments

11.3 Example 2.

Problem

1. *Kpq*	$(p \cdot q)$	given
2. *CNNpr*	$(\sim \sim p \supset r)$	given
Ars	$(r \lor s)$	to be proved

Strategy If you look at the conclusion, you will notice that it is an alternation. Since this alternation does not appear in the premises as a unit, it can only be gotten by using the rule of addition. In order to get it by the rule of addition, however, you must already have either *r* or *s* alone. So look for these in the premises. The variable *s* does not appear in them, but *r* does. It is the consequent of the second premise, so it can be gotten by modus ponens if you can get the antecedent of that premise. The formula you need to get, then, is the double negation of *p*. You know that you can get this from *p* which is a conjunct of the first premise. The variable *p*, therefore, can be gotten by simplification. And this is all you need to be able to write the proof.

Demonstration

1. *Kpq*	$(p \cdot q)$	given
2. *CNNpr*	$(\sim \sim p \supset r)$	given
Ars	$(r \lor s)$	to be proved
3. *p*	p	from 1 by simp.
4. *NNp*	$\sim \sim p$	from 3 by d.n.
5. *r*	r	from 2, 4 by m.p.
6. *Ars*	$(r \lor s)$	from 5 by add.

Structure

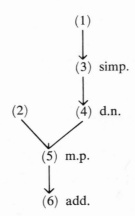

11.4 Example 3.

Problem

1. *Cpq*	$(p \supset q)$	given
2. *Cqr*	$(q \supset r)$	given
3. *Crs*	$(r \supset s)$	given
Cps	$(p \supset s)$	to be proved

Strategy   First notice that the conclusion is a conditional statement. The most natural transformation-rule to use to get such conclusions is assumption. To use this rule, you begin by assuming the antecedent of the conditional statement you want to get. In this case, the antecedent is the variable p. If you assume p, you should recognize at once that you can use it along with the first premise to get q by modus ponens. Once you get q, you can get r from the second premise by modus ponens; and when you get r, you can get s from the third premise by modus ponens. When you get s, you can discharge the assumption and get the conclusion you want.

Demonstration

1.	*Cpq*	$(p \supset q)$	given
2.	*Cqr*	$(q \supset r)$	given
3.	*Crs*	$(r \supset s)$	given
	Cps	$(p \supset s)$	to be proved
4.	$\ulcorner p$	$\ulcorner p$	assumed
5.	q	q	from 4, 1 by m.p.
6.	r	r	from 5,2 by m.p.
7.	$\lfloor s$	$\lfloor s$	from 6, 3 by m.p.
8.	*Cps*	$(p \supset s)$	from 4-7 by assump.

Structure

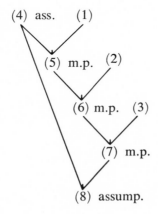

Problem

1. Cpq	$(p \supset q)$	given
2. $KNqNr$	$(\sim q \cdot \sim r)$	given
3. $CNrp$	$(\sim r \supset p)$	given
s	s	to be proved

Strategy An inspection of this argument-form reveals that the conclusion does not appear anywhere in the premises. Only the positive rule of absurdity allows you to draw such a conclusion. So the problem is to get a logical absurdity out of the premises. If you know the rules, and if you look at the premises carefully, you will quickly see that both q and its negation can easily be gotten. The negation of q can be gotten from the second premise by simplification. The variable q, however, can be gotten from the first premise by modus ponens if you can get p. This can be gotten from the third premise by modus ponens also if you can get the negation of r. But the negation of r is a conjunct of the second premise, so it can be simplified. Once you get both q and its negation, however, you have gotten a logical absurdity, so the conclusion can be written also.

Demonstration

1. Cpq	$(p \supset q)$	given
2. $KNqNr$	$(\sim q \cdot \sim r)$	given
3. $CNrp$	$(\sim r \supset p)$	given
s	s	to be proved
4. Nr	$\sim r$	from 2 by simp.
5. p	p	from 4, 3 by m.p.
6. q	q	from 5, 1 by m.p.
7. Nq	$\sim q$	from 2 by simp.
8. s	s	from 6, 7 by pos. abs.

Structure

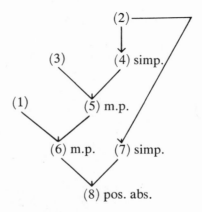

11.6 Example 5.

Problem

1. Cpq	$(p \supset q)$	given
2. $CKpqr$	$((p \cdot q) \supset r)$	given
3. $CpNr$	$(p \supset \sim r)$	given
Np	$\sim p$	to be proved

Strategy The conclusion of this argument-form is the negation of p. Now if you inspect the premises, you will notice that each time p appears, it is the antecedent of a conditional statement and p is not negated. So the only rule that can be used to get the negation of p from these premises is the negative rule of absurdity. To use it, however, you must assume p and try to get a logical absurdity. If you look at the premises again, you will see that a logical absurdity can easily be gotten from them if p is assumed, for from the first premise you can get q and from the third you can get the negation of r by two uses of modus ponens. Then you can conjoin p and q and use this conjunction with the second premise to get r by modus ponens. Both r and its negation can be gotten then if you assume p. So the negation of p follows.

Demonstration

1. Cpq	$(p \supset q)$	given
2. $CKpqr$	$((p \cdot q) \supset r)$	given
3. $CpNr$	$(p \supset \sim r)$	given
Np	$\sim p$	to be proved
4. ⌐p	⌐p	assumed
5. q	q	from 4, 1 by m.p.
6. Kpq	$(p \cdot q)$	from 4, 5 by conj.
7. r	r	from 6, 2 by m.p.
8. Nr	$\sim r$	from 4, 3 by m.p.
9. Np	$\sim p$	from 4-8 by neg. abs.

Structure

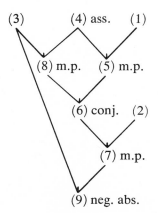

11.7 Example 6.

Problem

1. $CqNp$	$(q \supset \sim p)$	given
2. $CNpCqNr$	$(\sim p \supset (q \supset \sim r))$	given
3. $CANsNrNNq$	$((\sim s \vee \sim r) \supset \sim \sim q)$	given
4. $\underline{Ns}$	$\underline{\sim s}$	given
Nr	$\sim r$	to be proved

Strategy   Look at this argument-form. The conclusion is the consequent of the consequent of the second premise. To free this conclusion, you must first get the antecedent of the second premise, namely the negation of *p*. It is the consequent of the first premise; so to free it, you need the antecedent of that premise, namely *q*. If you look at the third premise, you will see that *q* can be gotten from the double negation of *q* which is the consequent of that premise. To get *q*, then, you must get the antecedent of the third premise. This antecedent is an alternation. One of its alternatives is the fourth premise; so the alternation needed can be gotten from the fourth premise by addition. All of these transformations allow you to free the consequent of the second premise. The conclusion you want is the consequent of this consequent; so to free the conclusion, you only need *q* which you already have.

Demonstration

1. $CqNp$	$(q \supset \sim p)$	given
2. $CNpCqNr$	$(\sim p \supset (q \supset \sim r))$	given
3. $CANsNrNNq$	$((\sim s \vee \sim r) \supset \sim \sim q)$	given
4. $\underline{Ns}$	$\underline{\sim s}$	given
Nr	$\sim r$	to be proved
5. $ANsNr$	$(\sim s \vee \sim r)$	from 4 by add.
6. NNq	$\sim \sim q$	from 5, 3 by m.p.
7. q	q	from 6 by d.n.
8. Np	$\sim p$	from 7, 1 by m.p.
9. $CqNr$	$(q \supset \sim r)$	from 8, 2 by m.p.
10. Nr	$\sim r$	from 9, 7 by m.p.

Structure

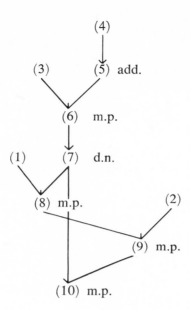

11.8 Example 7.

Problem

1. *Cpq*	$(p \supset q)$	given
2. *Cqr*	$(q \supset r)$	given
3. *Cst*	$(s \supset t)$	given
4. *Aps*	$(p \lor s)$	given
Art	$(r \lor t)$	to be proved

Strategy   Since the fourth premise is an alternation, the rule of cases must be used somewhere in this proof. To use the rule of cases, you must first assume *p* and derive the conclusion. Then you must assume *s* and derive the conclusion again. If you assume *p*, however, you can get *q* and then *r* by modus ponens. And from *r* you can get the conclusion by addition. If you assume *s*, you can get *t* by modus ponens, and then you can get the conclusion by using addition again.

Demonstration

1. *Cpq*	$(p \supset q)$	given
2. *Cqr*	$(q \supset r)$	given
3. *Cst*	$(s \supset t)$	given
4. *Aps*	$(p \lor s)$	given
Art	$(r \lor t)$	to be proved

59

			assumed
5.	p	p	assumed
6.	q	q	from 5, 1 by m.p.
7.	r	r	from 6, 2 by m.p.
8.	Art	$(r \lor t)$	from 7 by add.
9.	s	s	assumed
10.	t	t	from 9, 3 by m.p.
11.	Art	$(r \lor t)$	from 10 by add.
12.	Art	$(r \lor t)$	from 8, 11 by cases

Structure

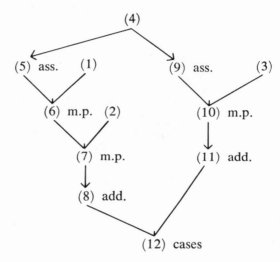

11.9 Example 8.

Problem

1.	$CApqr$	$((p \lor q) \supset r)$	given
2.	$CArqCpKCstCts$	$((r \lor q) \supset (p \supset ((s \supset t) \cdot$ $(t \supset s)))))$	given
3.	Kpt	$(p \cdot t)$	given
	$\overline{Est}$	$\overline{(s \equiv t)}$	to be proved

Strategy   Only the rule of material equivalence allows you to write this conclusion. To get it, you must first get

$KCstCts$ $\parallel$ $((s \supset t) \cdot (t \supset s))$

This formula is the consequent of the consequent of the second premise. To free what you need, you must have two additional formulas, namely p and the alternation of r and q. The variable p can easily be simplified from the third premise. The trick is to get the alternation of *r* and *q*. To do this, you must get either *r* or *q* by itself. If you look at the premises carefully, you will see that you cannot get *q*. So you must work for *r*. It is the consequent of the first premise. To free *r*, you need the antecedent of that premise. But since it is the alternation of *p* and *q*, and since you already have *p*, this alternation can be gotten by addition.

Demonstration

1. *CApqr*	$((p \lor q) \supset r)$	given
2. *CArqCpKCstCts*	$((r \lor q) \supset (p \supset ((s \supset t) \cdot ((t \supset s))))$	given
3. *Kpt*	$(p \cdot t)$	given
Est	$(s \equiv t)$	to be proved
4. *p*	*p*	from 3 by simp.
5. *Apq*	$(p \lor q)$	from 4 by add.
6. *r*	*r*	from 5, 1 by m.p.
7. *Arq*	$(r \lor q)$	from 6 by add.
8. *CpKCstCts*	$(p \supset ((s \supset t) \cdot (t \supset s)))$	from 7, 2 by m.p.
9. *KCstCts*	$((s \supset t) \cdot (t \supset s))$	from 4, 8 by m.p.
10. *Est*	$(s \equiv t)$	from 9 my m.e.

Structure

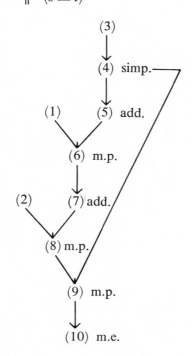

61

11.10 Example 9.

Problem

1.	$CpCpNq$	$(p \supset (p \supset \sim q))$	given
2.	Epq	$(p \equiv q)$	given
	$KNpNq$	$(\sim p \cdot \sim q)$	to be proved

Strategy   To prove this conclusion, you must get both the negation of p and the negation of q separately. If you had p, you could get the negation of q from the first premise, but since the negation of p is in the conclusion, you should not normally also look for p. So some other strategy must be found. To find it, look at the second premise. You can get

$$KCpqCqp \qquad \| \qquad ((p \supset q) \cdot (q \supset p))$$

from it by material equivalence. Now you should be able to see that using the negative rule of absurdity twice will allow you to write the conclusion:

Demonstration

1.	$CpCpNq$	$(p \supset (p \supset \sim q))$	given
2.	Epq	$(p \equiv q)$	given
	$KNpNq$	$(\sim p \cdot \sim q)$	to be proved
3.	$KCpqCqp$	$((p \supset q) \cdot (q \supset p))$	from 2 by m.e.
4.	Cpq	$(p \supset q)$	from 3 by simp.
5.	p	p	assumed
6.	$CpNq$	$(p \supset \sim q)$	from 5, 1 by m.p.
7.	Nq	$\sim q$	from 5, 6 by m.p.
8.	q	q	from 4, 5 by m.p.
9.	Np	$\sim p$	from 5-8 by neg. abs.
10.	Cqp	$(q \supset p)$	from 3 by simp.
11.	q	q	assumed
12.	p	p	from 10, 11 by m.p.
13.	$KpNp$	$(p \cdot \sim p)$	from 12, 9 by conj.
14.	Nq	$\sim q$	from 11-13 by neg. abs.
15.	$KNpNq$	$(\sim p \cdot \sim q)$	from 9, 14 by conj.

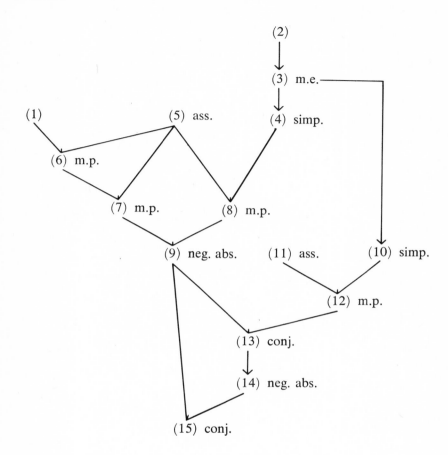

11.11 If you replace the numbers in the trees by the formulas on the lines in the demonstrations that correspond to the numbers, you will have another way of writing out a demonstration. For instance, the demonstration for the problem in example 9 can be written out like this:

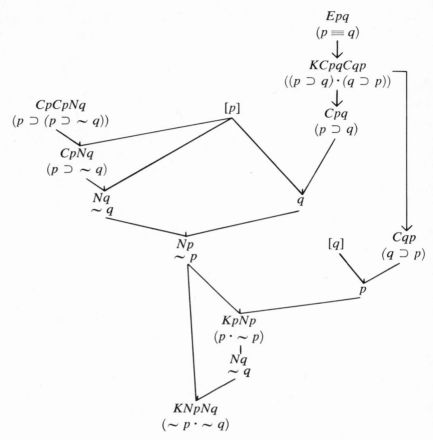

In trees, it is customary to put brackets around formulas that are being assumed.

11.12 In the preceding examples, the use of each of the twelve basic transformation-rules has again been illustrated. You have also seen how to analyze an argument logically in order to find out which transformation-rules will enable you to get the conclusion you want. This ability to analyze an argument, which is described in the strategies, is the primary ability you should try to acquire while studying logic, for in learning to analyze arguments logically, you are learning to think logically. Once you have thought through an argument, writing down the proof is really unnecessary. The reason for writing down the proof is so that you can then check to be sure that you have not made any errors in using the rules. Writing down the proofs, then, is nothing more than a learning device. When you have learned all the rules set out in this book and can use them to analyze arguments in your head, writing down proofs will no longer be necessary.

11.12.0 Exercise

Memorize the proofs of the nine examples.

11.12.1 Exercise

Analyze the following argument-forms and write out a paragraph telling how to demonstrate the conclusion of each and *then* write down the demonstrations so that you can be sure that you have not made any errors.

(1)	Epq	$(p \equiv q)$
	p	p
	q	q
(2)	Cpq	$(p \supset q)$
	Eqs	$(q \equiv s)$
	Cps	$(p \supset s)$
(3)	Apq	$(p \lor q)$
	Epq	$(p \equiv q)$
	Kpq	$(p \cdot q)$
(4)	Cpq	$(p \supset q)$
	$KsNr$	$(s \cdot \sim r)$
	Eqr	$(q \equiv r)$
	Np	$\sim p$
(5)	$CpCqr$	$(p \supset (q \supset r))$
	Cpq	$(p \supset q)$
	Cpr	$(p \supset r)$
(6)	$CpEqr$	$(p \supset (q \equiv r))$
	Cpr	$(p \supset r)$
	Cpq	$(p \supset q)$
(7)	$CpKqr$	$(p \supset (q \cdot r))$
	NNp	$\sim \sim p$
	$ANNrs$	$(\sim \sim r \lor s)$
(8)	Cpq	$(p \supset q)$
	$CCprCNsq$	$((p \supset r) \supset (\sim s \supset q))$
	$CNNqr$	$(\sim \sim q \supset r)$
	Ns	$\sim s$
	q	q

(9) *Epq*	$(p \equiv q)$
CpCqNr	$(p \supset (q \supset \sim r))$
CNrKst	$(\sim r \supset (s \cdot t))$
$\overline{Cps}$	$\overline{(p \supset s)}$
(10) *KApNNqr*	$((p \vee \sim \sim q) \cdot r)$
CKqrs	$((q \cdot r) \supset s)$
CrCpNt	$(r \supset (p \supset \sim t))$
$\overline{ANts}$	$\overline{(\sim t \vee s)}$

SECTION 12. Additional transformation-rules

12.1 Now that you have seen how the basic transformation-rules work, we will use them to prove some additional transformation-rules. These additional rules will be useful in working out more complicated problems, even though the only rules absolutely necessary are among the basic twelve. The point of having more rules is merely to make proving (and analyzing) shorter and easier. In order to think logically, you must know the basic rules. The more additional rules you learn, however, the easier your thinking will become.

12.1.1 Preliminary exercise

The rules proven in this section are listed below. Before you read the section, try to analyze and prove them. If you have mastered the previous sections, you shouldn't have much trouble with these. Their proofs are easy: A good way of learning, that is, studying, the skills you need to learn to do a demonstration is this: first try to do the demonstration without looking at the example in the book. Then if you can't do the demonstration, read through the example in the book, put the book aside, and try to do the demonstration again. Repeat this procedure over and over again until you can do the proof without referring to the book. Then go on to the next rule. You should use this method not only in this section but in sections 15 and 16 too.

(1) modus tollens (m.t.)

Cpq	$(p \supset q)$
Nq	$\sim q$
$\overline{Np}$	$\overline{\sim p}$

(2) hypothetical syllogism (h.s.)

Cpq	$(p \supset q)$
Cqr	$(q \supset r)$
$\overline{Cpr}$	$\overline{(p \supset r)}$

(3) constructive dilemma (c.d.)

$KCpsCqt$	Cps		$((p \supset s) \cdot (q \supset t))$	$(p \supset s)$
Apq	or Cqt		$(p \vee q)$	or $(q \supset t)$
$\overline{Ast}$	Apq		$\overline{(s \vee t)}$	$(p \vee q)$
	$\overline{Ast}$			$\overline{(s \vee t)}$

(4) commutation (comm.)

$$\frac{Apq}{Aqp} \text{ and } \frac{Aqp}{Apq} \qquad\qquad \frac{(p \vee q)}{(q \vee p)} \text{ and } \frac{(q \vee p)}{(p \vee q)}$$

(5) association (assoc.)

$$\frac{ApAqr}{AApqr} \text{ and } \frac{AApqr}{ApAqr} \qquad\qquad \frac{(p \vee (q \vee r))}{((p \vee q) \vee r)} \text{ and } \frac{((p \vee q) \vee r)}{(p \vee (q \vee r))}$$

12.2 Modus tollens (m.t.)

Transformation-rule

1. Cpq		$(p \supset q)$
Nq		$\sim q$
$\overline{Np}$		$\overline{\sim p}$

Strategy   The only way to prove this is to use negative absurdity, for if you assume p, you can get q from the first premise by modus ponens. But q and its negation (the second premise) together are logically absurd. So the negation of the assumption p follows.

Demonstration

1. Cpq	$(p \supset q)$	given
2. Nq	$\sim q$	given
$\overline{Np}$	$\overline{\sim p}$	to be proved
3. $\ulcorner p$	$\ulcorner p$	assumed
4. $\quad q$	$\quad q$	from 1, 3; m.p.
5. $\quad KqNq$	$\quad (q \cdot \sim q)$	from 2, 4; conj.
6. Np	$\sim p$	from 3-5; neg. abs.

Now that this transformation-rule has been proven, it can be used in any of the proofs that come later in this book. This rule is to be used exactly like the others: it is completely general, that is, the letters p and q stand for any well-formed formula. Any well-formed formula can serve as a substitute for these letters, but the same substitute must be put everywhere the letter being substituted for appears. Of course, all of the transformation-rules presented in this section can be used after they have been proven. All transformation-rules work in exactly the same way as the basic twelve.

12.3 Hypothetical syllogism (h.s.)

Transformation-rule

1. Cpq	$(p \supset q)$
2. Cqr	$(q \supset r)$
Cpr	$(p \supset r)$

Strategy Since the conclusion is a conditional statement, you must use the rule of assumption in this proof. To use it, you must assume p and derive r. This is easy enough, for when you assume p, you can get q from the first premise. When you get q, you can get r from the second. Then all you need to do is discharge the assumption.

Demonstration

1. Cpq	$(p \supset q)$		given
2. Cqr	$(q \supset r)$		given
Cpr	$(p \supset r)$		to be proved
3. $\ulcorner p$	$\ulcorner p$		assumed
4. $\quad q$	$\quad q$		1, 3; m.p.
5. $\llcorner r$	$\llcorner r$		2, 4; m.p.
6. Cpr	$(p \supset r)$		3-5; assump.

12.4 Constructive dilemma (c.d.)

Transformation-rule

1. Cps	$(p \supset s)$		
2. Cqt or $KCpsCqt$	$(q \supset t)$ or $((p \supset s) \cdot (q \supset t))$		
3. Apq $\quad Apq$	$(p \vee q)$ $\quad (p \vee q)$		
Ast $\quad Ast$	$(s \vee t)$ $\quad (s \vee t)$		

Strategy Because one premise is an alternation, you must use the law of cases to prove this rule. So you assume p, derive s by modus ponens, and then derive the conclusion by addition. Next assume q, derive t by modus ponens, and then derive the conclusion again by addition. Since you can prove the conclusion from both alternatives, you can write it. (The alternate statement of the rule merely requires two uses of simplification in its proof.)

Demonstration

1. Cps	$(p \supset s)$	given
2. Cqt	$(q \supset t)$	given
3. Apq	$(p \lor q)$	given
$\overline{Ast}$	$\overline{(s \lor t)}$	to be proved
4. $\ulcorner p$	$\ulcorner p$	assumed
5. $\;\; s$	s	4, 1; m.p.
6. $\llcorner Ast$	$(s \lor t)$	5; add.
7. $\ulcorner q$	$\ulcorner q$	assumed
8. $\;\; t$	t	7, 2; m.p.
9. $\llcorner Ast$	$(s \lor t)$	8; add.
Ast	$(s \lor t)$	6, 9; cases

12.5 Commutation (comm.)

Transformation-rule

1. Apq	$(p \lor q)$	
$\overline{Aqp}$	$\overline{(q \lor p)}$	

Strategy Since this rule has an alternation as its only premise, only the rule of cases can be used to prove it. So you first assume p and derive the conclusion by addition; then you assume q and also derive the conclusion by addition.

Demonstration

1. Apq	$(p \lor q)$	given
$\overline{Aqp}$	$\overline{(q \lor p)}$	to be proved
2. $\ulcorner p$	$\ulcorner p$	assumed
3. $\llcorner Aqp$	$\llcorner (q \lor p)$	2; add.
4. $\ulcorner q$	$\ulcorner q$	assumed
5. $\llcorner Aqp$	$\llcorner (q \lor p)$	4; add.
6. Aqp	$(q \lor p)$	3, 5; cases

12.6 Commutation (comm.)

Transformation-rule

1. Aqp	$(q \lor p)$	
$\overline{Apq}$	$\overline{(p \lor q)}$	

Strategy This proof goes just like the previous one, except that there is a q in this one everywhere there is a p in the other and there is a p in this one everywhere there is a q in the other.

SECTION 12. Additional transformation-rules

12.7 Association (assoc.)

Transformation-rule

$$1. \quad \frac{ApAqr}{AApqr} \qquad \left\| \quad \frac{(p \vee (q \vee r))}{((p \vee (q \vee r))} \right.$$

Strategy   The premise of this rule also is an alternation, so the rule of cases must be used. But you must use it twice, for one of the alternatives is itself an alternation:

Demonstration

1.	$ApAqr$	$(p \vee (q \vee r))$	given
	$AApqr$	$((p \vee q) \vee r)$	to be proved
2.	$\ulcorner p$	$\ulcorner p$	assumed
3.	$\quad Apq$	$\quad (p \vee q)$	2; add.
4.	$\quad AApqr$	$\quad ((p \vee q) \vee r$	3; add.
5.	$\ulcorner Aqr$	$\ulcorner (q \vee r)$	assumed
6.	$\quad \ulcorner q$	$\quad \ulcorner q$	assumed
7.	$\quad\quad Apq$	$\quad\quad (p \vee q)$	6; add.
8.	$\quad\quad AApqr$	$\quad\quad ((p \vee q) \vee r$	7; add.
9.	$\quad \ulcorner r$	$\quad \ulcorner r$	assumed
10.	$\quad\quad AApqr$	$\quad\quad ((p \vee q) \vee r)$	9; add.
11.	$\quad AApqr$	$\quad ((p \vee q) \vee r$	8, 10; cases
12.	$AApqr$	$((p \vee q) \vee r)$	4, 11; cases

The only things about this proof that may seem confusing are (1) why lines 4, 8, 10, 11, and 12 have the same formula written on them and (2) how addition is used to go from line 9 to line 10. The reason for the first is that lines 5–11 are by themselves a complete example of the use of the rule of cases. But since line 5 is itself only one alternative of a larger alternation, lines 5–11 are also only part of a use of the rule of cases. Line 10, on the other hand, follows from line 9 by addition, because the formula

$$Apq \qquad \left\| \quad (p \vee q) \right.$$

is a substitute for q and r is a substitute for p in

$$\frac{p}{Aqp} \qquad \left\| \quad \frac{p}{(q \vee p)} \right.$$

Transformation-rule

$$
\begin{array}{c|c}
1.\ \dfrac{A\,Apqr}{ApAqr} & \dfrac{((p \lor q) \lor r)}{p \lor (q \lor r)}
\end{array}
$$

Strategy   This rule must be proven like the last one. You must use the rule of cases twice.

Demonstration

1.	$A\,Apqr$	$((p \lor q) \lor r)$	given
	$ApAqr$	$(p \lor (q \lor r))$	to be proved
2.	$\vdash Apq$	$\vdash (p \lor q)$	assumed
3.	$\vdash p$	$\vdash p$	assumed
4.	$ApAqr$	$(p \lor (q \lor r))$	3; add.
5.	$\vdash q$	$\vdash q$	assumed
6.	Aqr	$(q \lor r)$	5; add.
7.	$ApAqr$	$(p \lor (q \lor r))$	6; add.
8.	$ApAqr$	$(p \lor (q \lor r))$	4, 7; cases.
9.	$\vdash r$	$\vdash r$	assumed
10.	Aqr	$(q \lor r)$	9; add.
11.	$ApAqr$	$(p \lor (q \lor r))$	10; add.
12.	$ApAqr$	$(p \lor (q \lor r))$	8, 11; cases

12.8.0 Exercise

Memorize the proofs for the following transformation-rules:
modus tollens
hypothetical syllogism
constructive dilemma
a rule of commutation
a rule of association

12.8.1 Exercise

Write a paragraph telling how to demonstrate the following additional transformation-rules and then demonstrate them.

(1) Repetition (rep.)

$$\frac{p}{p}$$

(2) Commutation (comm.)

$$\frac{Kpq}{Kqp} \qquad \qquad \Big\| \qquad \frac{(p \cdot q)}{(q \cdot p)}$$

and

$$\frac{Kqp}{Kpq} \qquad \qquad \Big\| \qquad \frac{(q \cdot p)}{(p \cdot q)}$$

(3) Association (assoc.)

$$\frac{KpKqr}{KKpqr} \qquad \qquad \Big\| \qquad \frac{(p \cdot (q \cdot r))}{((p \cdot q) \cdot r)}$$

and

$$\frac{KKpqr}{KpKqr} \qquad \qquad \Big\| \qquad \frac{((p \cdot q) \cdot r)}{(p \cdot (q \cdot r))}$$

(4) Assertion (assert.)

$$\frac{p}{CCpqq} \qquad \qquad \Big\| \qquad \frac{p}{((p \supset q) \supset q)}$$

(5) Absorption (abs.)

$$\frac{Cpq}{CpKpq} \qquad \qquad \Big\| \qquad \frac{(p \supset q)}{(p \supset (p \cdot q))}$$

(6) Simple Constructive Dilemma (s.c.d.)

$$\frac{\begin{matrix} Cpr \\ Cqr \\ Apq \end{matrix}}{r} \qquad \qquad \Big\| \qquad \frac{\begin{matrix} (p \supset r) \\ (q \supset r) \\ (p \vee q) \end{matrix}}{r}$$

(7) Exportation (exp.)

$$\frac{CKpqr}{CpCqr} \qquad \qquad \Big\| \qquad \frac{((p \cdot q) \supset r)}{(p \supset (q \supset r))}$$

(8) Importation (imp.)

$$\frac{CpCqr}{CKpqr} \qquad \qquad \Big\| \qquad \frac{(p \supset (q \supset r))}{((p \cdot q) \supset r)}$$

12.8.2 Exercise

(1) Take the rules of modus tollens, assertion, and absorption. Substitute q for p and p for q in these rules.

(2) Take the rules of hypothetical syllogism and simple constructive dilemma. In them substitute

$$Cpq \qquad \| \qquad (p \supset q)$$

for p,

$$Cpr \qquad \| \qquad (p \supset r)$$

for q, and

$$Cps \qquad \| \qquad (p \supset s)$$

for r.

(3) In the rule of repetition, substitute

$$KKpAqrNq \qquad \| \qquad ((p \cdot (q \vee r)) \cdot \sim q)$$

for p.

(4) In the rule of constructive dilemma, substitute

$$Kpq \qquad \| \qquad (p \cdot q)$$

for p,

$$Apq \qquad \| \qquad (p \vee q)$$

for q,

$$Cpq \qquad \| \qquad (p \supset q)$$

for r, and

$$Epq \qquad \| \qquad (p \equiv q)$$

for s.

(5) In the two rules of commutation and the two rules of association, substitute

$$CCpqq \qquad \| \qquad ((p \supset q) \supset q)$$

for q.

12.8.3 Exercise

Which of the rules proved in this section, including the exercises, can be used as replacement-rules? Why?

12.8.4 Exercise

(1) Take the rules of constructive dilemma. Replace the second premise and a variable in the conclusion.

(2) Look at the following argument-form:

$$CpNNCqr \qquad\qquad\qquad\| \qquad (p \supset \sim\sim (q \supset r))$$
$$KqKps \qquad\qquad\qquad\qquad\quad (q \cdot (p \cdot s))$$
$$\overline{NNr} \qquad\qquad\qquad\qquad\qquad \overline{\sim\sim r}$$

(a) Replace the consequent of the first premise.
(b) Replace the second premise.
(c) Replace the first conjunct of the formula that you get by replacing the second premise.
(d) Replace the conclusion.
(e) Take what you now have and in three steps prove the new conclusion.

(3) Can you replace the consequent of

$$CpCpKqr \qquad\qquad\qquad\| \qquad (p \supset (p \supset (q \cdot r)))$$

(4) Can you replace

$$CpCpKqr \qquad\qquad\qquad\| \qquad (p \supset (p \supset (q \cdot r)))$$

(5) Can you replace the consequent of

$$CpCKpqr \qquad\qquad\qquad\| \qquad (p \supset ((p \cdot q) \supset r))$$

(6) Can you replace the second p in

$$CpCKpqr \qquad\qquad\qquad\| \qquad (p \supset ((p \cdot q) \supset r))$$

(7) Can you replace the antecedent of the consequent of

$$CpCKpqr \qquad\qquad\qquad\| \qquad (p \supset ((p \cdot q) \supset r))$$

by using commutation and double negation?

(8) Take the formula

$$AKKpqrAqAApqr \qquad\qquad\| \qquad (((p \cdot q) \cdot r) \vee (q \vee ((p \vee q) \vee r)))$$

(a) Use commutation to replace

Kpq $\parallel$ $(p \cdot q)$

(b) Take what you get, and replace the first alternative, using associ-ation.

(c) Take what you now have, and replace the second q.

(d) Take what you now have, and replace the second alternative of the second alternative, using association.

(e) Now take the formula you have and commute it.

12.8.5 Exercise

Make up a substitution-instance for each transformation-rule presented in this chapter.

12.9 Second Summary of Rules

Transformation-rules	*Replacement-rules*
1. Conjunction	1. Material Equivalence
2. Simplification	2. Double Negation
3. Assumption	3. Commutation (2)
4. Modus Ponens	4. Association (2)
5. Addition	5. Exportation-Importation
6. Cases	
7. Negative Absurdity	
8. Positive Absurdity	
9. Modus Tollens	
10. Hypothetical Syllogism	
11. Constructive Dilemma	
12. Repetition	
13. Assertion	
14. Absorption	
15. Simple Constructive Dilemma	

You may use any of the above named rules in what follows.

SECTION 13. Proving tautological formulas

13.1   All transformation-rules (except those like assumption, cases, and negative absurdity which we represent by schemata) can be associated with tautological, conditional statements or logical equivalences. In other words, sometimes the rules are written as formulas rather than as argument-forms, and you can prove these formulas to be laws of logic in much the same way that you have been using to prove them as argument-forms. There is a slight difference, however, for when rules are written as formulas, you have no given premises to work from. To learn how to prove rules when they are written as formulas, you have to learn two techniques: one for tautological, conditional statements and another for logical equivalences.

13.2 Suppose, for example, you are asked to prove the formula

$$\overline{CpCCpqq} \qquad \Big\| \qquad \overline{(p \supset ((p \supset q) \supset q))}$$

(which you may recognize as another way of writing the law of assertion). How would you go about proving it? The method is very simple. You treat the formula exactly like any other argument-form that has a conditional statement as the conclusion. In other words, you would use the rule of assumption, assume the antecedent of the formula, and derive the consequent. For instance, in this case, you would begin by assuming

1. $\ulcorner p$ $\qquad \Big\| \qquad \ulcorner p$ $\qquad\qquad$ assumed

Now since the consequent is

$$CCpqq \qquad \Big\| \qquad ((p \supset q) \supset q)$$

which is another conditional statement, you can also assume its antecedent. This then gives you two lines to work from:

1. $\ulcorner p$ $\qquad\qquad \Big\| \qquad \ulcorner p$ $\qquad\qquad\qquad$ assumed
2. $\ulcorner Cpq$ $\qquad\qquad \ulcorner (p \supset q)$ $\qquad\qquad$ assumed

Now you can get q by modus ponens, and then you can discharge both of the assumptions. The complete proof looks like this:

	$\overline{CpCCpqq}$	$\overline{(p \supset ((p \supset q) \supset q))}$	to be proved
1.	$\ulcorner p$	$\ulcorner p$	assumed
2.	$\ulcorner Cpq$	$\ulcorner (p \supset q)$	assumed
3.	q	q	1, 2; m.p.
4.	$CCpqq$	$((p \supset q) \supset q)$	2–3; assump.
5.	$CpCCpqq$	$(p \supset ((p \supset q) \supset q))$	1–4; assump.

All transformation-rules when they are written as tautological, conditional statements can be proven in this way.

13.3 Two tautological statements can be gotten from any logical equivalence by applying the rules of material equivalence and simplification. So if you are called upon to prove a logical equivalence, you must first prove each of the tautological, conditional statements you can get from it, and finally, use the (converse) rule of material equivalence. For instance, suppose you are asked to prove the formula

$$\overline{ECKpqrCpCqr} \qquad \| \qquad \overline{(((p \cdot q) \supset r) \equiv (p \supset (q \supset r)))}$$

which is another way of writing the combined laws of exportation-importation and which is usually called the law of exportation. By using the method explained in the last paragraph, you first prove

$$CCKpqrCpCqr \qquad \| \qquad (((p \cdot q) \supset r) \supset (p \supset (q \supset r)))$$

Then, again using the same method, you prove

$$CCpCqrCKpqr \qquad \| \qquad ((p \supset (q \supset r)) \supset ((p \cdot q) \supset r))$$

Next, you use the (converse) rule of material equivalence to get the logical equivalence you set out to prove. The complete proof follows:

	$ECKpqrCpCqr$	to be proved
1.	$CKpqr$	assumed
2.	p	assumed
3.	q	assumed
4.	Kpq	2, 3; conj.
5.	r	1, 4; m.p.
6.	Cqr	3–5; assump.
7.	$CpCqr$	2–6; assump.
8.	$CCKpqrCpCqr$	1–7; assump.
9.	$CpCqr$	assumed
10.	Kpq	assumed
11.	p	10; simp.
12.	Cqr	11, 9; m.p.
13.	q	10; simp.
14.	r	12, 13; m.p.
15.	$CKpqr$	10–14; assump.
16.	$CCpCqrCKpqr$	9–15; assump.
17.	$ECKpqrCpCqr$	16; m.e.

$$\overline{(((p \cdot q) \supset r) \equiv (p \supset (q \supset r)))}$$ to be proved

1.	$\ulcorner ((p \cdot q) \supset r)$	assumed
2.	$\ulcorner p$	assumed
3.	$\ulcorner q$	assumed
4.	$(p \cdot q)$	2, 3; conj.
5.	r	1, 4; m.p.
6.	$(q \supset r)$	3–5; assump.
7.	$(p \supset (q \supset r))$	2–6; assump.
8.	$(((p \cdot q) \supset r) \supset (p \supset (q \supset r)))$	1–7; assump.
9.	$\ulcorner (p \supset (q \supset r))$	assumed
10.	$\ulcorner (p \cdot q)$	assumed
11.	p	10; simp.
12.	$(q \supset r)$	11, 9; m.p.
13.	q	10; simp.
14.	r	12, 13; m.p.
15.	$((p \cdot q) \supset r)$	10–14; assump.
16.	$(((p \supset (q \supset r)) \supset ((p \cdot q) \supset r)))$	9–15; assump.
17.	$(((p \cdot q) \supset r) \equiv (p \supset (q \supset r)))$	16; m.e.

13.3.1 Exercise

Prove that the following formulas are laws of logic.

(1) $CqCpq$	$(q \supset (p \supset q))$
(2) $CCpCpqCpq$	$((p \supset (p \supset q)) \supset (p \supset q))$
(3) $CpCNpq$	$(p \supset (\sim p \supset q))$
(4) $CCpqCArpArq$	$((p \supset q) \supset ((r \vee p) \supset (r \vee q)))$
(5) $CqEKpqp$	$(q \supset ((p \cdot q) \equiv p))$
(6) $EKCprCqrCApqr$	$(((p \supset r) \cdot (q \supset r)) \equiv ((p \vee q) \supset r))$
(7) $ECpqEKpqp$	$((p \supset q) \equiv ((p \cdot q) \equiv p))$
(8) $ECpqEApqq$	$((p \supset q) \equiv ((p \vee q) \equiv q))$
(9) $ECpEqrEKpqKpr$	$((p \supset (q \equiv r)) \equiv ((p \cdot q) \equiv (p \cdot r)))$
(10) $ECpCqrCqCpr$	$((p \supset (q \supset r)) \equiv (q \supset (p \supset r)))$

SECTION 14. The laws of thought

14.1   The rules that you can now use enable you to prove three formulas that are sometimes called the laws of thought. Individually, they are called the principle of identity, the principle of excluded middle, and the principle of non-contradiction.

14.2 The first of these—the principle of identity—is simply this:

$$\overline{Cpp} \qquad \| \qquad \overline{(p \supset p)}$$

Since it is a conditional statement, it can be proven by using assumption and repetition:

1.	$\ulcorner p$	$\ulcorner p$	assumed
2.	$\llcorner p$	$\llcorner p$	1; rep.
3.	Cpp	$(p \supset p)$	1–2; assump.

This principle, as you may have noticed, is the tautological, conditional statement that goes with the rule of repetition; so whenever you use that rule, you are in fact using this principle.

14.3 The second law of thought—the principle of excluded middle—looks like this:

$$\overline{ApNp} \qquad \| \qquad \overline{(p \lor \sim p)}$$

This law is perhaps the most useful of the three. To prove it you use this strategy: Because the formula has no premises, you must assume something (in order to have something to work on). But only two of the basic rules begin with assumptions and no new rules have been introduced that do. So the rule you have to use must be either assumption or negative absurdity. Assumption, however, only allows you to derive conditional statements. Since this formula is an alternation, you must therefore use the negative rule of absurdity. In fact, you must use it twice:

1.	$\ulcorner NApNp$	$\ulcorner \sim (p \lor \sim p)$	assumed
2.	$\ulcorner p$	$\ulcorner p$	assumed
3.	$ApNp$	$(p \lor \sim p)$	2; add.
4.	$KApNpNApNp$	$((p \lor \sim p) \cdot \sim (p \lor \sim p))$	3, 1; conj.
5.	Np	$\sim p$	2–4; neg. abs.
6.	$ApNp$	$(p \lor \sim p)$	5; add.
7.	$KApNpNApNp$	$((p \lor \sim p) \cdot \sim (p \lor \sim p))$	6, 1; conj.
8.	$NNApNp$	$\sim \sim (p \lor \sim p)$	1–7; neg. abs.
9.	$ApNp$	$(p \lor \sim p)$	8; d.n.

The reason that you must use negative absurdity twice in this demonstration is easily seen. Line 1, although it is something to work with, doesn't fit any of the rules you have to work with so far except double negation. You need something else to work with too. This means that you must also assume something else. Since what we want to derive is

$$ApNp \qquad \| \qquad (p \lor \sim p)$$

so that it and the formula on line 1 together are logically absurd, you must derive either p or its negation. But you can do this by assuming either p or its negation and using the negative rule of absurdity again.

14.3.1 Exercise

(1) Prove the principle of excluded middle by assuming the negation of p where p was assumed in the preceding paragraph.
(2) The principle of identity can also be proven by using the negative rule of absurdity. Prove it this way.

14.4   Finally, the law of non-contradiction goes

$$\overline{NKpNp} \qquad \| \qquad \overline{\sim(p \cdot \sim p)}$$

It must also be proven by using the negative rule of absurdity, but you'll need the positive rule of absurdity too:

1. ⌐$KpNp$	⌐$(p \cdot \sim p)$	assumed
2. q	q	1; pos. abs.
3. Nq	$\sim q$	1; pos. abs.
4. $NKpNp$	$\sim(p \cdot \sim p)$	1–3; neg. abs.

14.5   The usefulness of the principle of identity has already been explained, since it goes with the rule of repetition. But what use have the other two laws of thought? Both are tautological, so you can never go wrong by using them. To see how they are useful, look at the following argument-form:

1. Cpq	$(p \supset q)$
2. $CNpq$	$(\sim p \supset q)$
q	q

If you remember the rules you have already proven, you should see that this argument-form looks a lot like the rule of simple constructive dilemma. Only the premise that is an alternation is missing. If it were present, it would have to be

$$ApNp \qquad \| \qquad (p \lor \sim p)$$

But since this formula is the principle of excluded middle, you can use it as line 3 to then get q by simple constructive dilemma. You can justify line 3 by merely writing 'excluded-middle' or an abbreviation for it.

14.6 The use of the principle of non-contradiction can be illustrated in a similar way. In subsection 9.9, which explained why the negative rule of absurdity always works, the following illustration was used. Suppose that you assume a formula

$$\ulcorner p \qquad\qquad \| \qquad\qquad \ulcorner p$$

and eventually derive a logical absurdity from it.

$$\left\lfloor \begin{array}{l} \cdot \\ \cdot \\ \cdot \\ KqNq \end{array} \right. \qquad\qquad \| \qquad\qquad \left\lfloor \begin{array}{l} \cdot \\ \cdot \\ \cdot \\ (q \cdot \sim q) \end{array} \right.$$

By the rule of assumption, you can write

$$CpKqNq \qquad\qquad \| \qquad\qquad (p \supset (q \cdot \sim q))$$

Now suppose for the moment that you were not allowed to use the negative rule of absurdity. Since you can now use modus tollens, and since you know that formulas like

$$NKqNq \qquad\qquad \| \qquad\qquad \sim(q \cdot \sim q)$$

are tautological, you can set up this argument-form:

$$\begin{array}{l} CpKqNq \\ \underline{NKqNq} \\ Np \end{array} \qquad\qquad \| \qquad\qquad \begin{array}{l} (p \supset (q \cdot \sim q)) \\ \underline{\sim(q \cdot \sim q)} \\ \sim p \end{array}$$

In other words, you can use the rules of assumption and modus tollens, and the principle of non-contradiction to prove the negative rule of absurdity.

14.6.1 Exercise

By using the rule of assumption and the rule of simple constructive dilemma, prove the rule of cases.

14.6.2 Exercise

Take the principle of identity. Then first making the proper substitutions and next the appropriate replacements, turn it into the tautological, conditional statements that go with the following transformation-rules:
(1)   converse material equivalence

(2) material equivalence
(3) converse double negation
(4) double negation
(5) the four rules of commutation
(6) the four rules of association
(7) exportation
(8) importation

14.7   The point of this section is this: if you can prove that something is tautological, you can use it either as a transformation-rule or as a line in any proof. Of course, unless you need to use a tautology that is familiar, chances are that you will not recognize the tautologies that you need without proving them. The principle of excluded middle and the principle of non-contradiction are so familiar to anyone who has studied logic, however, that there is no reason why they should not be used whenever they can be.

14.8 Third Summary of Rules and Principles

Transformation-rules	*Replacement-rules*	*Principles*
1. Conjunction	1. Material Equiva-lence	1. Identity
2. Simplification		2. Excluded Middle
3. Assumption	2. Double Negation	3. Non-contradiction
4. Modus Ponens	3. Commutation (2)	
5. Addition	4. Association(2)	
6. Cases	5. Exportation-Im-portation	
7. Negative Absurdity		
8. Positive Absurdity		
9. Modus Tollens		
10. Hypothetical Syllogism		
11. Constructive Dilemma		
12. Repetition		
13. Assertion		
14. Absorption		
15. Simple Constructive Dilemma		

You may use any of the above named rules and principles in what follows.

15.1   In this section, we will use the rules (and principles) that have already been proven to prove a final group of transformation-rules. The purpose of this section is twofold: to acquaint you with some more rules that will make analyzing arguments and proving their conclusions easier and to illustrate for you the many proof techniques that you must master if you are to be able to use your knowledge skillfully. Again, the more of the following rules and proof techniques you learn, the easier your thinking will be.

15.1.1 Preliminary exercise

The rules proven in this section are listed below. Before you read through their proofs, try to analyze and prove them yourself. If, after studying them, you think you can prove any of them, write out a strategy for each proof and then write out the proofs to make sure you have not made any errors in your analyses. Again, to learn the skills needed to prove these, you should first try to prove them by yourself. If you cannot prove them, read the proofs in the book, put the book aside, and try the proofs again. Repeat this procedure until you can prove every transformation-rule listed in this paragraph without having to refer to the book. Prove these transformation-rules in the order that they are given in, for after they are proven in the book, they are used in subsequent proofs.

(1)   disjunctive syllogism (d.s.)

$$\frac{Apq}{q} \quad \text{or} \quad \frac{Apq}{p} \qquad \Bigg\| \quad \frac{(p \vee q)}{q} \quad \text{or} \quad \frac{(p \vee q)}{p}$$
$$\frac{Np}{} \qquad \frac{Nq}{} \qquad \qquad \frac{\sim p}{} \qquad \frac{\sim q}{}$$

(2)   transposition (trans.)

$$\frac{Cpq}{CNqNp} \quad \text{and} \quad \frac{CNqNp}{Cpq} \qquad \Bigg\| \quad \frac{(p \supset q)}{(\sim q \supset \sim p)} \quad \text{and} \quad \frac{(\sim q \supset \sim p)}{(p \supset q)}$$

(3)   material implication (m.i.)

$$\frac{Cpq}{ANpq} \quad \text{and} \quad \frac{ANpq}{Cpq} \qquad \Bigg\| \quad \frac{(p \supset q)}{(\sim p \vee q)} \quad \text{and} \quad \frac{(\sim p \vee q)}{(p \supset q)}$$

(4)   De Morgan's laws (d.m.)

$$\frac{Kpq}{NANpNq} \quad \text{and} \quad \frac{NANpNq}{Kpq} \qquad \Bigg\| \quad \frac{(p \cdot q)}{\sim(\sim p \vee \sim q)} \quad \text{and} \quad \frac{\sim(\sim p \vee \sim q)}{(p \cdot q)}$$

$$\frac{Apq}{NKNpNq} \quad \text{and} \quad \frac{NKNpNq}{Apq} \qquad \Bigg\| \quad \frac{(p \vee q)}{\sim(\sim p \cdot \sim q)} \quad \text{and} \quad \frac{\sim(\sim p \cdot \sim q)}{(p \vee q)}$$

(5) distribution (dist.)

$$\frac{ApKqr}{KApqApr} \text{ and } \frac{KApqApr}{ApKqr} \quad \bigg\| \quad \frac{(p \lor (q \cdot r))}{((p \lor q) \cdot (p \lor r))} \text{ and } \frac{((p \lor q) \cdot (p \lor r))}{(p \lor (q \cdot r))}$$

$$\frac{KpAqr}{AKpqKpr} \text{ and } \frac{AKpqKpr}{KpAqr} \quad \bigg\| \quad \frac{(p \cdot (q \lor r))}{((p \cdot q) \lor (p \cdot r))} \text{ and } \frac{((p \cdot q) \lor (p \cdot r))}{(p \cdot (q \lor r))}$$

$$\frac{CpKqr}{KCpqCpr} \text{ and } \frac{KCpqCpr}{CpKqr} \quad \bigg\| \quad \frac{(p \supset (q \cdot r))}{((p \supset q) \cdot (p \supset r))} \text{ and } \frac{((p \supset q) \cdot (p \supset r))}{(p \supset (q \cdot r))}$$

15.2 Disjunctive syllogism (d.s.)

Transformation-rule

1. Apq		$(p \lor q)$
2. Np		$\sim p$
q		q

Strategy Because the first premise of this argument-form is an alternation, you must use the rule of cases to prove it. When you assume p, however, this assumption and the second premise will allow you to get q by the positive rule of absurdity; and when you assume q, you can get q by repetition.

Demonstration

1.	Apq	$(p \lor q)$	given
2.	Np	$\sim p$	given
	q	q	to be proved
3.	$\ulcorner p$	$\ulcorner p$	assumed
4.	$KpNp$	$(p \cdot \sim p)$	2, 3; conj.
5.	q	q	4; pos. abs.
6.	$\ulcorner q$	$\ulcorner q$	assumed
7.	q	q	6, repetition
8.	q	q	5, 7; cases

15.3 Alternate disjunctive syllogism (d.s.)

Transformation-rule

1. Apq		$(p \lor q)$
2. Nq		$\sim q$
p		p

Strategy The proof for this version of disjunctive syllogism is identical to the other except that p substitutes for q and *vice versa*.

15.4 Transposition (trans.)

Transformation-rule

1. $\dfrac{Cpq}{CNqNp}$ $\left\|\ \dfrac{(p \supset q)}{(\sim q \supset \sim p)}\right.$

Strategy   Since this conclusion is a conditional statement, you need to use the rule of assumption and modus tollens to prove this transformation-rule:

Demonstration

1.	$\dfrac{Cpq}{CNqNp}$	$\dfrac{(p \supset q)}{(\sim q \supset \sim p)}$	given / to be proved
2.	$\ulcorner Nq$	$\ulcorner \sim q$	assumed
3.	$\lfloor Np$	$\lfloor \sim p$	1, 2; m.t.
4.	$CNqNp$	$(\sim q \supset \sim p)$	2-3; assump.

15.5 (Additional rule of) transposition (trans.)

Transformation-rule

1. $\dfrac{CNqNp}{Cpq}$ $\left\|\ \dfrac{(\sim q \supset \sim p)}{(p \supset q)}\right.$

Strategy   The proof for this is very much like the last except that you must also use double negation:

1.	$\dfrac{CNqNp}{Cpq}$	$\dfrac{(\sim q \supset \sim p)}{(p \supset q)}$	given / to be proved
2.	$\ulcorner p$	$\ulcorner p$	assumed
3.	$\mid NNp$	$\mid \sim \sim p$	2; d.n.
4.	$\mid NNq$	$\mid \sim \sim q$	3, 1; m.t.
5.	$\lfloor q$	$\lfloor q$	4; d.n.
6.	Cpq	$(p \supset q)$	2-5; assump.

15.6 Material implication (m.i.)

Transformation-rule

1. $\dfrac{Cpq}{ANpq}$ $\left\|\ \dfrac{(p \supset q)}{(\sim p \vee q)}\right.$

Strategy   The thing to notice about this conclusion is that it can be gotten from the negation of *p* by addition or from *q* by addition. But

SECTION 15. Additional transformation-rules

neither of these is available. The variable q, however, can be gotten by modus ponens if p is available. So if either p or the negation of p is available, you can get this conclusion. The alternation of p and its negation is the principle of excluded middle, and you know that you can use that. If you add it as line 2, you can use cases to get the conclusion:

Demonstration

1.	Cpq		$(p \supset q)$	given
	$ANpq$		$(\sim p \vee q)$	to be proved
2.	$ApNp$		$(p \vee \sim p)$	excluded-middle
3.	$\lceil p$		$\lceil p$	assumed
4.	$\mid q$		$\mid q$	1, 3; m.p.
5.	$\lfloor ANpq$		$\lfloor (\sim p \vee q)$	4; add.
6.	$\lceil Np$		$\lceil \sim p$	assumed
7.	$\lfloor ANpq$		$\lfloor (\sim p \vee q)$	6; add.
8.	$ANpq$		$(\sim p \vee q)$	5, 7; cases

15.7 (Additional rule of) material implication (m.i.)

Transformation-rule

1.	$ANpq$		$(\sim p \vee q)$
	Cpq		$(p \supset q)$

Strategy   Since the conclusion is a conditional statement, all you need to use is assumption and disjunctive syllogism:

Demonstration

1.	$ANpq$		$(\sim p \vee q)$	given
	Cpq		$(p \supset q)$	to be proved
2.	$\lceil p$		$\lceil p$	assumed
3.	$\mid NNp$		$\mid \sim \sim p$	2; d.n.
4.	$\lfloor q$		$\lfloor q$	3, 1; d.s.
5.	Cpq		$(p \supset q)$	2-4; assump.

15.8 De Morgan's law (d.m.)

Transformation-rule

1.	Kpq		$(p \cdot q)$
	$NANpNq$		$\sim (\sim p \vee \sim q)$

Strategy Because this conclusion is negated, the rule must be proven by using the negative rule of absurdity. Only simplification, disjunctive syllogism, and double negation are also needed.

Demonstration

1.	Kpq	$(p \cdot q)$	given
	$NANpNq$	$\sim(\sim p \lor \sim q)$	to be proved
2.	$\lceil ANpNq$	$\lceil (\sim p \lor \sim q)$	assumed
3.	$\mid p$	p	1; simp.
4.	$\mid NNp$	$\sim\sim p$	3; d.n.
5.	$\mid Nq$	$\sim q$	4, 2; d.s.
6.	$\lfloor q$	q	1; simp.
7.	$NANpNq$	$\sim(\sim p \lor \sim q)$	2-6; neg. abs.

15.9 (Additional) De Morgan's law (d.m.)

Transformation-rule

1.	$NANpNq$	$\sim(\sim p \lor \sim q)$
	Kpq	$(p \cdot q)$

Strategy To prove this conclusion, you must prove p and q separately. But in the premise, both are negated; therefore, you must use the negative rule of absurdity twice to prove it.

Demonstration

1.	$NANpNq$	$\sim(\sim p \lor \sim q)$	given
	Kpq	$(p \cdot q)$	to be proved
2.	$\lceil Np$	$\lceil \sim p$	assumed
3.	$\mid ANpNq$	$(\sim p \lor \sim q)$	2; add.
4.	$\mid KANpNqNANpNq$	$((\sim p \lor \sim q) \cdot$	1, 3; conj.
		$\sim(\sim p \lor \sim q))$	
5.	NNp	$\sim\sim p$	2-4; neg. abs.
6.	p	p	5; d.n.
7.	$\lceil Nq$	$\lceil \sim q$	assumed
8.	$\mid ANpNq$	$(\sim p \lor \sim q)$	7; add.
9.	$\mid KANpNqNANpNq$	$((\sim p \lor \sim q) \cdot$	1, 9; conj.
		$\sim(\sim p \lor \sim q))$	
10.	NNq	$\sim\sim q$	7-9; neg. abs.
11.	q	q	10; d.n.
12.	Kpq	$(p \cdot q)$	6, 11; conj.

SECTION 15. Additional transformation-rules

15.10 (Additional) De Morgan's law (d.m.)

Transformation-rule

1. Apq ‖ $(p \lor q)$
   $NKNpNq$ ‖ $\sim(\sim p \cdot \sim q)$

Strategy　This De Morgan's law is proven very much like the one in 15.8:

Demonstration

1. Apq	‖	$(p \lor q)$	given
$NKNpNq$	‖	$\sim(\sim p \cdot \sim q)$	to be proved
2. $\lceil KNpNq$	‖	$\lceil (\sim p \cdot \sim q)$	assumed
3. $\quad Np$	‖	$\quad \sim p$	2; simp.
4. $\quad q$	‖	$\quad q$	1, 3; d.s.
5. $\quad Nq$	‖	$\quad \sim q$	2; simp.
6. $NKNpNq$	‖	$\sim(\sim p \cdot \sim q)$	2-5; neg. abs.

15.11 (Additional) De Morgan's law (d.m.)

Transformation-rule

1. $NKNpNq$ ‖ $\sim(\sim p \cdot \sim q)$
   Apq ‖ $(p \lor q)$

Strategy　Because this conclusion is an alternation that nothing can be assumed from, and since the premise is not very useful as it stands, you must again use the negative rule of absurdity to prove this rule:

Demonstration

1. $NKNpNq$	‖	$\sim(\sim p \cdot \sim q)$	given
Apq	‖	$(p \lor q)$	to be proved
2. $\lceil NApq$	‖	$\lceil \sim(p \lor q)$	assumed
3. $\quad KNpNq$	‖	$\quad (\sim p \cdot \sim q)$	2; d.m. (from 15.9)
4. $\quad KKNpNqNKNpNq$	‖	$\quad ((\sim p \cdot \sim q) \cdot \sim(\sim p \cdot \sim q))$	1, 3; conj.
5. $NNApq$	‖	$\sim\sim(p \lor q)$	2-4; neg. abs.
6. Apq	‖	$(p \lor q)$	5; d.n.

15.12 Distribution (dist.)

Transformation-rule

1.	$ApKqr$	$(p \vee (q \cdot r))$	given
	$KApqApr$	$((p \vee q) \cdot (p \vee r))$	to be proved
2.	$\neg p$	$\neg p$	assumed
3.	Apq	$(p \vee q)$	2; add.
4.	Apr	$(p \vee r)$	2; add.
5.	$KApqApr$	$((p \vee q) \cdot (p \vee r))$	3, 4; conj.
6.	$\neg Kqr$	$\neg (q \cdot r)$	assumed
7.	q	q	6; simp.
8.	Apq	$(p \vee q)$	7; add.
9.	r	r	6; simp.
10.	Apr	$(p \vee r)$	9; add.
11.	$KApqApr$	$((p \vee q) \cdot (p \vee r))$	8, 10; conj.
12.	$KApqApr$	$((p \vee q) \cdot (p \vee r))$	5, 11; cases

15.13 Distribution (dist.)

Transformation-rule

1.	$KApqApr$	$((p \vee q) \cdot (p \vee r))$
	$ApKqr$	$(p \vee (q \cdot r))$

Strategy   Because this premise is a conjunction of alternations, you can prove this rule by first simplifying and then using the rule of cases twice. It is a difficult proof to see through, for it is not easy to see that the second time you use the rule of cases, you must use it inside the scope of the assumption of the second alternative of the first time you use the rule of cases. To see why you must do this, look at the following: you need

$ApKqr$ $\|$ $(p \vee (q \cdot r))$

which can be gotten from p by addition and from the conjunction of q and r by addition. If you simplify

Apq $\|$ $(p \vee q)$

from the first premise and use the rule of cases on it, you will assume p. And that will give you the conclusion by addition. But you must complete the argument by cases and assume q. You cannot get

$ApKqr$ $\|$ $(p \vee (q \cdot r))$

SECTION 15. Additional transformation-rules

out of q, however, unless you can conjoin it to r. But how can you get r? Only by assuming it as part of another argument by cases that begins from

$Apr \qquad \| \quad (p \lor r)$

Since you must conjoin q and r, however, to be able to get the conclusion of this transformation-rule, the second use of the rule of cases must be done inside the scope of q when it is assumed as the *second* part of the first use of the rule of cases. Once you understand this explanation, you can write out the following proof:

Demonstration

1.	$KApqApr$	$((p \lor q) \cdot (p \lor r))$	given
	$\overline{ApKqr}$	$\overline{(p \lor (q \cdot r))}$	to be proved
2.	Apq	$(p \lor q)$	1; simp.
3.	$\ulcorner p$	$\ulcorner p$	assumed
4.	$\lfloor ApKqr$	$\lfloor (p \lor (q \cdot r))$	3; add.
5.	Apr	$(p \lor r)$	1; simp.
6.	$\ulcorner q$	$\ulcorner q$	assumed
7.	$\quad \ulcorner p$	$\quad \ulcorner p$	assumed
8.	$\quad \lfloor ApKqr$	$\quad \lfloor (p \lor (q \cdot r))$	7; add.
9.	$\quad \ulcorner r$	$\quad \ulcorner r$	assumed
10.	$\quad \mid Kqr$	$\quad \mid (q \cdot r)$	6, 9; conj.
11.	$\quad \lfloor ApKqr$	$\quad \lfloor (p \lor (q \cdot r))$	10; add.
12.	$\lfloor ApKqr$	$\lfloor (p \lor (q \cdot r))$	8, 11; cases
13.	$ApKqr$	$(p \lor (q \cdot r))$	4, 12; cases

15.14 Distribution (dist.)

Transformation-rule

1.	$KpAqr$	$(p \cdot (q \lor r))$
	$\overline{AKpqKpr}$	$\overline{((p \cdot q) \lor (p \cdot r))}$

Strategy   Since the premise of this rule is equivalent to two premises (because it is a conjunction that can be simplified), and since one of the implicit premises is an alternation, you can use cases to prove the rule:

Demonstration

1.	$KpAqr$	$(p \cdot (q \lor r))$	given
	$\overline{AKpqKpr}$	$\overline{((p \cdot q) \lor (p \cdot r))}$	to be proved
2.	p	p	1; simp.
3.	Aqr	$(q \lor r)$	1; simp.

4.	$\ulcorner q$	$\ulcorner q$		assumed
5.	Kpq	$(p \cdot q)$		2, 4; conj.
6.	$AKpqKpr$	$((p \cdot q) \vee (p \cdot r))$		5; add.
7.	$\ulcorner r$	$\ulcorner r$		assumed
8.	Kpr	$(p \cdot r)$		2, 7; conj.
9.	$AKpqKpr$	$((p \cdot q) \vee (p \cdot r))$		8; add.
10.	$AKpqKpr$	$((p \cdot q) \vee (p \cdot r))$		6, 9; cases

15.15 Distribution (dist.)

Transformation-rule

$$1. \quad \frac{AKpqKpr}{KpAqr} \qquad \left\| \quad \frac{((p \cdot q) \vee (p \cdot r))}{(p \cdot (q \vee r))} \right.$$

Strategy Again, since the premise is an alternation, the obvious strategy is to use the rule of cases:

Demonstration

1.	$\dfrac{AKpqKpr}{KpAqr}$	$\dfrac{((p \cdot q) \vee (p \cdot r))}{(p \cdot (q \vee r))}$		given to be proved
2.	$\ulcorner Kpq$	$\ulcorner (p \cdot q)$		assumed
3.	p	p		2; simp.
4.	q	q		2; simp.
5.	Aqr	$(q \vee r)$		4; add.
6.	$KpAqr$	$(p \cdot (q \vee r))$		5, 3; conj.
7.	$\ulcorner Kpr$	$\ulcorner (p \cdot r)$		assumed
8.	p	p		7; simp.
9.	r	r		7; simp.
10.	Aqr	$(q \vee r)$		9; add.
11.	$KpAqr$	$(p \cdot (q \vee r))$		10, 8; conj.
12.	$KpAqr$	$(p \cdot (q \vee r))$		6, 11; cases

15.16 Distribution (dist.)

Transformation-rule

$$1. \quad \frac{CpKqr}{KCpqCpr} \qquad \left\| \quad \frac{(p \supset (q \cdot r))}{((p \supset q) \cdot (p \supset r))} \right.$$

Strategy This rule is most easily proven by using the rule of material implication to change the premise into an alternation and then using the rule of distribution that was proven in subsection 15.12:

91

Demonstration

1. *CpKqr*	$(p \supset (q \cdot r))$	given
$\overline{KCpqCpr}$	$\overline{((p \supset q) \cdot (p \supset r))}$	to be proved
2. *ANpKqr*	$(\sim p \vee (q \cdot r))$	1; m.i.
3. *KANpqANpr*	$((\sim p \vee q) \cdot (\sim p \supset r))$	2; dist. (from 15.12)
4. *KCpqCpr*	$((p \supset q) \cdot (p \supset r))$	3; m.i. (twice)

15.17 Distribution (dist.)

Transformation-rule

1. *KCpqCpr*	$((p \supset q) \cdot (p \supset r))$
$\overline{CpKqr}$	$\overline{(p \supset (q \cdot r))}$

Strategy   The strategy for proving this rule is like the strategy for proving the last, except that you must use the rule of distribution that was proven in subsection 15.13:

Demonstration

1. *KCpqCpr*	$((p \supset q) \cdot (p \supset r))$	given
$\overline{CpKqr}$	$\overline{(p \supset (q \cdot r))}$	to be proved
2. *KANpqANpr*	$((\sim p \vee q) \cdot (\sim p \vee r))$	1; m.i. (twice)
3. *ANpKqr*	$(\sim p \vee (q \cdot r))$	2; dist. (from 15.13)
4. *CpKqr*	$(p \supset (q \cdot r))$	3; m.i.

15.17.0 Exercise

Memorize the proofs of the following transformation-rules:
disjunctive syllogism (15.2)
material implication (15.6)
material implication (15.7)
De Morgan's law (15.8)
De Morgan's law (15.9)
distribution (15.13)
distribution (15.16)

15.17.1 Exercise

Write a paragraph telling how to and then demonstrate the following additional transformation-rules:
(1) Idempotency (id.)

$$\frac{Kpp}{p} \text{ and } \frac{p}{Kpp} \qquad \qquad \left\| \qquad \frac{(p \cdot p)}{p} \text{ and } \frac{p}{(p \cdot p)} \right.$$

$$\frac{App}{p} \text{ and } \frac{p}{App} \qquad \left\| \qquad \frac{(p \lor p)}{p} \text{ and } \frac{p}{(p \lor p)} \right.$$

(2) Commutation (comm.)

$$\frac{Epq}{Eqp} \text{ and } \frac{Eqp}{Epq} \qquad \left\| \qquad \frac{(p \equiv q)}{(q \equiv p)} \text{ and } \frac{(q \equiv p)}{(p \equiv q)} \right.$$

(3) Destructive Dilemma (d.d.)

$$\begin{array}{c} Cpq \\ Crs \\ ANqNs \\ \hline ANpNr \end{array} \qquad \left\| \qquad \begin{array}{c} (p \supset q) \\ (r \supset s) \\ (\sim q \lor \sim s) \\ \hline (\sim p \lor \sim r) \end{array} \right.$$

(4) Distribution (dist.)

$$\frac{ApCqr}{CApqApr} \text{ and } \frac{CApqApr}{ApCqr} \qquad \left\| \qquad \frac{(p \lor (q \supset r))}{((p \lor q) \supset (p \lor r))} \text{ and} \right.$$
$$\frac{((p \lor q) \supset (p \lor r))}{(p \lor (q \supset r))}$$

$$\frac{ApAqr}{AApqApr} \text{ and } \frac{AApqApr}{ApAqr} \qquad \left\| \qquad \frac{(p \lor (q \lor r))}{((p \lor q) \lor (p \lor r))} \text{ and} \right.$$
$$\frac{((p \lor q) \lor (p \lor r))}{(p \lor (q \lor r))}$$

$$\frac{CpAqr}{ACpqCpr} \text{ and } \frac{ACpqCpr}{CpAqr} \qquad \left\| \qquad \frac{(p \supset (q \lor r))}{((p \supset q) \lor (p \supset r))} \text{ and} \right.$$
$$\frac{((p \supset q) \lor (p \supset r))}{(p \supset (q \lor r))}$$

$$\frac{KpKqr}{KKpqKpr} \text{ and } \frac{KKpqKpr}{KpKqr} \qquad \left\| \qquad \frac{(p \cdot (q \cdot r))}{((p \cdot q) \cdot (p \cdot r))} \text{ and} \right.$$
$$\frac{((p \cdot q) \cdot (p \cdot r))}{(p \cdot (q \cdot r))}$$

$$\frac{CpCqr}{CCpqCpr} \text{ and } \frac{CCpqCpr}{CpCqr} \qquad \left\| \qquad \frac{(p \supset (q \supset r))}{((p \supset q) \supset (p \supset r))} \text{ and} \right.$$
$$\frac{((p \supset q) \supset (p \supset r))}{(p \supset (q \supset r))}$$

93

SECTION 15. Additional transformation-rules

$$\frac{ApEqr}{EApqApr} \text{ and } \frac{EApqApr}{ApEqr}$$

$$\frac{(p \lor (q \equiv r))}{((p \lor q) \equiv (p \lor r))} \text{ and}$$

$$\frac{((p \lor q) \equiv (p \lor r))}{(p \lor (q \equiv r))}$$

$$\frac{CpEqr}{ECpqCpr} \text{ and } \frac{ECpqCpr}{CpEqr}$$

$$\frac{(p \supset (q \equiv r))}{((p \supset q) \equiv (p \supset r))} \text{ and}$$

$$\frac{((p \supset q) \equiv (p \supset r))}{(p \supset (q \equiv r))}$$

(5) Alternate material equivalence (m.e.)

$$\frac{Epq}{AKpqKNpNq} \text{ and } \frac{AKpqKNpNq}{Epq}$$

$$\frac{(p \equiv q)}{((p \cdot q) \lor (\sim p \cdot \sim q))} \text{ and}$$

$$\frac{((p \cdot q) \lor (\sim p \cdot \sim q))}{(p \equiv q)}$$

(6) Alternate material implication (m.i.)

$$\frac{Cpq}{NKpNq} \text{ and } \frac{NKpNq}{Cpq}$$

$$\frac{(p \supset q)}{\sim(p \cdot \sim q)} \text{ and } \frac{\sim(p \cdot \sim q)}{(p \supset q)}$$

15.17.2 Exercise

By using the methods explained in section 13, prove the following formulas:

(1) Tautology-elimination (t.e.)

$EKpAqNqp$ $\qquad \| \ ((p \cdot (q \lor \sim q)) \equiv p)$

(2) Absurdity-purification (a.p)

$EKpKqNqKqNq$ $\qquad \| \ ((p \cdot (q \cdot \sim q)) \equiv (q \cdot \sim q))$

(3) Contradiction-elimination (c.e.)

$EApKqNqp$ $\qquad \| \ ((p \lor (q \cdot \sim q)) \equiv p)$

15.17.3 Exercise

Write the transformation-rules that can be gotten from the three laws of logic that are to be proved in subsection 15.17.2.

15.17.4 Exercise

Write out a paragraph telling how to and then demonstrate the following additional laws of logic:

(1) Transitive law of material equivalence (t.m.e.)

$$CKEpqEqrEpr \qquad \| \qquad (((p \equiv q) \cdot (q \equiv r)) \supset (p \equiv r))$$

(2) Association (assoc.)

$$\frac{EpEqr}{EEpqr} \text{ and } \frac{EEpqr}{EpEqr} \qquad \| \qquad \frac{(p \equiv (q \equiv r))}{((p \equiv q) \equiv r)} \text{ and } \frac{((p \equiv q) \equiv r)}{(p \equiv (q \equiv r))}$$

15.17.5 Exercise

(1) Take the rules of disjunctive syllogism, transposition, material implication, De Morgan's laws, tautology-elimination, and absurdity-purification. In each substitute q for p and p for q.

(2) Take the transitive law of material equivalence, the rules of distribution, and the rule of association for material equivalence. In each, substitute

$$Apq \qquad \| \qquad (p \lor q)$$

for p,

$$Nq \qquad \| \qquad \sim q$$

for q, and

$$Kpq \qquad \| \qquad (p \cdot q)$$

for r.

(3) In the rules of idempotency, substitute

$$ApKqr \qquad \| \qquad (p \lor (q \cdot r))$$

for p.

(4) Make up the proper substitutions in the rule of destructive dilemma that are needed to turn it into a simple rule of destructive dilemma.

(5) Make a substitution instance for each of the transformation-rules presented in this section (including the exercises).

15.17.6 Exercise

Which of the rules proved in this section (including the exercises) can be used as replacement-rules? Why?

15.17.7 Exercise

Look at the following two formulas:

$$ApCNqr \qquad\qquad \big\| \qquad\qquad (p \vee (\sim q \supset r))$$
$$KqKrANpNp \qquad\qquad \qquad\qquad (q \cdot (r \cdot (\sim p \vee \sim p)))$$

(a) Replace the second alternative of the first premise by using transposition.

(b) Replace the second conjunct of the second conjunct of the second premise by using idempotency.

(c) From the formulas you now have, derive

$$CNrq \qquad\qquad \big\| \qquad\qquad (\sim r \supset q)$$

(d) Replace this conclusion by using the alternative rule of material implication.

(e) Replace what you now have with another formula by using De Morgan's law.

(f) Use the rule of distribution on each of the two formulas listed above.

(g) Use the rule of association on the second formula listed above.

(h) Use the rule of commutation on each of the two formulas listed above.

(i) Use the rule of double negation on a variable.

(j) Use the rule of double negation on a compound formula.

15.17.8 Exercise

You have proven ten distribution-rules. There are six other formulas that look like the distribution-rules, which, however, cannot be proven. They are:

(1) $EKpCqrCKpqKpr$ $\big\|$ $((p \cdot (q \supset r)) \equiv ((p \cdot q) \supset (p \cdot r)))$

(2) $EKpEqrEKpqKpr$ $((p \cdot (q \equiv r)) \equiv ((p \cdot q) \equiv (p \cdot r)))$

(3) $EEpAqrAEpqEpr$ $((p \equiv (q \vee r)) \equiv ((p \equiv q) \vee (p \equiv r)))$

(4) $EEpKqrKEpqEpr$ $((p \equiv (q \cdot r)) \equiv ((p \equiv q) \cdot (p \equiv r)))$

(5) $EEpCqrCEpqEpr$ $((p \equiv (q \supset r)) \equiv ((p \equiv q) \supset (p \equiv r)))$

(6) $EEpEqrEEpqEpr$ $((p \equiv (q \equiv r)) \equiv ((p \equiv q) \equiv (p \equiv r)))$

Write a paragraph for each of these explaining why they cannot be proven.

Transformation-rules	*Replacement-rules*
1. Conjunction	1. Material Equivalence (2)
2. Simplification	2. Double Negation
3. Assumption	3. Commutation (3)
4. Modus Ponens	4. Association (3)
5. Addition	5. Exportation-Importation
6. Cases	6. Transposition
7. Negative Absurdity	7. Material Implication (2)
8. Positive Absurdity	8. De Morgan's Laws (2)
9. Modus Tollens	9. Distribution (10)
10. Hypothetical Syllogism	10. Idempotency (2)
11. Constructive Dilemma	11. Tautology-Elimination
12. Repetition	12. Absurdity-Purification
13. Assertion	13. Contradiction-Elimination
14. Absorption	
15. Simple Constructive Dilemma	
16. Disjunctive Syllogism	*Principles*
17. Destructive Dilemma	1. Identity
18. Transitive Law of Material Equivalence	2. Excluded Middle
	3. Non-Contradiction

15.19   Although there are fifty-one items on the preceding list, they fall into a small number of neat groups:

(1) Some allow you to introduce truth-functors,
(2) Some allow you to eliminate truth-functors,
(3) Some allow you to change one truth-functor into aonther,
(4) Some allow you to change the order of formulas,
(5) Some allow you to regroup formulas,
(6) Some are what are known as dilemmas,
(7) Some allow you to distribute formulas,
(8) One allows you to repeat a formula,
(9) One allows you to make a connected chain of formulas,
(10) One allows you to eliminate tautological parts of formulas, and
(11) One allows you to eliminate non-absurd parts of logical absurdities.

There is, thus, an appropriate rule for every situation that you are likely to run into. If you have learned these rules, you now have at your fingertips all of the transformation-rules that you are likely to need in order to think logically and evaluate arguments of the kind we are dealing with in this chapter.

16.1 If you have mastered the preceding sections, using the rules to show that the conclusions of the argument-forms presented in this section are connected by laws of logic to the premises of those argument-forms should be very easy. In this section, you will be taught—by a sequence of examples—to use these rules on ordinary argument-forms. In general, this section will be developed like the others that it is similar to. But there is one important difference: Because you have more than twice as many transformation-rules to work with than you ordinarily need, there is more than one way to demonstrate each conclusion. So in trying to demonstrate the conclusions, you may find a proof that is different from the one given in the text. There is nothing wrong with that just as long as you are certain that you have not made any errors in using the rules.

16.1.1 Preliminary exercise

The argument-forms proven in this section are listed below. Analyze each one, and try to write out a paragraph that tells you how to go about proving the conclusion. Work at thinking through the problems rather than at writing down the proofs. Only write down the proof after you have worked out in your head how to go about developing the proof. Remember, the only reason there is for writing down proofs is to check your thinking to be sure that you have used the transformation-rules correctly. The point to learning logic is to learn to think logically rather than to write out proofs. Again, if you are unable to figure out how to prove a conclusion, read through the example in the text, put the book aside, and try to prove the conclusion again. Repeat this procedure for any problems that give you trouble until you can work them without having to refer to the book. When you have mastered the examples, then move on to the exercises at the end of the section.

$$(1) \quad CpCqr$$
$$Nr$$
$$\overline{ANpNq}$$

$$(p \supset (q \supset r))$$
$$\sim r$$
$$\overline{(\sim p \lor \sim q)}$$

$$(2) \quad ANpq$$
$$CNrNq$$
$$\overline{Cpr}$$

$$(\sim p \lor q)$$
$$(\sim r \supset \sim q)$$
$$\overline{(p \supset r)}$$

$$(3) \quad CpKqr$$
$$Nr$$
$$\overline{Np}$$

$$(p \supset (q \cdot r))$$
$$\sim r$$
$$\overline{\sim p}$$

(4) $ANpCqr$ $(\sim p \vee (q \supset r))$
      $KpNr$ $(p \cdot \sim r)$
      $\overline{Nq}$ $\overline{\sim q}$

(5) $KCspCtq$ $((s \supset p) \cdot (t \supset q))$
      Nr $\sim r$
      $CpCqr$ $(p \supset (q \supset r))$
      $\overline{ANsNt}$ $\overline{(\sim s \vee \sim t)}$

(6) $CNKpqKrs$ $(\sim(p \cdot q) \supset (r \cdot s))$
      $CpNp$ $(p \supset \sim p)$
      $\overline{r}$ $\overline{r}$

(7) $CpAqr$ $(p \supset (q \vee r))$
      Nr $\sim r$
      $\overline{CNqNp}$ $\overline{(\sim q \supset \sim p)}$

(8) $CKpqKrs$ $((p \cdot q) \supset (r \cdot s))$
      $NCqr$ $\sim(q \supset r)$
      $\overline{Np}$ $\overline{\sim p}$

(9) Np $\sim p$
      $\overline{EqApq}$ $\overline{(q \equiv (p \vee q))}$

(10) Cpq $(p \supset q)$
       Crs $(r \supset s)$
       Cqt $(q \supset t)$
       $CNuNs$ $(\sim u \supset \sim s)$
       $CtNu$ $(t \supset \sim u)$
       $CNrNp$ $(\sim r \supset \sim p)$
       $\overline{Np}$ $\overline{\sim p}$

16.2 Example 1.

Problem

1. $CpCqr$ $(p \supset (q \supset r))$ given
2. Nr $\sim r$ given
   $\overline{ANpNq}$ $\overline{(\sim p \vee \sim q)}$ to be proved

Strategy You should see immediately that the first premise is a prime candidate for importation. If you import it, it will be another conditional statement, but it will have the conjunction of p and q as its antecedent and r as its consequent. That sets up a modus tollens argument that the negation of the conjunction of p and q follows from. But this negation is equivalent to the conclusion by De Morgan's law:

Demonstration

3. $CKpqr$	$((p \cdot q) \supset r)$	1; imp.
4. $NKpq$	$\sim(p \cdot q)$	2, 3; m.t.
5. $ANpNq$	$(\sim p \lor \sim q)$	4; d.m.

16.3 Example 2.

Problem

1. $ANpq$	$(\sim p \lor q)$	given
2. $CNrNq$	$(\sim r \supset \sim q)$	given
Cpr	$(p \supset r)$	to be proved

Strategy The most natural way to prove this would be to use the rule of assumption. But there is another fairly obvious way too, namely, by using hypothetical syllogism. The first premise can be changed into a conditional statement by using material implication, and the second can be put into the proper order by using transposition:

3. Cpq	$(p \supset q)$	1; m.i.
4. Cqr	$(q \supset r)$	2; trans.
5. Cpr	$(p \supset r)$	3, 4; h.s.

16.4 Example 3.

Problem

1. $CpKqr$	$(p \supset (q \cdot r))$	given
2. Nr	$\sim r$	given
Np	$\sim p$	to be proved

First strategy Since the conclusion is the negated antecedent of the first premise, and since one of the variables in the consequent of that premise is unnecessary, the first premise can be distributed and then simplified. Then modus tollens will give you the conclusion:

Demonstration

3. $KCpqCpr$	$((p \supset q) \cdot (p \supset r))$	1: dist.
4. Cpr	$(p \supset r)$	3; simp.
5. Np	$\sim p$	4, 2; m.t.

Second strategy In order to use modus tollens on the first premise, you can try to make the negation of the consequent out of the second premise. You can do this by using addition and De Morgan's law:

Demonstration

3. *ANqNr*	$(\sim q \lor \sim r)$	2; add.
4. *NKqr*	$\sim(q \cdot r)$	3; d.m.
5. *Np*	$\sim p$	4, 1; m.t.

16.5 Example 4.

Problem

1. *ANpCqr*	$(\sim p \lor (q \supset r))$	given
2. *KpNr*	$(p \cdot \sim r)$	given
Nq	$\sim q$	to be proved

Strategy First find *q* in the premises. It is the antecedent of a conditional statement that is itself part of an alternation. So to prove the conclusion, you must first free the conditional sentence by using disjunctive syllogism and then use modus tollens. To use these, however, you must have *p* and the negation of *r*. They can be simplified from the second premise:

Demonstration

3. *p*	p	2; simp.
4. *NNp*	$\sim \sim p$	3; d.n.
5. *Cqr*	$(q \supset r)$	4, 1; d.s.
6. *Nr*	$\sim r$	2; simp.
7. *Nq*	$\sim q$	5, 6; m.t.

16.6 Example 5.

Problem

1. *KCspCtq*	$((s \supset p) \cdot (t \supset q))$	given
2. *Nr*	$\sim r$	given
3. *CpCqr*	$(p \supset (q \supset r))$	given
ANsNt	$(\sim s \lor \sim t)$	to be proved

Strategy The conclusion and the first premise of this problem should remind you of destructive dilemma. The task then is to try to make the missing part of a destructive dilemma from the second and third premises.

You can do this by using the strategy that you used on the first example:

Demonstration

4. *CKpqr*	$((p \cdot q) \supset r)$	3; imp.
5. *NKpq*	$\sim(p \cdot q)$	2, 4; m.t.
6. *ANpNq*	$(\sim p \vee \sim q)$	5; d.m.
7. *ANsNt*	$(\sim s \vee \sim t)$	6, 1; d.d.

16.7 Example 6.

Problem

1. *CNKpqKrs*	$(\sim(p \cdot q) \supset (r \cdot s))$	given
2. *CpNp*	$(p \supset \sim p)$	given
r	*r*	to be proved

Strategy First find *r* in the premises. It is part of a conjunction—which can always be simplified—that is the consequent of a conditional statement. So you must first free the conjunction by modus ponens. To use modus ponens, however, you must build the antecedent of the first premise from the second premise. This can be done by using material implication, idempotency, addition, and DeMorgan's law:

Demonstration

3. *ANpNp*	$(\sim p \vee \sim p)$	2; m.i.
4. *Np*	$\sim p$	3; idem.
5. *ANpNq*	$(\sim p \vee \sim q)$	4; add.
6. *NKpq*	$\sim(p \cdot q)$	5; d.m.
7. *Krs*	$(r \cdot s)$	6, 1; m.p.
8. *r*	*r*	7; simp.

16.8 Example 7.

Problem

1. *CpAqr*	$(p \supset (q \vee r))$	given
2. *Nr*	$\sim r$	given
CNqNp	$(\sim q \supset \sim p)$	to be proved

Strategy Again it would seem natural enough to use the rule of assumption on this problem. But to begin the proof by assuming the negation of *q* would not be very helpful. So let's try another strategy. First rearrange the first premise to isolate *r*. This can be done by using material implication and association. Then you can use disjunctive syllogism and transposition to get the conclusion:

Demonstration

3. $ANpAqr$	$(\sim p \lor (q \lor r))$	1; m.i.
4. $AANpqr$	$((\sim p \lor q) \lor r)$	3; assoc.
5. $ANpq$	$(\sim p \lor q)$	4, 2; d.s.
6. Cpq	$(p \supset q)$	5; m.i.
7. $CNqNp$	$(\sim q \supset \sim p)$	6; trans.

16.9 Example 8.

Problem

1. $CKpqKrs$	$((p \cdot q) \supset (r \cdot s))$	given
2. $NCqr$	$\sim(q \supset r)$	given
Np	$\sim p$	to be proved

Strategy By distributing the first premise, you can get rid of the superfluous s. What is left can then be rearranged to form a premise that when combined with the second premise is a modus tollens argument:

Demonstration

3. $KCKpqrCKpqs$	$(((p \cdot q) \supset r) \cdot ((p \cdot q) \supset s))$	1; dist.
4. $CKpqr$	$((p \cdot q) \supset r)$	3; simp.
5. $ANKpqr$	$(\sim(p \cdot q) \lor r)$	4; m.i.
6. $AANpNqr$	$((\sim p \lor \sim q) \lor r))$	5; d.m.
7. $ANpANqr$	$(\sim p \lor (\sim q \lor r))$	8, 2; m.t.
8. $CpCqr$	$(p \supset (q \supset r))$	7; m.i.
9. Np	$\sim p$	6; assoc.

16.10 Example 9.

1. Np	$\sim p$	given
$EqApq$	$(q \equiv (p \lor q))$	to be proved

Strategy The key to solving a problem like this is recognition—being able to recognize what you can prove from what is given and being able to see what more is needed. The negation of p is not a very powerful premise, but assertion allows you to prove half of what is needed. If you can recognize that the other half can be proven from the principle of excluded middle, the problem is solved, since you can always use a tautology as a line in a proof:

Demonstration

2. $CCNpqq$	$((\sim p \supset q) \supset q)$	1; assert.
3. $CANNpqq$	$((\sim \sim p \vee q) \supset q)$	2; m.i.
4. $CApqq$	$((p \vee q) \supset q)$	3; d.n.
5. $ANqq$	$(\sim q \vee q)$	ex. mid.
6. $AANqqp$	$((\sim q \vee q) \vee p)$	5; add.
7. $ANqAqp$	$(\sim q \vee (q \vee p))$	6; assoc.
8. $ANqApq$	$(\sim q \vee (p \vee q))$	7; comm.
9. $CqApq$	$(q \supset (p \vee q))$	8; m.i.
10. $EqApq$	$(q \equiv (p \vee q))$	4, 9; m.e.

16.11 Example 10

Problem

1. Cpq	$(p \supset q)$	given
2. Crs	$(r \supset s)$	given
3. Cqt	$(q \supset t)$	given
4. $CNuNs$	$(\sim u \supset \sim s)$	given
5. $CtNu$	$(t \supset \sim u)$	given
6. $CNrNp$	$(\sim r \supset \sim p)$	given
Np	$\sim p$	to be proved

Strategy   There is only one way—unless you use negative absurdity—to prove a conclusion like this from a series of conditional statements. The key to doing it is this: you must set up a series of hypothetical syllogisms that ends with the following formula:

$$CpNp \qquad \| \quad (p \supset \sim p)$$

The negation of p can be gotten from this by material implication and idempotency. To set up the series of hypothetical syllogisms, you must start with a premise that has p as its antecedent and end with one that has the negation of p as its consequent. In between, you match up consequents with antecedents:

Demonstration

7. Cpt	$(p \supset t)$	1, 3; h.s.
8. $CpNu$	$(p \supset \sim u)$	7, 5; h.s.
9. $CpNs$	$(p \supset \sim s)$	8, 4; h.s.
10. $CNsNr$	$(\sim s \supset \sim r)$	2; trans.

11. CpNr	$(p \supset \sim r)$	9, 10; h.s.
12. CpNp	$(p \supset \sim p)$	11, 6; h.s.
13. ANpNp	$(\sim p \lor \sim p)$	12; m.i.
14. Np	$\sim p$	13; idem.

16.12 Sometimes you can simplify a proof considerably if you can change the conclusion of an argument into a conditional statement by using one of the replacement-rules and then using the rule of assumption on it. For it stands to reason that if you can prove something that is logically equivalent to a conclusion, you can get the conclusion from what you've proven by using the appropriate replacement-rule. There is no limit to the ingenuity you can use to demonstrate conclusions just so long as you can justify every move you make by citing a transformation or replacement-rule.

16.12.1 Exercise

If you have not already done so, prove example 7 by using the rule of assumption.

16.12.2 Exercise

The principle of excluded middle can be proven from line 4 of the demonstration in example 9. Try to do it. In others words, work the following problem:

1. CApqq	$((p \lor q) \supset q)$	given
ANqq	$(\sim q \lor q)$	to be proved.

16.12.3 Exercise

Write out a paragraph telling how to and then demonstrate the conclusions of the following argument-forms.

(1) CArpq
Nq
—————
Nr

$((r \lor p) \supset q)$
$\sim q$
—————
$\sim r$

(2) Cpq
ANqr
Nr
—————
Np

$(p \supset q)$
$(\sim q \lor r)$
$\sim r$
—————
$\sim p$

(3) Cpp
—————
Epp

$(p \supset p)$
—————
$(p \equiv p)$

(4) $CpKqr$ $(p \supset (q \cdot r))$
Nq $\sim q$
$CNpCst$ $(\sim p \supset (s \supset t))$
—————————————
Cst $(s \supset t)$

(5) $KCqpCrp$ $((q \supset p) \cdot (r \supset p))$
$KCNqrCpNr$ $((\sim q \supset r) \cdot (p \supset \sim r))$
—————————————
Kpq $(p \cdot q)$

(6) Apr $(p \lor r)$
$ANrs$ $(\sim r \lor s)$
$AqNs$ $(q \lor \sim s)$
—————————————
Apq $(p \lor q)$

(7) $CNqKpr$ $(\sim q \supset (p \cdot r))$
Crs $(r \supset s)$
Csq $(s \supset q)$
—————————————
Cpq $(p \supset q)$

(8) Cpr $(p \supset r)$
$AqNr$ $(q \lor \sim r)$
$CqKsNs$ $(q \supset (s \cdot \sim s))$
Ns $\sim s$
—————————————
Epq $(p \equiv q)$

(9) Cpq $(p \supset q)$
$AsNq$ $(s \lor \sim q)$
$KCstCsr$ $((s \supset t) \cdot (s \supset r))$
$ANtNr$ $(\sim t \lor \sim r)$
—————————————
$AKNpNqq$ $((\sim p \cdot \sim q) \lor q)$

(10) Cpq $(p \supset q)$
—————————————
$CpApq$ $(p \supset (p \lor q))$

(11) $KCpqCpr$ $((p \supset q) \cdot (p \supset r))$
—————————————
$CpEqr$ $(p \supset (q \equiv r))$

(12) $CpNq$ $(p \supset \sim q)$
$CNqr$ $(\sim q \supset r)$
$CNpNq$ $(\sim p \supset \sim q)$
—————————————
r r

(13) Cpq $(p \supset q)$
Crs $(r \supset s)$

Apr	$(p \lor r)$
$CpNs$	$(p \supset \sim s)$
$CrNq$	$(r \supset \sim q)$
$\overline{EsNq}$	$\overline{(s \equiv \sim q)}$
(14) $AAqNrs$	$((q \lor \sim r) \lor s)$
$ANqNANrq$	$(\sim q \lor \sim (\sim r \lor q))$
$\overline{ANrs}$	$\overline{(\sim r \lor s)}$
(15) $ANpKqr$	$(\sim p \lor (q \cdot r))$
$CNrKqp$	$(\sim r \supset (q \cdot p))$
$\overline{r}$	$\overline{r}$
(16) $KpCqr$	$(p \cdot (q \supset r))$
$\overline{CKpqKpr}$	$\overline{((p \cdot q) \supset (p \cdot r))}$
(17) $KpEqr$	$(p \cdot (q \equiv r))$
$\overline{EKpqKpr}$	$\overline{((p \cdot q) \equiv (p \cdot r))}$
(18) $KEpqEpr$	$((p \equiv q) \cdot (p \equiv r))$
$\overline{EpKqr}$	$\overline{(p \equiv (q \cdot r))}$
(19) $EpCqr$	$(p \equiv (q \supset r))$
$\overline{CEpqEpr}$	$\overline{((p \equiv q) \supset (p \equiv r))}$
(20) $EpAqr$	$(p \equiv (q \lor r))$
$\overline{AEpqEpr}$	$\overline{((p \equiv q) \lor (p \equiv r))}$

SECTION 17. English as a model of the system

17.1 Now that you have learned how to use the rules and how to write out demonstrations, learning how to apply this knowledge to arguments is easy. That is your next job. You should begin by reviewing chapter 1, section 5, paragraph 2, where the five truth-functors were first explained. In that paragraph, the truth-functors were associated with certain English words that were said to usually indicate the linguistic acts that the five functors stand for. In this section, you will learn how to symbolize arguments and other English words that indicate the linguistic acts that the truth-functors stand for.

17.2 Usually the task of translating an argument into symbols is an easy one. Most of the time, the English words that usually indicate the truth-functors are the ones that are used. For instance, look at the following argument:

> If Plato were a student of Socrates, Plato must have lived in Athens.
> Plato was a student of Socrates.
> ___
> Therefore Plato must have lived in Athens.

If you symbolize the simple sentence "Plato was a student of Socrates" by the constant s (which is taken from the word *student*), and the simple sentence "Plato must have lived in Athens" by the constant l (which is taken from the word *lived*), then you would symbolize the argument like this:

The argument comes out like this because the word *if* is usually replaced by the sign for material implication. Notice that every simple declarative sentence (sometimes called a proposition) is assigned a constant and that each different simple declarative sentence is assigned a different constant. Of course, when the same simple sentence occurs in the same argument more than once, it is assigned the same constant each time. Because each simple sentence is assigned a constant, the kind of logic presented in this chapter is called *sentential* or *propositional* logic. The letters s and l are called *statement-constants* because they stand for specific statements. (Recall that the letters p, q, and r, etc. that we have been using all along are called statement-variables because they stand for any declarative sentences whatsoever.) Once it has been symbolized, you should recognize the argument cited above as an example of modus ponens. Since this argument exemplifies a law of logic, the argument is reasoned well.

17.3 A slightly more complicated argument is this:

> Either Aristotle or Plato wrote the *Republic*.
> Aristotle was the teacher of Alexander and did not write the *Republic*.
> ___
> Therefore Plato wrote the *Republic*.

If you symbolize the simple sentence "Aristotle wrote the *Republic*" with the constant a, the simple sentence "Plato wrote the *Republic*" with the constant p, the simple sentence "Aristotle was the teacher of Alexander" with the constant t, and the simple sentence "Aristotle did not write the

Republic" with the constant *a* negated, the argument-form comes out
like this:

Aap	‖	$(a \vee p)$
$\underline{KtNa}$		$\underline{(t \cdot \sim a)}$
p		p

It comes out like this because the word *not* is usually replaced by the sign
for negation, the words *either . . . or . . .* are usually replaced by the sign
for alternation, and the word *and* is usually replaced by the sign for conjunction. (Notice that although the letter *p* is used in this argument-form,
it is being used as a constant and not as a variable.) Having symbolized
this argument, you should easily see how to show that the conclusion
follows from the premises by using the rules of simplification and disjunctive syllogism.

17.4   Unfortunately, the truth-functors do not merely replace the basic
words *not, and, or, if-then,* and *if and only if.* And sometimes arguments
are written with a lot of complexity. So you must learn how to decipher
such arguments. To help you, five groups of English words are presented
in subsections 17.5–17.13: one list of each of the truth-functors. Your
knowledge of the English language and how to symbolize sentences that
contain these words and phrases should enable you to correctly symbolize
most arguments that are propositional.

17.5   In section 5 of chapter 1, you learned that the sign for negation is
most often replaced by the phrase *it is false that* and the word *not.* Another
obvious way of indicating negation, however, is with a prefix. The most
common prefixes for negation are these:

> a-
> il-
> im-
> in-
> ir-
> non-
> um-
> un-

All of these can be used to indicate negation, but negation is often indicated
by conjunctions and conjunctive adverbs. Many of these conjunctions and
conjunctive adverbs appear in the lists that follow.

SECTION 17. English as a model of the system

17.6   A conjunction is a word whose main job is to join words or groups of words. Conjunctions are used in a variety of situations and are of two main types: coordinating and subordinating.

17.7   Coordinating conjunctions are normally used to connect sentential elements of the same grammatical class: that is, noun to noun, adverb to adverb, clause to clause, etc. In logic, they are always understood to connect clause to clause. The main coordinating conjunctions are *and, but, or,* and *for.* But many adverbs also act like conjunctions. Coordinating conjunctions and conjunctive adverbs can be divided into the following six classes: copulative, adversitive, disjunctive, causal, illative, and explanatory. Of these, the first three, namely, copulative, adversitive, and disjunctive, are important in logic. The class of explanatory conjunctions has no logical role, while the causal conjunction *for* is the sign of a premise and illative conjunctions such as *consequently, therefore, hence, so,* and *thus,* are signs for conclusions. Copulative and adversitive conjunctions usually are replaced by the sign for conjunction; disjunctive conjunctions, as you might guess, are usually replaced by the sign for alternation. Lists of the most frequently used copulative, adversitive, and disjunctive conjunctions follow. (Some temporal conjunctions are also listed since they often act like copulative conjunctions.)

17.8 Translations for conjunction.

p-and-*q*	not-*p*-and-not-*q*
both *p* and *q*.	not *p* nor *q*.
p as well as *q*.	not *p*, not *q*.
not only *p* but *q*.	no *p* nor *q*.
p, q too.	never *p* or *q*.
p moreover *q*.	neither *p* nor *q*.
p besides *q*.	nor *p* nor *q*.
p likewise *q*.	
p, further *q*.	
p furthermore *q*.	
p, even *q*.	
p, let alone *q*.	
in the first place *p*, next, *q*.	
first *p*, secondly *q*.	
p, finally *q*.	
p, then *q*.	
first *p*, then *q*.	
now *p*, now *q*.	
p but then *q*.	

_p_-and-_q_

  _p_ but _q_.

  _p_ only _q_.

  _p_ still _q_.

  _p_ yet _q_.

  _p_ and yet _q_.

  _p_, however, _q_.

  _p_, on the other hand _q_.

  _p_, on the contrary _q_.

  _p_, rather _q_.

  _p_ notwithstanding _q_.

  _p_ nevertheless _q_.

  _p_ none the less _q_.

  _p_, all the same _q_.

  _p_ though _q_.

  _p_ for all that _q_.

  _p_, at the same time _q_.

  _p_ in the meantime _q_.

  _p_ while _q_.

  _p_ when _q_.

  _p_ whereas _q_.

  _p_ as _q_.

  _p_ as soon as _q_.

  _p_ as long as _q_.

  _p_ as often as _q_.

  _p_ whenever _q_.

  _p_ whensoever _q_.

  _p_ so surely as _q_.

  the time that _p_, _q_.

  by the time that _p_, _q_.

  the moment _p_, _q_.

  the day _p_, _q_.

  the week _p_, _q_.

  the month _p_, _q_.

  the year _p_, _q_.

  everytime that _p_, _q_.

  _p_ directly _q_.

  _p_ immediately _q_.

  _p_ instantly _q_.

  _p_ since _q_.

  _p_ after _q_.

SECTION 17. English as a model of the system

<u>*p*-and-*q*</u>
p before *q*.
p till *q*.
p until *q*.
no sooner than *p*, *q*.
scarcely *p*, *q*.
hardly *p* when *q*.
scarcely *p* but *q*.

p along with *q*.
p together with *q*.

17.9 Translations for alternation.

<u>*p*-or-*q*</u>
either *p* or *q*.
p or else *q*.
p otherwise *q*.

17.10 Subordinating conjunctions are used to connect adverb or noun clauses to some sentential element in the main clause in complex sentences. Only those conjunctions and conjunctive adverbs that connect some adverb clauses to main clauses are important logically. Adverb clauses, like adverbs, usually modify verbs. So they can indicate time, place, manner, cause, concession, condition, result, purpose, and comparison. Not all of these have a logical role, however. The major conjunctions that do, indicate condition. A list of the most frequently used conjunctions of condition follows. Conjunctions of condition are usually replaced by the sign for material implication. (You should now understand why formulas that have the symbol for material implication as their main truth-functor are called conditional statements.)

17.11 Translations for material implication.

<u>if-*p*-then-*q*</u>	<u>if-not-*p*-then-*q*</u>
if *p*, *q*.	*q* if not *p*.
q if *p*.	*q* unless *p*.
q on condition that *p*.	*q* only that *p*.
q provided that *p*.	*q* saving *p*.
q provided only *p*.	*q* except *p*.
q providing that *p*.	*q* but for *p*.
p so that *q*.	*q* but that *p*.
p so as *q*.	
p so *q*.	

if-*p*-then-*q*

q so long as *p*.
q in the case that *p*.
q in the event that *p*.
q suppose *p*.
q supposing *p*.
q once *p*.
p only if *q*.
q is a necessary condition for *p*.
p is a sufficient condition for *q*.
when *p* then *q*.
q whenever *p*.

17.12 Other grammatical constructions sometimes replace so-called if-clauses. Sometimes the if-clause is replaced by a wish: "Could I see her once more, all my desires would be fulfilled" means "If I could see her once more, all my desires would be fulfilled." If-clauses are also often replaced by two independent sentences that are sometimes but not always linked by a conjunction. For instance, "Give him an inch and he'll take a mile" means "If you give him an inch, he'll take a mile." Likewise, "Do it once, you will never regret it" means "If you do it once, then you'll never regret it." "Do that at once, or else you will be punished" means "If you do not do that at once, then you will be punished." "Love me, love my dog" means "If you love me, then love my dog." "He cannot be in his right mind; otherwise, he would not make such wild statements" means "If he were in his right mind, he would not make such wild statements." And "We'd have done better only we ran against a hard wind" means "If we had not run against a hard wind, we would have done better." All such sentences should be translated into conditional statements.

17.13 Translations for material equivalence.

p-if and only if-*q*

p is equivalent to *q*.
p is the same as *q*.
p is identical to *q*.
to say that *p* is to say that *q*.
to be *p* is to be *q*.
p is a necessary and sufficient condition for *q*.

17.14 You have probably noticed that the same word often has different uses in English; so before you decide how to symbolize a sentence, you must decide how the relevant word is being used. The lists that you have

113

just read are not meant to convey the impression that every time you run across a certain word you can symbolize it in the same way. The lists are merely meant to teach you to distinguish between different kinds of conjunctions and conjunctive adverbs and the uses that these kinds of words are put to. That is what you must learn to recognize if you are to symbolize sentences correctly.

17.14.1 Exercise

You should now be able to symbolize and demonstrate all of the following arguments:

(1) Socrates must have been very intelligent provided that Plato was a student of his. Of course, Plato was Socrates' student; so Socrates must have been very intelligent or else he had a strong personality.

(2) Either Aristotle was a student of Socrates or Plato as well as Xenophon was. So Xenophon must have been, since Aristotle was not.

(3) To say that Aristophanes was a philosopher is to say that Sophocles was. But Sophocles was not; so Aristophanes was not.

(4) Anaximines must have known of Thales unless Anaximines was not a Milesian. But Anaximines must have known of Thales if and only if Anaximander did. Therefore Anaximander knew of Thales in the event that Anaximines was a Milesian.

(5) Either Thales or Anaximines thought that everything was made of water, while Heraclitus thought everything was made of fire. Since Anaximines did not think that things were made of water, Thales did.

(6) Protagoras was a relativist supposing that he thought that man is the measure of all things. But Protagoras was not a relativist; otherwise, Plato refuted Protagoras' views. Protagoras did, of course, think that man is the measure of all things; he even thought that he could teach men how to be virtuous. So it follows that Plato refuted Protagoras' views.

(7) Socrates thought of the theory of forms; otherwise Plato did. And Plato thought of the theory if and only if no other student of Socrates did. Socrates did not think of it, but he was Plato's teacher. Thus no other student of Socrates thought of the theory either.

(8) Empedocles was neither a monist nor an idealist so long as he believed that love and hate moved matter. But if Empedocles believed that love and hate moved matter only if he was not a monist, he must have been a pluralist. Still if he believed that love and hate moved matter only if he was not an idealist, he must not have been a materialist either. But either he was a materialist or Democritus was. So Empedocles was a pluralist and Democritus was a materialist.

(9) Not only Xenophanes but Parmenides also was monist. For after all, to call Xenophanes an Eleatic is to call Parmenides one, and if Xenophanes and Parmenides were Eleatics, they were both monists and held that the universe was one in its essential nature. But neither Xenophanes nor Parmenides were Eleatics only if they were followers of the Milesian Thales. Yet they sought the one changeless stuff that underlies all change if they were his followers. Still, if they sought that one changeless stuff, they were monists.

(10) Any philosopher who is a monist is one who believes one stuff underlies all differences. But if one believes that, to be a materialist is not to be an idealist. So being a materialist provided one is a monist is the same as not being an idealist so long as one is not a monist.

17.15　The application of logic to language is called an *interpretation* of logic, and the language to which the logic is applied is called a *model.* You get an interpretation of logic by assigning meanings to the primitive symbols. If you use language as a model, you assign words to the primitive symbols. In a sense, that's what this section is all about—assigning words to symbols so that language can be a model of our logical system. Of course, when you assign meanings to the primitive symbols, you must do it so that the formulas of the system become true statements; otherwise, the model would not be any good. Language is not the only model for this logical system, but it is the only model described in this book.

17.16　Many students of logic have the idea that the truth-tables that define particular truth-functors were chosen so that they could be modeled by the words that we have associated with these truth-functors. The idea that these students have is this: First there was language, then logic, and logic was made to mirror language. Although there is some truth to this idea, it unfortunately gives students the wrong picture of relating logic to language. In reality, the situation is this: There are sixteen ways of writing a truth-table with four lines of values:

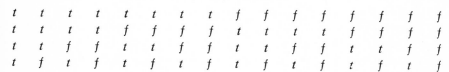

In other words, each of these sixteen columns can serve as the main column of values in a four-lined truth-table. So each of these columns can be used to define a truth-functor. The problem, then, is not one of

SECTION 17. English as a model of the system

finding a truth-table that can convey the meanings of certain words but rather of finding words that fit the truth-tables. Some words can be found that seem to fit the tables perfectly. Other words fit the tables approximately, and some tables do not seem to fit any words. Logical systems, however, have been put together that utilize different truth-functors than the ones used in this book. Because logical systems can be built by using different truth-functors, the following symbols and names have sometimes been used for some of them.

Bpq	$(p \subset q)$	converse implication
t	t	
t	t	
f	f	
t	t	
Dpq	$(p \mid q)$	non-conjunction
f	f	"Sheffer's stroke"
t	t	
t	t	
t	t	
Jpq	$(p \not\equiv q)$	material non-equivalence
f	f	exclusive alternation
t	t	exclusive disjunction
t	f	
f	f	
Lpq	$(p \mathrel{\not\supset} q)$	material non-implication
f	f	
t	t	
f	f	
f	f	
Mpq	$(p \not\subset q)$	converse non-implication
f	f	
f	f	
t	t	
f	f	
Xpq	$(p \mathrel{\not\vee} q)$	non-alteration
f	f	non-disjunction
f	f	
f	f	
t	t	

17.16.1 Exercise

Try to model these truth-functors with English words.

17.16.2 Exercise

The following terms have been introduced in this chapter. You should know the meaning of each one.

law of logic

replacement-rule

argument-schema

deduction

proof

propositional logic

interpretation

scope of an assumption

substitution-instance

formalism

demonstration

statement-constant

sentential logic

model

Chapter THREE **MONADIC PREDICATE LOGIC**

SECTION 18. The shortcomings of propositional logic

18.1   The propositional logic that you have been studying only sets out the features of very elementary kinds of reasoning. This reasoning is so elementary that it was almost completely overlooked for centuries, even though it is the base that more complicated reasoning is built on.

18.2   It is easy to see that propositional logic cannot be used to work out the logical connections in reasoning that is only slightly more complicated than propositional reasoning. For example, propositional logic cannot be used to work out the logical connections in the following argument:

> Some men are philosophers.
> All philosophers seek wisdom.
> _____
> Some men seek wisdom.

As an example of propositional logic, this argument would have to be taken as a sequence of three different simple sentences. But then the logical connections between these three sentences would be blotted out.

The reason for this is that the logical connections between these three sentences are the result of the connection between the predicate of one premise and the subject of the other. Propositional logic does not allow us to show such connections.

18.3   In order to show these connections and also use propositional logic as the basis for this new kind of reasoning, we must rewrite the sentences used in this new kind of reasoning so that each subject term and each predicate term become the predicates of simple sentences. It is because subject and predicate terms are made into predicates that this new kind of logic is called *predicate logic*.

SECTION 19. Predicates

19.1   How are the sentences in this new kind of logic to be rewritten? The answer is by putting in a new subject for the new predicates. But this new subject cannot be something specific, for any new specific subject would create the whole problem over again: in order to get the kind of simple sentences that we need to work with, the new specific subject would also have to be turned into a predicate. So the new subject that we put in must be something general.

19.2   For instance, take the sentence "All philosophers seek wisdom." We must get two sentences out of it—one using each of the following two predicates:

_____ is a philosopher.
_____ seeks wisdom.

These are partial statement-forms that are made up of a subject-marker and a predicate. If we replace the subject-marker by a symbol, say the letter x, the two partial statement-forms are these:

x is a philosopher.
x seeks wisdom.

Now if we can find a way of saying that we mean all of the things that this generic subject can stand for, we can rewrite the original sentence as a combination of these two partial statement-forms. (The things that a generic subject stands for are often called its *universe of discourse*.) But we can say "all of the things that this generic subject stands for" merely by saying "for all x." So the sentence "All philosophers seek wisdom" can be rewritten as this:

For all x, if x *is* a philosopher, then x seeks wisdom.

This new sentence is made up of (1) the phrase *for all x,* (2) the truth-functor indicated by the words *if . . . then . . .* , and (3) two partial statement-forms. (The phrase *for all x* is called the *universal quantifier* because it says that the quantity of things being referred to in the universe of discourse is universal, that is, everything.)

19.3 Now let's take the other premise as another example, for this premise comes out a little bit different. The sentence "Some men are philosophers" must also be rewritten by using two sentences (actually, logicians call these *propositional functions,* since they don't become sentences until the *x* is replaced by a specific subject):

> *x* is a man.
> *x* is a philosopher.

But now we must find a way of saying "some of the things that this generic subject stands for." We can do it by saying merely "for some *x.*" So the sentence "Some men are philosophers" can be rewritten

> For some *x, x* is a man and *x* is a philosopher.

This new sentence is made up of (1) the phrase *for some x,* (2) the truth-functor indicated by the word *and,* and (3) two partial statement-forms. The phrase *for some x* is called the *particular quantifier* because it says that the quantity of things being referred to in the universe of discourse that the subject *x* stands for is partial; that is, not total. The words *particular* and *partial* are etymologically related.

19.4 The complete argument that we have been using as an example now comes out like this:

> For some *x, x* is a man and *x* is a philosopher.
> For all *x,* if *x* is a philosopher, then *x* seeks wisdom.
> _____
> So for some *x, x* is a man and *x* seeks wisdom.

Now you should be able to see how the transformation-rules you learned in the last chapter can be used to work out the logical connections in this argument, for if you leave off (for the time being) the phrases *for some x* and *for all x,* the argument has this form:

> *p* and *q*
> if *q* then *r*
> _____
> *p* and *r*

MONADIC PREDICATE LOGIC

In symbols this is,

$$\frac{\begin{array}{c} Kpq \\ Cqr \end{array}}{Kpr} \qquad \Bigg\| \qquad \frac{\begin{array}{c} (p \cdot q) \\ (q \supset r) \end{array}}{(p \cdot r)}$$

The conclusion can be gotten by using simplification, modus ponens, and conjunction.

SECTION 20. New symbols

20.1   Of course, we cannot merely leave off the phrases *for some x* and *for all x* in working out arguments, for to leave them off would be to change the meanings of the sentences involved. Furthermore, there is an advantage in working with completely abstract rather than partial statement-forms, as you saw in the previous chapters. So, we must expand our sets of symbols if we are to lay out argument-forms in predicate logic as we laid out the argument-forms of propositional logic. Two kinds of symbols, not counting the parentheses used in Principia Notation, are needed in propositional logic: symbols for variables and symbols for the truth-functors. We will still use the symbols for the truth-functors just as we have been using them, but now we need new symbols for (1) predicates, (2) subjects, and (3) the quantifiers, for some x and for all x. The new symbols we will use are these:

For the universal quantifier, for all x, we will use the symbol Πx. For the particular quantifier, for some x, we will use the symbol Σx. For subjects we will use lower case letters within parentheses. And for predicates, we will use capital letters (which are always followed by subject-symbols). You will always be able to tell predicates apart from truth-functors, because predicates will always be followed by subject-symbols. You will also always be able to tell statement-variables from subject-symbols, for subject-symbols are always surrounded by parentheses.

For the universal quantifier, for all x, we will use the symbol (x). For the particular quantifier, we will use the symbol $(\exists x)$. For subjects, we will use lower case letters within parentheses. And for predicates, we will use capital letters (which are always followed by subject-symbols). You will always be able to tell statement-variables from subject-symbols, for subject-symbols will always be surrounded by parentheses. Of course, we still need other pairs of parentheses to punctuate formulas.

20.2　The various kinds of symbols that you now have to work with are these:

(1)	statement-variables:		$p, q, r, s, \ldots$	
(2)	truth-functors:	$N, K, A, C, E.$	$\sim, \cdot, \vee, \supset, \equiv.$
(3)	punctuation marks:		$(,).$
(4)	quantifiers:	$\Pi x, \Sigma x.$	$(x), (\exists x).$
(5)	predicates:		$P( ), Q( ), R( ), \ldots$
(6)	subject, generic:		$(x).$
	subjects, specific:		$(a), (b), (c), \ldots$

(The parentheses that follow predicate-symbols are the same ones that surround subject-symbols.) Now since we have these new symbols, we must extend our recursive definition of a well-formed formula. The new definition goes like this: (Again the Greek letters α and β that are used in writing this definition are variables that stand for any symbolic expression, well-informed or not.)

(1) Statement-variables standing alone are well-formed.

(2) Predicate-variables with specific subjects standing alone are well-formed.

(3) If $\alpha(x)$ is a formula in which x is not quantified, that is, is free, then
　　(a) the universal quantification of $\alpha(x)$ is well-formed, and
　　(b) the particular quantification of $\alpha(x)$ is well-formed.

(4) If α is well-formed, then the negation of α is well-formed.

(5) If α and β are each well-formed, then
　　(a) the conjunction of α and β is well-formed,
　　(b) the alternation of α and β is well-formed,
　　(c) the material implication of α and β is well-formed, and
　　(d) the material equivalence of α and β is well-formed.

(6) Nothing else is well-formed.

20.2.1 Exercise

Which of the following are well-formed?

(1) $\Pi x C F(a) G(a)$	$(x)(F(a) \supset G(a))$
(2) $\Pi x C F(x) G(a)$	$(x)(F(x) \supset G(a))$
(3) $\Sigma x K F(x) G(x)$	$(\exists x)(F(x) \cdot G(x))$
(4) $\Pi a F(a)$	$(a)F(a)$
(5) $\Pi \Sigma(x)$	$( )\exists(x)$
(6) $\Pi F(a) G(a)$	$(F(a) ( ) G(a))$
(7) $P(x)$	$P(x)$
(8) $K P(a) G(a)$	$(P(a) \cdot G(a))$
(9) $K p F(a)$	$(p \cdot F(a))$
(10) $A p \Pi x E F(x) N G(x)$	$(p \vee (x)(F(x) \equiv \sim G(x))$

20.3 Given these symbols, we can now completely symbolize the argument that was used as an example in the last section:

$$
\begin{array}{c}
\Sigma x KM(x)P(x) \\
\Pi x CP(x)S(x) \\
\hline
\Sigma x KM(x)S(x)
\end{array}
\qquad \| \qquad
\begin{array}{c}
(\exists x)\,(M(x) \cdot P(x)) \\
(x)\,(P(x) \supset S(x)) \\
\hline
(\exists x)\,(M(x) \cdot S(x))
\end{array}
$$

The first formula (which is called particular because it is quantified with the particular quantifier) says something like this: "Some *m*'s are *p*'s." The second formula (which is called universal because it is quantified with the universal quantifier) says something like "All *p*'s are *s*'s." Now, if we again leave off the quantifiers, you can compare this new way of symbolizing arguments with the way used in subsection 19.4 where we tried to show the logical connections in this argument. There, we symbolized it like this:

$$
\begin{array}{c}
Kpq \\
Cqr \\
\hline
Kpr
\end{array}
\qquad \| \qquad
\begin{array}{c}
(p \cdot q) \\
(q \supset r) \\
\hline
(p \cdot r)
\end{array}
$$

Now the argument-form looks like this:

$$
\begin{array}{c}
KM(x)P(x) \\
CP(x)S(x) \\
\hline
KM(x)S(x)
\end{array}
\qquad \| \qquad
\begin{array}{c}
(M(x) \cdot P(x)) \\
(P(x) \supset S(x)) \\
\hline
(M(x) \cdot S(x))
\end{array}
$$

The only difference is that now symbols like $M(x)$, $P(x)$, and $S(x)$ take the place of p, q, and r. In other words, symbols like $M(x)$ which are combinations of a predicate and a subject-symbol are used just like the statement-variables of the last chapter. Remember that statement-variables are sometimes called propositional variables. These new symbols like $M(x)$ are used just like propositional variables. They are called propositional functions, because they become statement forms whenever (1) they are quantified or (2) the generic subject x is replaced by a specific subject. So to work out the logical connections in the argument-form cited in this paragraph, you could merely simplify the propositional function $P(x)$ from the first premise, use it together with the second premise to get the propositional function $S(x)$ by modus ponens, simplify the propositional function $M(x)$ from the first premise and then conjoin the two propositional functions $M(x)$ and $S(x)$.

SECTION 21. Quantification-rules

21.1 If it were not for the quantifiers that stand in front of these formulas, you could easily get the conclusion from the premises by using the trans-

123

formation-rules that you learned in the last chapter. So if you are going to be able to use those rules, we must work out ways of taking the quantifiers from the premises and putting quantifiers back on conclusions after they have been derived. Before we can work these ways out, however, you must understand what the quantifiers mean.

21.2   The universal quantifier says *'for all x'*. When it is attached to a formula, the quantifier shows that the formula is about all, that is, each and every one, of the things in the universe of discourse that x directs your attention to. For instance, suppose we say that all ancient Greeks were pagans. The universe of discourse is all persons who lived in Greece in ancient times. If a census had been taken, we might have a list of all their names. Suppose we did have, and suppose the list began like this:

Abaris
Acesimbrotus
Achaemenes
Achelous
Acheron
.
.
.

Then instead of writing the sentence "All ancient Greeks were pagans," we could instead write:

Abaris was a pagan, and
Acesimbrotus was a pagan, and
Achaemenes was a pagan, and
Achelous was a pagan, and
Acheron was a pagan, and
etc.

When we had named every ancient Greek whose name is on the census list and said that he was a pagan, we would have written a very long sentence that said the same thing as the short sentence "All ancient Greeks were pagans."

21.3   Now a sentence like "Abaris was a pagan" is specific and concrete. A sentence like "All ancient Greeks were pagans" is general. Because such sentences are general, they are called generalizations, and specific sentences like "Abaris was a pagan" are called instances of the generalization "All ancient Greeks were pagans." So, there are generalizations and instances

MONADIC PREDICATE LOGIC

of generalizations. It should now be easy for you to see what a universally quantified sentence means from the previous example, which showed that a universal generalization can be replaced by a very long conjunction of instances of the generalization.

21.4   Now if you take the sentence "For all x, x is an F," you can see that it means that

a is an F, and
b is an F, and
c is an F, and
d is an F, and
etc.

(where the letters a, b, c, and d etc. are the names of the things in the universe of discourse that the subject x stands for). So the phrase *for all x* attached to a formula is a way of abbreviating a conjunction, and the formula

$$\Pi x F(x) \qquad\qquad \| \qquad\qquad (x)F(x)$$

(which is to be read "For all x, x is an F") is an abbreviation for the conjunction

$$\ldots KKKF(a)F(b)F(c)F(d) \ldots \quad \| \quad (((F(a) \cdot F(b)) \cdot F(c)) \cdot F(d)) \ldots$$

21.5   Another kind of generalization is called particular. Take, for example, the sentence "Some ancient Greeks were philosophers." It too has as its universe of discourse all persons who lived in Greece in ancient times. This sentence, however, does not direct your attention to each and every one of them; instead, it merely directs your attention to some of them. So if we had a list of all the persons who lived in Greece in ancient times, we could replace the sentence "Some ancient Greeks were philosophers" by the very long sentence:

Abaris was a philosopher, or
Acesimbrotus was a philosopher, or
Achaemenes was a philosopher, or
Achelous was a philosopher, or
Acheron was a philosopher, or
etc.

Again, when we had named every ancient Greek whose name is on the list and said that he was a philosopher, we would have written a very long sentence that said the same thing as the short sentence "Some ancient Greeks were philosophers." In other words, a particular generalization can be replaced by a very long alternation of instances of the generalization.

21.6 So now if you take the sentence "For some x, x is an F," you can easily see that it means that

a is an F, or
b is an F, or
c is an F, or
d is an F, or
etc.

(where the letters a, b, c, and d etc. again are the names of the things in the universe of discourse that the subject x stands for). The phrase *for some x* attached to a formula is a way of abbreviating an alternation, and the formula

$$\Sigma x F(x) \qquad\qquad \| \qquad\qquad (\exists x)F(x)$$

(which is to be read "For some x, x is an F") is an abbreviation for the alternation

$$\ldots AAAF(a)F(b)F(c)F(d) \ldots \qquad \| \qquad (((F(a) \vee F(b)) \vee F(c)) \vee F(d)) \ldots$$

21.7 Since a universally quantified formula is an abbreviation for a conjunction and a particularly quantified formula is an abbreviation for an alternation, these quantifiers can be changed into each other by using De Morgan's laws. After all, if

$$\Pi x F(x) \qquad\qquad \| \qquad\qquad (x)F(x)$$

means

$$\ldots KKKF(a)F(b)F(c)F(d) \ldots \qquad \| \qquad (((F(a) \cdot F(b)) \cdot F(c)) \cdot F(d)) \ldots$$

then

$$N\Pi x F(x) \qquad\qquad \| \qquad\qquad \sim(x)F(x)$$

must mean

$$\ldots NKKKF(a)F(b)F(c)F(d) \ldots \qquad \| \qquad \sim(((F(a) \cdot F(b)) \cdot F(c)) \cdot F(d)) \ldots$$

By De Morgan's law this last formula can be replaced by the following one:

$$\ldots AAANF(a)NF(b)NF(c) \qquad \| \qquad (((\sim F(a) \lor \sim F(b)) \lor$$
$$NF(d) \ldots \qquad\qquad\qquad\qquad \sim F(c)) \lor \sim F(d)) \ldots$$

And this formula can be abbreviated by

$$\Sigma x NF(x) \qquad\qquad \| \qquad\qquad (\exists x) \sim F(x)$$

Similarly, if

$$\Sigma x F(x) \qquad\qquad \| \qquad\qquad (\exists x) F(x)$$

means

$$\ldots AAAF(a)F(b)F(c)F(d) \ldots \| \quad (((F(a) \lor F(b)) \lor F(c)) \lor F(d)) \ldots$$

then

$$N\Sigma x F(x) \qquad\qquad \| \qquad\qquad \sim(\exists x)F(x)$$

must mean

$$\ldots NAAAF(a)F(b)F(c)F(d) \ldots \| \sim(((F(a) \lor F(b)) \lor F(c)) \lor F(d)) \ldots$$

By De Morgan's law this last formula can be replaced by this:

$$\ldots KKKNF(a)NF(b) \qquad \| \qquad (((\sim F(a) \cdot \sim F(b)) \cdot$$
$$NF(c)NF(d) \ldots \qquad\qquad\qquad \sim F(c)) \cdot \sim F(d)) \ldots$$

And this formula can be abbreviated by

$$\Pi x NF(x) \qquad\qquad \| \qquad\qquad (x) \sim F(x)$$

So, we can write out the following replacement-rules for quantifiers:

$$\frac{\Pi x F(x)}{N\Sigma x NF(x)} \text{ and } \frac{N\Sigma x NF(x)}{\Pi x F(x)} \qquad\qquad \frac{(x)F(x)}{\sim(\exists x)\sim F(x)} \text{ and } \frac{\sim(\exists x)\sim F(x)}{(x)F(x)}$$

$$\frac{\Pi x NF(x)}{N\Sigma x F(x)} \text{ and } \frac{N\Sigma x F(x)}{\Pi x NF(x)} \qquad\qquad \frac{(x)\sim F(x)}{\sim(\exists x)F(x)} \text{ and } \frac{\sim(\exists x)F(x)}{(x)\sim F(x)}$$

$$\frac{N\Pi x F(x)}{\Sigma x NF(x)} \text{ and } \frac{\Sigma x NF(x)}{N\Pi x F(x)} \qquad\qquad \frac{\sim(x)F(x)}{(\exists x)\sim F(x)} \text{ and } \frac{(\exists x)\sim F(x)}{\sim(x)F(x)}$$

$$\frac{N\Pi x NF(x)}{\Sigma x F(x)} \text{ and } \frac{\Sigma x F(x)}{N\Pi x NF(x)} \qquad\qquad \frac{\sim(x)\sim F(x)}{(\exists x)F(x)} \text{ and } \frac{(\exists x)F(x)}{\sim(x)\sim F(x)}$$

127

SECTION 21. Quantification-rules

Now that you see what the quantifiers mean, we can work out rules for taking quantifiers off and putting them on formulas.

21.8 Let's take the universal quantifier first. Suppose you had an argument-form that has

$$\Pi x F(x) \qquad \| \qquad (x)F(x)$$

as its only premise. The question is, what conclusions can be derived from it? If you write the premise out in terms of what it means, you get this:

$$\underline{\ldots KKKF(a)F(b)F(c)F(d)\ldots} \qquad \| \qquad \underline{(((F(a) \cdot F(b)) \cdot F(c)) \cdot F(d))\ldots}$$

By the rule of simplification, however, you know that you can write down any one of these conjuncts; so you can conclude, for example,

$$\overline{F(a)} \qquad \| \qquad \overline{F(a)}$$

The rule then that allows us to take the universal quantifier off of a formula is nothing more than an abbreviated rule of simplification. It is usually called *universal instantiation* (u.i.), and it can be written like this:

$$\frac{\Pi x F(x)}{F(a)} \qquad \| \qquad \frac{(x)F(x)}{F(a)}$$

This rule merely means that if you have a universally quantified formula, you can write a similar formula without the quantifier that names an individual in the universe of discourse instead of the generic subject x. Formulas about a specific individual in the universe of discourse are called *singular formulas* (because they are about a single subject). So the rule of universal instantiation says that if you have a universal formula, you can write a singular formula that is an instance of the universal formula.

21.9 Suppose now that you had an argument-form that has only a singular formula as the premise. Again the question is, what conclusions can be derived from it? Let's see what can be gotten from a formula like this:

$$\underline{F(a)} \qquad \| \qquad \underline{F(a)}$$

Since such formulas work just like statement-variables, only a few of our transformation-rules can be used on it. The important one is addition, for it allows us to derive the following formula:

$$\overline{\ldots AAAF(a)F(b)F(c)F(d)\ldots} \qquad \| \qquad \overline{(((F(a) \vee F(b)) \vee F(c)) \vee F(d))\ldots}$$

MONADIC PREDICATE LOGIC

And we know that this can be abbreviated by

$$\overline{\Sigma x F(x)} \qquad \| \qquad \overline{(\exists x)F(x)}$$

The rule then that allows us to put a particular quantifier on a formula is nothing more than an abbreviated rule of addition. It is called *particular generalization* (p.g.) and can be written like this:

$$\frac{F(a)}{\Sigma x F(x)} \qquad \| \qquad \frac{F(a)}{(\exists x)F(x)}$$

It allows you to derive a particularly quantified formula from a singular formula.

21.10 You now have a rule for taking off the universal quantifier and a rule for putting on the particular quantifier. Before you can work out arguments that have quantifiers in them, that is, *quantificational arguments*, you must have a rule for putting on the universal quantifier and a rule for taking off the particular quantifier. These rules, unfortunately, are more complicated than the former two.

21.11 Suppose, for instance, that the singular formula $F(a)$ is a line of a demonstration and is not inside the scope of an assumption. When would the line

$$\Pi x F(x) \qquad \| \qquad (x)F(x)$$

follow? The inference just asked about is this: when can you go from

$$\begin{matrix} \cdot \\ \cdot \\ \cdot \\ F(a) \end{matrix} \qquad \| \qquad \begin{matrix} \cdot \\ \cdot \\ \cdot \\ F(a) \end{matrix}$$

to

$$\ldots KKKF(a)F(b)F(c)F(d) \ldots ? \qquad \| \qquad (((F(a) \cdot F(b)) \cdot F(c)) \cdot F(d)) \ldots ?$$

The answer is only when $F(b)$, $F(c)$, $F(d)$, etc. are also possible lines of the demonstration, for the only basic rule you can use to get a conjunction is the rule of conjunction, and to use it, all the conjuncts must be given. So the question is, how can you show that although only $F(a)$ is given, $F(b)$, $F(c)$, $F(d)$ etc. could be lines if you wanted them to be? The answer is that you can do it if the subject a is an arbitrarily chosen member of the universe of discourse that the x in

$$\Pi x F(x) \qquad \| \qquad (x)F(x)$$

stands for.

21.12 But what does it mean to say that the subject a is an arbitrarily chosen member of the universe of discourse? It means that you could have chosen any other member of the universe of discourse—b, c, d, etc. —that you wanted and that the choice would not have made any difference as far as the demonstration goes. For instance, look at the rule of universal instantiation again. Remember, it is an abbreviated rule of simplification. So if you have

$$\Pi x F(x) \qquad \| \qquad (x)F(x)$$

you can get $F(a)$, $F(b)$, $F(c)$, $F(d)$, etc., for it makes no difference which conjunct you simplify. The transformation from

$$\Pi x F(x) \qquad \| \qquad (x)F(x)$$

to any one of them is equally correct. In other words, it makes no difference what the subject of the predicate F is. When it makes no difference, the subject of such a predicate can be chosen arbitrarily. Now if we want a rule that allows us to go from a singular formula like $F(a)$ to a generalization like

$$\Pi x F(x) \qquad \| \qquad (x)F(x)$$

we must find a way of requiring that the subject of the singular formula be an arbitrarily chosen member of the universe of discourse. We can do this by writing what are called restrictions on the subject of the singular formula from which we are going to derive the generalization.

21.13 The restrictions that we need in order to make this rule work are not hard to write, for if the subject of the singular formula that we are to derive the generalization from must be an arbitrarily chosen member of the universe of discourse, we must not allow anything to be predicated of it that we could not predicate of any other member of the universe of discourse. In other words, the subject of the singular formula can't be the subject of any special predicate. And in order to insure that it isn't, all we have to do is make sure the subject of the singular formula is not the subject of a premise or an undischarged assumption. So if you remember the need for these restrictions, we can write a rule that allows you to put the universal quantifier on a formula. It is called *universal generalization* (u.g.) and is written as follows:

$$\frac{F(a)}{\Pi x F(x)} \qquad\qquad \frac{F(a)}{(x)F(x)}$$

when a is the subject of neither a premise nor an undischarged assumption. The rule is an abbreviated rule of conjunction.

21.14 If you have been paying close attention, you probably have noticed that we used the rules of simplification and conjunction to justify the new rules of universal instantiation and universal generalization. Simplification and conjunction, of course, form a basic pair of rules that allow you to take out and put in the symbol for conjunction. Since a universally quantified formula is an abbreviation for a conjunction, using simplification and conjunction as we did is the natural thing to do. We also, however, used the rule of addition to justify the new rule of particular generalization. And since the law of cases goes with addition to form another basic pair of rules that allow you to take out and put in the symbol for alternation, it seems natural that we should use cases to justify the one rule that is still needed. This rule will allow you to take the particular quantifier off of a formula and is called *particular instantiation* (p.i.)

21.15 In order to explain this rule, let's suppose you have an argument-form with this premise:

$$\underline{\Sigma x F(x)} \qquad\qquad \underline{(\exists x)F(x)}$$

What kind of formula could follow from this premise? Of course, you can get other formulas from it by using replacement-rules. But let's forget about these for the moment and try to see what else you might get and how you would have to go about getting it. This premise means this:

$$\ldots AAAF(a)F(b)F(c)F(d)\ldots \qquad \|(((F(a) \vee F(b)) \vee F(c)) \vee F(d))\ldots$$

Since this formula is an alternation, you must be able to get the same formula from every alternative; otherwise, you cannot get anything from it except by using replacement-rules and addition. If you are to get the

131

same formula from every alternative, however, you must use the law of cases on this alternation. So what you do is assume $F(a)$ and work out the demonstration just as you would if you were using the law of cases and derive some formula that we will represent by the Greek letter ψ:

$$\Sigma x F(x) \qquad\qquad\qquad (\exists x)F(x)$$

$$\begin{array}{c} \lceil F(a) \\ \cdot \\ \cdot \\ \cdot \\ \cdot \\ \lfloor \quad \psi \end{array} \qquad\qquad \Bigg\| \qquad\qquad \begin{array}{c} \lceil F(a) \\ \cdot \\ \cdot \\ \cdot \\ \lfloor \quad \psi \end{array}$$

Now if you can also derive the formula that ψ stands for from every other alternative, you can write the formula that ψ stands for outside the scope of the assumptions.

21.16 But, of course, you never really know what all of the alternatives are; so you can't work them out one by one. What you must do instead is let the demonstration of the formula that ψ stands for from the assumption of one alternative be a stand-in for the demonstrations of the formula that ψ stands for from all the other possible alternatives. But how can you do this unless you know what all the other possible alternatives are and that you can derive the formula that ψ stands for from them? Again the answer is by putting restrictions on the kind of assumption you can make.

21.17 And again, it is not hard to work out these restrictions. First of all, the alternative you assume must be arbitrarily chosen. This means that the subject of the formula that you are going to assume must have no conditions attached to it. Since you attach conditions to a subject by making it the subject of a predicate, the subject of the formula you are going to assume must not be the subject of any other formula that is written in the demonstration anywhere earlier than the assumption. In other words, the subject you choose cannot already be the subject of a premise, an undischarged assumption, or a line in the demonstration that is outside the scope of a discharged assumption. Second, the formula that ψ stands for cannot have the same subject as the assumed alternative, for if it did, the formula that ψ stands for would be about the subject of the alternative that you chose to assume rather than about any alternative. And unless the formula that ψ stands for can be derived from any alternative, the demonstration cannot serve as a stand-in for all the other possible demonstrations.

21.18 With all of this in mind, the rule can now be written out:

where the subject a does not appear anywhere in the part of the demonstration that comes before the assumption (unless it's within the scope of a discharged assumption) and where the Greek letter ψ stands for any derived formula that does not have a as its subject.

21.19 These quantification-rules are completely general, just as all the other transformation-rules are. That is, the predicate-symbol $F(\ )$ can be thought of as a symbol for any predicate or any larger formula that has at least one predicate symbol in it. To point up the generality of these rules, they are usually written with Greek letters that stand for entire formulas of any size. For instance, let the Greek letter ϕ stand for any well-formed formula. If the formula that ϕ stands for has at least one predicate variable in it, we put parentheses after the ϕ and within them we put the subject of that predicate. So $\phi(a)$ stands for a well-formed formula that has at least one predicate-variable in it with the subject a. The quantification-rules, when written out with Greek letters, look like this: (quantifier replacement rules—q.r.)

$$\frac{\Pi x\phi(x)}{N\Sigma xN\phi(x)} \text{ and } \frac{N\Sigma xN\phi(x)}{\Pi x\phi(x)} \qquad \frac{(x)\phi(x)}{\sim(\exists x)\sim\phi(x)} \text{ and } \frac{E\sim(x)\sim\phi(x)}{(x)\phi(x)}$$

$$\frac{\Pi xN\phi(x)}{N\Sigma x\phi(x)} \text{ and } \frac{N\Sigma x\phi(x)}{\Pi xN\phi(x)} \qquad \frac{(x)\sim\phi(x)}{\sim(\exists x)\phi(x)} \text{ and } \frac{\sim(\exists x)\phi(x)}{(x)\sim\phi(x)}$$

$$\frac{N\Pi x\phi(x)}{\Sigma xN\phi(x)} \text{ and } \frac{\Sigma xN\phi(x)}{N\Pi x\phi(x)} \qquad \frac{\sim(x)\phi(x)}{(\exists x)\sim\phi(x)} \text{ and } \frac{(\exists x)\sim\phi(x)}{\sim(x)\phi(x)}$$

$$\frac{N\Pi xN\phi(x)}{\Sigma x\phi(x)} \text{ and } \frac{\Sigma x\phi(x)}{N\Pi xN\phi(x)} \qquad \frac{\sim(x)\sim\phi(x)}{(\exists x)\phi(x)} \text{ and } \frac{(\exists x)\phi(x)}{\sim(x)\sim\phi(x)}$$

$$\text{(u.i.)} \qquad \frac{\Pi x\phi(x)}{(a)} \qquad\qquad\qquad \frac{(x)\phi(x)}{\phi(a)}$$

$$\text{(p.g.)} \qquad \frac{\phi(a)}{\Sigma x\phi(x)} \qquad\qquad\qquad \frac{\phi(a)}{(\exists x)\phi(x)}$$

SECTION 21. Quantification-rules

(u.g.)

$$\frac{\phi(a)}{\Pi x \phi(x)} \qquad\qquad \frac{\phi(a)}{(x)\phi(x)}$$

where a is the subject of neither a premise nor an undischarged assumption.

(p.i.)

where the subject a does not appear anywhere in the part of the demonstration that comes before the assumption (unless it's inside the scope of a discharged assumption) and where ψ stands for any derived formula that does not have a as its subject.

21.20   Once these rules have been written out like this, it is easy to exemplify them. For instance, look at the following sequence of transformations:

1.	$N\Sigma xNKJ(x)L(x)$	$\sim(\exists x)\sim(J(x) \cdot L(x))$	given
2.	$\Pi xCF(x)G(x)$	$(x)(F(x) \supset G(x))$	given
3.	$N\Pi xNKF(x)H(x)$	$\sim(x)\sim(F(x) \cdot H(x))$	given
4.	$\Sigma xKF(x)H(x)$	$(\exists x)(F(x) \cdot H(x))$	3; q.r.
5.	$KF(a)H(a)$	$(F(a) \cdot H(a))$	assumed
6.	$CF(a)G(a)$	$(F(a) \supset G(a))$	2; u.i.
7.	$F(a)$	$F(a)$	5; simp.
8.	$G(a)$	$G(a)$	6, 7; m.p.
9.	$\Sigma xG(x)$	$(\exists x)G(x)$	8; p.g.
10.	$\Sigma xG(x)$	$(\exists x)G(x)$	4-9; p.i.
11.	$\Pi xKJ(x)L(x)$	$(x)(J(x) \cdot L(x))$	1; q.r.
12.	$KJ(a)L(a)$	$(J(a) \cdot L(a))$	11; u.i.
13.	$J(a)$	$J(a)$	12; simp.
14.	$\Pi xJ(x)$	$(x)J(x)$	13; u.g.
15.	$N\Sigma xNJ(x)$	$\sim(\exists x)\sim J(x)$	14; q.r.
16.	$KN\Sigma xNJ(x)\Sigma xG(x)$	$(\sim(\exists x)\sim J(x) \cdot (\exists x)G(x))$	15, 10; conj.

21.21 To understand how the restrictions on the rules work, look first at lines 1 through 5. Line 5 is all right because the subject of the formula on that line does not appear earlier in the sequence of transformations.

21.22 Now look at lines 2, and 4 through 9:

2.	$\Pi x CF(x)G(x)$		$(x)(F(x) \supset G(x))$
4.	$\Sigma x KF(x)H(x)$		$(\exists x)(F(x) \cdot H(x))$
5.	⌐$KF(a)H(a)$		⌐$(F(a) \cdot H(a))$
6.	$CF(a)G(a)$		$(F(a) \supset G(a))$
7.	$F(a)$		$F(a)$
8.	$G(a)$		$G(a)$
9.	$\Sigma x G(x)$		$(\exists x)G(x)$

It is not too hard to see that the subject of the formulas on lines 5 through 8 can be replaced by any other subject and the transformations are still correct. So you can easily set up the rest of an argument by cases, for you can write out the following transformations if you want to:

5′.	⌐$KF(b)H(b)$		⌐$(F(b) \cdot H(b))$
6′.	$CF(b)G(b)$		$(F(b) \supset G(b))$
7′.	$F(b)$		$F(b)$
8′.	$G(b)$		$G(b)$
9′.	$\Sigma x G(x)$		$(\exists x)G(x)$

5″.	⌐$KF(c)H(c)$		⌐$(F(c) \cdot (H(c))$
6″.	$CF(c)G(c)$		$(F(c) \supset G(c))$
7″.	$F(c)$		$F(c)$
8″.	$G(c)$		$G(c)$
9″.	$\Sigma x G(x)$		$(\exists x)G(x)$

You can keep writing this sequence of transformations over and over for a different subject as many times as you like. It is because of this possibility that lines 5 through 9 can serve as a stand-in for all the others. And since those lines can serve as a stand-in for all the others, line 10 can be written outside of the scope of the assumption.

21.23 Finally, look at lines 13 and 14. Line 14 is all right because the subject of the formula on line 13 is the subject of neither a premise nor an undischarged assumption. (Notice however that the subject of the formula on line 13 is the subject of the discharged assumption.)

21.24 If you understand these new rules, you now have all of the rules you need to work out problems in *monadic predicate-logic*, that is, logic about predicate-symbols that are followed by only one subject-symbol.

21.25 Fifth Summary of Rules and Principles

Transformation Rules

1. Conjunction
2. Simplification
3. Assumption
4. Modus Ponens
5. Addition
6. Cases
7. Negative Absurdity
8. Positive Absurdity
9. Modus Tollens
10. Hypothetical Syllogism
11. Constructive Dilemma
12. Repetition
13. Assertion
14. Absorption
15. Simple Constructive Dilemma
16. Disjunctive Syllogism
17. Destructive Dilemma
18. Transitive Law of Material Equivalence
19. Universal Instantiation
20. Particular Generalization
21. Universal Generalization
22. Particular Instantiation

Replacement Rules

1. Material Equivalence (2)
2. Double Negation
3. Commutation (3)
4. Association (3)
5. Exportation-Importation
6. Transposition
7. Material Implication (2)
8. De Morgan's Laws (2)
9. Distribution (10)
10. Idempotency (2)
11. Tautology-Elimination
12. Absurdity-Purification
13. Contradiction-Elimination
14. Quantifier-Replacement (4)

Principles

1. Identity
2. Excluded Middle
3. Non-Contradiction

SECTION 22. Correct and incorrect uses of the rules

22.1 In this section, you will find a number of examples that illustrate both the correct and incorrect uses of quantifier-rules.

22.2 Example 1.

Problem

$$1. \frac{L(a)}{\Sigma x L(x)} \qquad \Big\| \qquad \frac{L(a)}{(\exists x) L(x)}$$

Comment   Because there is no restriction on the use of particular generalization, this conclusion follows from the premise by that rule.

22.3 Example 2.

Problem

1. $\dfrac{L(a)}{\Pi x L(x)}$ $\biggm\|$ $\dfrac{L(a)}{(x)L(x)}$

Comment   This conclusion does not follow from the premise; because a is the subject of a premise, this problem violates one of the restrictions on universal generalization.

22.4 Example 3.

Problem

1. $\Pi x CL(x)M(x)$ $\biggm\|$ $(x)(L(x) \supset M(x))$
2. $\Pi x CM(x)N(x)$ $(x)(M(x) \supset N(x))$
   $\overline{\Pi x CL(x)N(x)}$ $\overline{(x)(L(x) \supset N(x))}$

Comment   To get this conclusion, the premise must first be instantiated. The rule of universal instantiation allows you to do this. After getting a formula for the instantiated subject that looks like the conclusion, the rule of universal generalization must be used:

3. $CL(a)M(a)$ $\biggm\|$ $(L(a) \supset M(a))$ 1; u.i.
4. $CM(a)N(a)$ $(M(a) \supset N(a))$ 2; u.i.
5. $CL(a)N(a)$ $(L(a) \supset N(a))$ 3, 4; h.s.
6. $\Pi x CL(x)N(x)$ $(x)(L(x) \supset N(x))$ 5; u.g.

Step 6 is allowed because the subject of the formula on line 5 is the subject of neither a premise nor an undischarged assumption.

22.5 Example 4.

Problem

1. $\Pi x CL(x)M(x)$ $\biggm\|$ $(x)(L(x) \supset M(x))$
2. $\Pi x CM(x)N(x)$ $(x)(M(x) \supset N(x))$
   $\overline{\Sigma x CL(x)N(x)}$ $\overline{(\exists x)(L(x) \supset N(x))}$

Comment   This problem is almost identical to the last one, except that the last step must be done by using the rule of particular generalization instead of universal generalization. Since particular generalization has no restrictions on its use, this inference can be done correctly.

22.6 Example 5.

Problem

1. $\Pi x CL(x)M(x)$	$(x)\,(L(x) \supset M(x))$
2. $\Sigma x KL(x)N(x)$	$(\exists x)\,(L(x) \cdot N(x))$
$\Pi x KM(x)N(x)$	$(x)\,(M(x) \cdot N(x))$

Comment Let's suppose that this problem can be done correctly even though it can't. What you would do is instantiate the premises, work out the demonstration, and then use universal generalization. It would probably go like this:

3.	$\ulcorner KL(a)N(a)$	$\ulcorner (L(a) \cdot N(a))$	assumed (from 2)
4.	$CL(a)M(a)$	$(L(a) \supset M(a))$	1; u.i.
5.	$L(a)$	$L(a)$	3; simp.
6.	$M(a)$	$M(a)$	4, 5; m.p.
7.	$N(a)$	$N(a)$	3; simp.
8.	$KM(a)N(a)$	$(M(a) \cdot N(a))$	6, 7; conj.
9.	$\Pi x KM(x)N(x)$	$(x)(M(x) \cdot N(x))$	8; u.g.
10.	$\Pi x KM(x)N(x)$	$(x)(M(x) \cdot N(x))$	2-9; p.i.

Of course step 9 is wrong, for the formula on line 8 has as its subject the subject of the undischarged assumption on line 3, and the rule of universal generalization cannot be used on formulas that have the subjects of undischarged assumptions.

22.7 Example 6.

Look at the same problem again. Notice that in working out the demonstration, we instantiated the second premise first. The reason was to avoid a different error, for suppose we do instantiate the first premise first and then the second:

3. $CL(a)M(a)$	$(L(a) \supset M(a))$	1; u.i.
4. $\ulcorner KL(a)N(a)$	$\ulcorner (L(a) \supset M(a))$	assumed (from 2)

Now however step 4 is wrong, for the subject of the formula on line 4 is also the subject of the formula on line 3, but the rule of particular instantiation says that the subject of the assumed formula cannot be the subject of any formula that shows up earlier in the demonstration. The correct instantiation of the second premise would have to have a different subject:

3'. $CL(a)M(a)$	$(L(a) \supset M(a))$	1; u.i.
4'. $\ulcorner KL(b)N(b)$	$\ulcorner L(b) \cdot N(b))$	assumed (from 2)

But now $L(b)$ and $L(a)$ do not match up, so modus ponens can no longer be carried out. If you can't use modus ponens, however, you can't work out the proof.

22.8 Example 7.

Problem

1. $\Pi x CL(x)M(x)$	$(x)\,(L(x) \supset M(x))$
2. $\Sigma x KL(x)N(x)$	$(\exists x)\,(L(x) \cdot N(x))$
$\Sigma x KM(x)N(x)$	$(\exists x)\,(M(x) \cdot N(x))$

Comment   This problem can be done correctly if you follow the right order in instantiating the premises. Because of the restrictions on the use of particular instantiation, you must instantiate the second premise first.

3.	$\ulcorner KL(a)N(a)$	$\ulcorner (L(a) \cdot N(a))$	assumed (from 2)
4.	$\;\;CL(a)M(a)$	$\;\;(L(a) \supset M(a))$	1; u.i.
5.	$\;\;L(a)$	$\;\;L(a)$	3; simp.
6.	$\;\;M(a)$	$\;\;M(a)$	4, 5; m.p.
7.	$\;\;N(a)$	$\;\;N(a)$	3; simp.
8.	$\;\;KM(a)N(a)$	$\;\;(M(a) \cdot N(a))$	6, 7; conj.
9.	$\;\;\Sigma x KM(x)N(x)$	$\;\;(\exists x)\,(M(x) \cdot N(x))$	8; p.g.
10.	$\Sigma x KM(x)N(x)$	$(\exists x)\,(M(x) \cdot N(x))$	2-9; p.i.

Steps 4 and 9 are all right because the rules of universal instantiation and particular generalization have no restrictions on their uses.

22.9 Example 8.

Problem

1. $\Sigma x KL(x)M(x)$	$(\exists x)\,(L(x) \cdot M(x))$
2. $\Sigma x KM(x)N(x)$	$(\exists x)\,(M(x) \cdot N(x))$
$\Sigma x KL(x)N(x)$	$(\exists x)\,(L(x) \cdot N(x))$

Comment   This problem cannot be done correctly. Because of the restrictions on the rule of particular instantiation, the premises must be instantiated with different subjects. When that is done, however, the result cannot be generalized:

3.	$\ulcorner KL(a)M(a)$	$\ulcorner (L(a) \cdot M(a))$	assumed (from 1)
4.	$\;\;\ulcorner KM(b)N(b)$	$\;\;\ulcorner (M(b) \cdot M(a))$	assumed (from 2)
5.	$\;\;\;\;L(a)$	$\;\;\;\;L(a)$	3; simp.
6.	$\;\;\;\;N(b)$	$\;\;\;\;N(b)$	4; simp.
7.	$\;\;\;\;KL(a)N(b)$	$\;\;\;\;(L(a) \cdot N(b))$	5, 6; conj.

139

The formula on line 7 cannot be generalized, because it names two different subjects, while all of the quantifier-rules as they are written in this chapter name only one subject.

22.10 Example 9.

Problem

1. $L(a)$	$L(a)$
2. $\Pi x CL(x)M(x)$	$(x)\,(L(x) \supset M(x))$
$M(a)$	$M(a)$

Comment To work out this problem, you only need to instantiate the second premise and use the rule of modus ponens.

3. $CL(a)M(a)$	$(L(a) \supset M(a))$	2; u.i.
4. $M(a)$	$M(a)$	1, 3; m.p.

22.11 Example 10.

Problem

1. $L(a)$	$L(a)$
2. $\Pi x CL(x)M(x)$	$(x)\,(L(x) \supset M(x))$
$\Sigma x M(x)$	$(\exists x)M(x)$

Comment This problem is similar to the last, except that its conclusion is a generalization. Since the rule of particular generalization has no restrictions on its use, this conclusion can be gotten from line 4 of the previous example:

3. $CL(a)M(a)$	$(L(a) \supset M(a))$	
4. $M(a)$	$M(a)$	
5. $\Sigma x M(x)$	$(\exists x)M(x)$	4; p.g.

22.12 Example 11.

Problem

1. $L(a)$	$L(a)$
2. $\Pi x CL(x)M(x)$	$(x)\,(L(x) \supset M(x))$
$\Pi x M(x)$	$(x)M(x)$

Comment Although the premises of this problem are identical to those of the last two, this conclusion cannot be gotten from them, for the subject of the formula on line 4 of the last two demonstrations is the subject of the first premise. So the rule of universal generalization cannot be used.

22.13 Example 12.

Problem

1. $NL(a)$
2. $\underline{\Sigma x A L(x) M(x)}$
   $M(a)$

$\sim L(a)$
$\underline{(\exists x)\,(L(x) \vee M(x))}$
$M(a)$

Comment This problem cannot be done correctly, for when the second premise is instantiated, some subject other than a must be named. So the subject of $M(\ )$ can never be a.

22.13.1 Exercise

Write out a paragraph analyzing each of the following argument-forms and then demonstrate their conclusions:

1. $\underline{\Sigma x K P(x) R(x)}$
   $\Sigma x K R(x) P(x)$

$\underline{(\exists x)\,(P(x) \cdot R(x))}$
$(\exists x)\,(R(x) \cdot P(x))$

2. $\underline{\Pi x C P(x) N R(x)}$
   $\Pi x C R(x) N P(x)$

$\underline{(x)\,(P(x) \supset \sim R(x))}$
$(x)\,(R(x) \supset \sim P(x))$

3. $\Pi x C Q(x) N R(x)$
   $\underline{\Pi x C P(x) Q(x)}$
   $\Pi x C P(x) N R(x)$

$(x)\,(Q(x) \supset \sim R(x))$
$\underline{(x)\,(P(x) \supset Q(x))}$
$(x)\,(P(x) \supset \sim R(x))$

4. $\Pi x C R(x) Q(x)$
   $\underline{\Pi x C P(x) N Q(x)}$
   $\Pi x C P(x) N R(x)$

$(x)\,(R(x) \supset Q(x))$
$\underline{(x)\,(P(x) \supset \sim Q(x))}$
$(x)\,(P(x) \supset \sim R(x))$

5. $\Pi x C R(x) Q(x)$
   $\underline{\Pi x C Q(x) N P(x)}$
   $\Pi x C P(x) N R(x)$

$(x)\,(R(x) \supset Q(x))$
$\underline{(x)\,(Q(x) \supset \sim P(x))}$
$(x)\,(P(x) \supset \sim R(x))$

6. $\Sigma x K Q(x) N R(x)$
   $\underline{\Pi x C Q(x) P(x)}$
   $\Sigma x K P(x) N R(x)$

$(\exists x)\,(Q(x) \cdot \sim R(x))$
$\underline{(x)\,(Q(x) \supset P(x))}$
$(\exists x)\,(P(x) \cdot \sim R(x))$

7. $\Pi x C R(x) N Q(x)$
   $\underline{\Sigma x K P(x) Q(x)}$
   $\Sigma x K P(x) N R(x)$

$(x)\,(R(x) \supset \sim Q(x))$
$\underline{(\exists x)\,(P(x) \cdot Q(x))}$
$(\exists x)\,(P(x) \cdot \sim R(x))$

8. $\Pi x E P(x) R(x)$
   $\underline{P(a)}$
   $\Sigma x R(x)$

$(x)\,(P(x) \equiv R(x))$
$\underline{P(a)}$
$(\exists x) R(x)$

22.13.2 Exercise

Write out a paragraph telling how to and then demonstrate the following formulas:

1. $EN\Pi xCP(x)R(x)\Sigma xKP(x)NR(x)$ ‖ $(\sim (x)\,(P(x) \supset R(x)) \equiv$
   $(\exists x)\,(P(x)\cdot \sim R(x)))$

2. $EN\Sigma xKP(x)R(x)\Pi xCP(x)NR(x)$ ‖ $(\sim(\exists x)\,(P(x)\cdot R(x)) \equiv$
   $(x)\,(P(x) \supset \sim R(x)))$

SECTION 23. English as a model of the system

23.1 The only task that is left is to learn to use these new methods on arguments. To do this, however, you must be able to translate arguments expressed in English into symbols. In this section, you will learn how to symbolize various kinds of sentences. When you have learned how to symbolize them, you should have no trouble symbolizing predicate arguments correctly.

23.2 Basically, there are three different kinds of sentences that need to be taken into account. These are universal, particular, and singular sentences, for these are the only kinds of sentences that the techniques of monadic predicate logic allow you to work with. But sentences of these kinds are not always written in the same standard ways.

23.3 You have already seen how the universal sentence "All philosophers seek wisdom" is to be symbolized. As you remember, it comes out "For all x, if x is a philosopher, x seeks wisdom." That is the standard way of symbolizing universal sentences. Universal sentences can also be negative. "No philosopher is vicious" is an example of one that is. Its standard translation is "For all x, if x is a philosopher, x is not vicious."

23.4 You have also already seen how particular sentences are to be symbolized. The sentence "Some men are philosophers," you remember, comes out "For some x, x is a man and x is a philosopher." Such sentences can also be negative. An example is "Some men are not philosophers." Its standard translation is "For some x, x is a man and x is not a philosopher."

23.5 You must be careful not to symbolize particular sentences with the symbol for material implication. To do so would be to weaken a particular sentence's meaning. For example, "Some men are philosophers" means that some things are both men and philosophers. If you made the mistake of symbolizing it with the symbol for material implication, it would come out like this:

$$\Sigma x CM(x)P(x) \qquad \| \qquad (\exists x)\, (M(x) \supset P(x))$$

Translated back into English, this sentence merely means that some things are either not men or philosophers. Anything that is not a man makes such a sentence true, but anything that is not a man does not make the sentence "Something is both a man and a philosopher" true.

23.6 You make an error of the same kind if you misplace the negation sign in symbolizing universal, negative sentences. The sentence "No philosopher is vicious" means "For all x, if x is a philosopher, x is not vicious." The sentence does not mean "For all x, it is false that if x is a philosopher, x is vicious." This last sentence would be symbolized like this:

$$\Pi x NCP(x)V(x) \qquad \| \qquad (x)\sim(P(x) \supset V(x))$$

When this is translated back into English, this formula means that everything is either a philosopher or vicious. And that says much more than the sentence "No philosopher is vicious" does.

23.7 Singular sentences, of course, are the easiest of all to symbolize. The sentence "Socrates is a philosopher" comes out merely as $P(s)$. Such sentences can also be negative. "Socrates is not a sophist" comes out

$$NS(s) \qquad \| \qquad \sim S(s)$$

23.8 Quantifiers, however, are not always expressed in the same way either. In addition to the words *all* and *no*, the universal quantifier is expressed by the following words: *every, everything, everyone, any, anything, anyone, each, who, he who, who so, whoever*, and their negative counterparts. In addition to the word *some*, the particular quantifier is expressed by the words *something, at least one, there exists, there are, a few, many, one, two, three*, etc.

23.9 Sometimes the quantifiers are left out completely. For example, the sentence "Philosophers are thoughtful" means all philosophers are thoughtful. Yet the sentence "Philosophers are alive" merely means some philosophers are alive. The full meaning of sentences without quantifiers must be gotten from the contexts in which such sentences are found.

23.10 Finally, sometimes the quantifiers are expressed by the articles *a, an,* and *the*. For instance, the sentence "A philosopher is a lover of wisdom" means all philosophers are lovers of wisdom; yet, the sentence "A philosopher is illogical" means some philosopher is illogical. Again it is the context that tells what is meant. Similarly, the sentence "The human being is a mammal" means all human beings are mammals, but the sentence "The human being who was the teacher of Plato was executed in Athens" is a singular sentence, since the phrase "The human being who was the teacher of Plato" is a description of a specific person. Such phrases are called *definite descriptions*.

23.11 Sentences such as "Not all philosophers are idealists" and "There are no living sophists" are sentences that negate quantifiers. The first means some philosophers are not idealists, and the second means all sophists are dead. You can, of course, symbolize them in the following respective ways:

$$N\Pi xCP(x)I(x) \qquad \qquad \sim (x)\,(P(x) \supset I(x))$$
$$N\Sigma xKP(x)L(x) \qquad \qquad \sim(\exists x)\,(P(x) \cdot L(x))$$

Then you can work them out by using the quantifier replacement-rules.

23.12 Sometimes universal, particular, and singular sentences are written in more complicated ways. Sometimes they are merely disordered. For example, "Idealists are all dreamers" means all idealists are dreamers. Similarly, "All is thought well that is logical" means all that is logical is thought well. Sometimes universal, particular, and singular sentences have compound subjects and predicates. The sentence "Philosophers are both intelligent and knowing" means "For all x, if x is a philosopher, then x is intelligent and x is knowing." Similarly, the sentence "All ontologists are either monists or pluralists" means "For all x, if x is an ontologist, then x is a monist or x is a pluralist." But what about the sentence "Philosophers and mathematicians are logicians"? It means "For all x, if x is a philosopher *or* if x is a mathematician, then x is a logician," for you do not have to be both a philosopher and a mathematician to be a logician.

23.13 Certain sentences like "All the great philosophers except Democritus are not materialists" are called *exceptive propositions* because they point out exceptions. The sentence refers to all the great philosophers *except* Democritus. These exceptive sentences mean two things. This one means (1) that if x is a great philosopher and x is not Democritus, then x is not a materialist; and (2) that if x is a great philosopher and x is not a materialist, then x is not Democritus. Such a pair of sentences can be written with the sign of material equivalence and should be universally quantified. The sentences mean, then, that "For all x, if x is a great philosopher, then x is not Democritus if and only if x is not a materialist." Other ways of expressing the same sentence are these: "All the great philosophers but Democritus are not materialists" and "Of all the great philosophers, Democritus alone is a materialist." Each of these is to be symbolized just like the first one. Not all exceptive sentences are universally quantified material equivalences, however. Some are conjunctions of particular sentences. For example, the sentence "Most philosophers are wise" means that some philosophers are wise and some are not. Other ways of writing such conjunctions follow: "Almost all philosophers are wise"; "Not quite all philosophers are wise"; "All but a few philosophers are wise"; and "Almost every philosopher is wise."

23.14 Another special kind of sentence is called *exclusive*, because such sentences exclude something. For example, the sentence "Only philosophers deserve to be honored" *excludes* from those who are honorable all except philosophers. This sentence means that if one deserves to be honored, he is a philosopher. But it does not mean that all philosophers deserve to be honored, for some of them may not be honorable. So this sentence must be symbolized, "For all x, if x deserves to be honored, x is a philosopher." Other ways of writing the same sentence are these: "None but philosophers deserve to be honored"; "Philosophers alone deserve to be honored"; and "Philosophers exclusively deserve to be honored." All of these are to be symbolized in the same way.

23.15 Sometimes universal sentences are definitions, and definitions can be symbolized as universally quantified material equivalences. For instance the word *philosopher* is often defined as *lover of wisdom*. So you can say that a philosopher is a lover of wisdom and mean "For all x, x is a philosopher if and only if x is a lover of wisdom."

23.16 On rare occasions, sentences must be rewritten if they are going to be symbolized correctly. Whenever you must rewrite sentences, the three words *times, places,* and *cases* are very useful. These words are often called *parameters*. To understand how to use them, take a sentence like "Socrates always wins an argument." It means "Whenever Socrates argues, he wins." And this in turn can be translated into this: "For all x, if x is a time when Socrates argues, x is a time when Socrates wins." The word *times* used in this way allows us to turn the original sentence into a standard universal sentence. The words *places* and *cases* can be used in similar ways. The sentence "Where there are no philosophers, there is little wisdom" can be changed into a standard universal sentence by using the parameter *places*. It goes like this: "For all x, if x is a place where

145

there are no philosophers, then x is a place where there is little wisdom." Finally, consider this sentence: "A philosopher dishonors his profession whenever he argues poorly." Its standard translation is "For all x, if x is a case of a philosopher's arguing poorly, then x is a case of a philosopher's dishonoring his profession." Of course, when you are symbolizing sentences, you must symbolize synonymous expressions with the same predicate variable.

23.16.1 Exercise

Symbolize the following arguments and demonstrate their conclusions:

1. All members of the Academy are Platonists. Some members of the Academy concerned themselves only with ethics. So some Platonists concerned themselves only with ethics.

2. None of the great sages except Thales was an important philosopher. Yet many of the great sages in addition to Thales were famous for their wisdom. So some who were famous for their wisdom were not important philosophers.

3. He who believes in reified abstractions is a Platonist. Anyone who is a Platonist is not a relativist. So believers in reified abstractions are not relativists.

4. Philosophers are lovers and seekers of wisdom. Yet a seeker of wisdom is a zetetic. So philosophers are zetetics.

5. Phyrro alone of all the great Greek philosophers was a skeptic. So most great Greek philosophers were not skeptics. (Since most great Greek philosophers were not Phyrro.)

6. There are no living peripatetics. Demetrius was a peripatetic. So Demetrius is dead.

7. No philosopher who is either a poor logician or an immoral person can be respected. So no philosopher who is immoral can be respected.

8. All sophists are teachers of rhetoric. Sophistic teachers of rhetoric are dishonest. Any sophistic teacher of rhetoric who is dishonest is a scoundrel. So all sophists are scoundrels.

9. Platonists and Aristotelians are philosophers. Speusippus was a Platonist and Theophrastus was an Aristotelian. So Speusippus and Theophrastus were philosophers.

10. If he were unbiased, anyone on the jury who knew Socrates would have voted to free him. And everyone on the jury would have been unbiased except those who were criticized by Socrates or were friends of his accusers Meletus, Anytus, and Lyco. But no one on the jury was ever criticized by Socrates nor were they friends of the accusers. Yet not every-

one on the jury voted to free Socrates. So not everyone on the jury knew him.

23.16.2 Exercise

The following terms have been introduced in this chapter. You should know the meaning of each.

predicate logic	definite description
quantifier	exceptive proposition
universal quantifier	exclusive proposition
particular quantifier	parameter
universal formula	universe of discourse
particular formula	propositional function
singular formula	generalization
quantifier replacement-rules	instance of a generalization
quantificational argument	universal generalization
monadic predicate logic	particular generalization

Chapter FOUR **INVALIDITY AND UNSOUNDNESS**

SECTION 24. Validity

24.1 Until now, you have had, for the most part, to deal only with good reasoning, that is, with reasoning in which conclusions follow from their premises. Logicians call such reasoning valid. A feature of all of such reasoning is this: conclusions must be true whenever their premises are true. This feature is usually used as a definition of validity, and what this defiinition means can be explained in two ways.

24.2 First, you will remember that in chapter 2, the reason the laws of logic always work was explained. These explanations are based on the truth-tables that define the truth-functors. We said, for instance, that if

$$Kpq \qquad\qquad \| \qquad\qquad (p \cdot q)$$

has the truth-value t, we know that p and q each must also have that truth-value, for a conjunction has the value t only if both of its conjuncts have the value t. So if we have

$$Kpq \qquad \| \qquad (p \cdot q)$$

we can write down either p or q by itself. Whichever we do write down must have the value t. In other words, if the premise is the conjunction of p and q, and if that conjunction has the value t, the conclusion, if it is one of the conjuncts, must also have the value t. When you derive p from the conjunction of p and q, your reasoning is valid. Of course, all of the transformation-rules lay out valid ways of reasoning, and any argument-form whose conclusion can be gotten from its premises by using transformation-rules also lays out a valid way of reasoning. So, in chapters 2 and 3, you were shown one way of finding out if an argument-form is valid (that is, lays out a valid way of reasoning), and in learning how to find this out, you were shown the basic methods and principles of valid reasoning.

24.3 But there is another way to understand the definition of validity. Since the explanations of why the laws of logic always work are based on the truth-tables that define the truth-functors, truth-tables can also be used to show that reasoning is valid. You should remember that most of the laws of logic that you learned are tautological. (The only exceptions are the three complicated laws of assumption, cases, and negative absurdity.) The reason that laws of logic are tautological is this: As you know, most of the transformation-rules can be written as conditional statements: The premises of a transformation-rule are conjoined and made into an antecedent while the conclusion is made into a consequent. The rule of simplification, then, can be written like this:

$$CKpqp \qquad \| \qquad ((p \cdot q) \supset p)$$

Now why is this tautological? The answer is because it is impossible for the value of the consequent to be f whenever the value of the antecedent is t. But this last sentence is just another way of writing the definition of validity that was given in subsection 24.1. So all tautological reasoning is valid. If you want to find out if an argument-form is valid then, you can write it out as a formula and make a truth-table. If the formula is tautological, it lays out a valid way of reasoning. For instance, look at a truth-table for modus tollens.

$CKCpqNqNp$		$(((p \supset q) \cdot \sim q) \supset \sim p)$
$t\,f\,t\,t\,t\,f\,t\,f\,t$	$\|$	$t\quad t\quad t\,f\,f\,t\quad t\quad f\,t$
$t\,f\,f\,t\,f\,t\,f\,f\,t$	$\|$	$t\quad f\quad f\,f\,t\,f\quad t\quad f\,t$
$t\,f\,t\,f\,t\,f\,t\,t\,f$	$\|$	$f\quad t\quad t\,f\,f\,t\quad t\quad t\,f$
$t\,t\,t\,f\,f\,t\,f\,t\,f$	$\|$	$f\quad t\quad f\,t\,t\,f\quad t\quad t\,f$

149

SECTION 24. Validity

25.1 Unfortunately, not all reasoning is valid; people sometimes reason invalidly. It is important not only to be able to recognize invalid reasoning but also to be able to show that such reasoning is invalid. In this section, you will be taught four ways to do this.

25.2 The first way is analyzing arguments. If you have learned the methods and principles that were put forth in chapters 2 and 3, you should be able to recognize most of the invalid reasoning you are likely to come across. For instance, look at the following argument-form:

$$
\begin{array}{c}
Cpq \\
ANqr \\
Asp \\
\underline{s} \\
r
\end{array}
\qquad \qquad
\begin{array}{c}
(p \supset q) \\
(\sim q \vee r) \\
(s \vee p) \\
\underline{s} \\
r
\end{array}
$$

If you tried to analyze this argument-form, you would probably do it in the following way. First you would look for r in the premises. You would see that it is one of the alternatives in the second premise. So you would know that you can get it only if you can get the negation of the other alternative. So you would go looking for q. You would find it as the consequent of the first premise. To get it, you need the antecedent. So you would go looking for p. It is one of the alternatives in the third premise. To get it you need the negation of the other alternative. So you would go looking for the negation of s. But you would not find it; instead, you would find s. So you would conclude that it is impossible to get r from those premises by using the transformation-rules you know. The argument-form must be invalid.

25.3 Analyzing arguments is the method you should use most often to recognize invalid reasoning. Unfortunately, arguments can be written that are very difficult to analyze, so you cannot always rely on this method. Furthermore, to show someone who did not know the transformation-rules that an invalid argument-form is invalid might prove to be difficult. One way to do this is to make up what is known as a counterexample.

25.4 The key to making up a counterexample is the definition of validity. Reasoning is valid, you remember, if the conclusion must be true whenever the premises are true. So if some chain of reasoning has a false conclusion and true premises, it must be invalid. If you want to show that an argument is invalid then, all you need to do is make up another argument that has the same form as the one you think is invalid but that also has premises that can be true whenever the conclusion is false. For instance, suppose someone presented this argument:

If Plato's theory of forms were true, Plato would have known what justice is. Since the theory of forms is false, he did not know what justice is.

The form of this argument is this:

Cpq $\|$ $(p \supset q)$
$\dfrac{Np}{Nq}$ $\dfrac{\sim p}{\sim q}$

To show that this argument is invalid, all you have to do is make up another argument that has the same form but that has premises that can be true when the conclusion is false—in other words, make up a counterexample. Thinking of counterexamples for this argument is easy; for instance, look at this one:

If Plato had a daughter, he was a father. Since he had no daughter, he was not a father.

The premises of this argument can be true when the conclusion is false, for the conclusion is false if Plato had a son and the premises are true if he did not have a daughter.

25.5   To be able to think of a counterexample for every invalid argument, however, is a very hard job. Luckily, you do not need to. What you can do instead is make a truth-table. In subsection 24.4, we pointed out that all tautological reasoning is valid. So whenever reasoning is invalid, it is not tautological. For instance, look at the argument-form that was used as an example in the last paragraph:

Cpq $\|$ $(p \supset q)$
$\dfrac{Np}{Nq}$ $\dfrac{\sim p}{\sim q}$

By using the method you learned in chapter 1, you can turn this into the following formula:

$CKCpqNpNq$ $\|$ $(((p \supset q) \cdot \sim p) \supset \sim q)$

If you build a truth-table for this formula, the table comes out like this:

CKCpqNpNq		$(((p \supset q) \cdot \sim p) \supset \sim q)$
t f t t t f t f t	‖	t t t f f t t f t
t f f t f f t t f	‖	t f f f f t t t f
f t t f t t f f t	‖	f t t t t f f f t
t t t f f t f t f	‖	f t f t t f t t f

Now look at the third line of this table:

CKCpqNpNq		$(((p \supset q) \cdot \sim p) \supset \sim q)$
f t t f t t f f t	‖	f t t t t f f f t

This has the value f because the antecedent has the value t and the consequent has the value f. Since the antecedent was made by conjoining the premises of the argument-form, and the consequent is the conclusion of the argument-form, this line shows that the premises can be true when the conclusion is false. In effect, this line is an abstract counterexample for the argument-form we are testing.

25.6   So another way of showing that an argument-form is invalid is by making up an abstract counterexample. To do this, all you have to do is assign truth-values to the parts of the argument-form so that the conclusion is false and the premises are true. The procedure for doing this never varies. First, you give the conclusion the value f by assigning its parts the appropriate values. Then, by using those values, choose values for the remaining parts of the argument so that each premise has the value t. For example, take the argument-form we just made a truth-table for:

Cpq		$(p \supset q)$
Np	‖	$\sim p$
___		___
Nq		$\sim q$

To give the conclusion the value f, we must give q the value t. If q has the value t, however, the first premise must have the value t. So all you have to do is give the second premise the value t by giving p the value f. This shows that the argument-form is invalid, for the premises have the value t and the conclusion has the value f.

25.7   If you tried to use this procedure on a valid argument-form, you would find that you could not make the value of each of the premises t when the value of the conclusion is f. The reason for this is merely that all tautological argument-forms are valid. For instance, look at modus ponens:

$$Cpq \qquad\qquad\qquad (p \supset q)$$
$$\frac{p}{q} \qquad\qquad\qquad \frac{p}{q}$$

If you give the conclusion q the value f, you must give p the value f if the first premise is to have the value t. But then the value of the second premise is f. On the other hand, if you give p the value t to give the second premise the value t, the first premise has the value f. You cannot give each of the premises the value t when the conclusion has the value f. The argument-form, therefore, must be valid.

25.7.1 Exercise

Look at the following argument-forms. (1) Analyze them to see why they are invalid, (2) assign truth-values to show that they are invalid, and (3) try to make up a counterexample for each one.

(1) Cpq $(p \supset q)$
     $\dfrac{q}{p}$ $\dfrac{q}{p}$

(2) Cpq $(p \supset q)$
     Cpr $(p \supset r)$
     $\overline{Cqr}$ $\overline{(q \supset r)}$

(3) Apq $(p \lor q)$
     $\dfrac{p}{Nq}$ $\dfrac{p}{\sim q}$

(4) Cpq $(p \supset q)$
     Crs $(r \supset s)$
     Aqs $(q \lor s)$
     $\overline{Apr}$ $\overline{(p \lor r)}$

(5) Cps $(p \supset s)$
     $CsNp$ $(s \supset \sim p)$
     $\overline{EsNp}$ $\overline{(s \equiv \sim p)}$

(6) Epq $(p \equiv q)$
     $NKNpNq$ $\sim(\sim p \cdot \sim q)$
     $\overline{NKpq}$ $\overline{\sim(p \cdot q)}$

25.8   These methods work for invalid quantificational arguments too. But applying the method of assigning truth-values is a little bit more complicated. The reason for this complication is that quantificational arguments are about different numbers of individuals. Some of these arguments are about all of the individuals in the universe of discourse, some are about some of those individuals, and others are about only one individual. So we must find a way of laying out an argument that shows the number of individuals we are testing for. You will find that some arguments are valid in universes that have a certain number of individuals in them and invalid in universes with a greater number of individuals.

25.9   To lay out argument-forms so that they show the number of individuals they are being tested for, you must remember that a universally quantified formula stands for a conjunction and that a particularly quantified formula stands for an alternation. Remembering this, look at the following argument-form:

$$\begin{array}{ll} \Pi x CR(x)Q(x) & \qquad\qquad (x)(R(x) \supset Q(x)) \\ \Sigma x KP(x)Q(x) & \qquad\qquad (\exists x)(P(x) \cdot Q(x)) \\ \hline \Sigma x KP(x)R(x) & \qquad\qquad (\exists x)(P(x) \cdot R(x)) \end{array}$$

To test it for a universe of one individual, you merely write it out like this:

$$\begin{array}{ll} CR(a)Q(a) & \qquad\qquad (R(a) \supset Q(a)) \\ KP(a)Q(a) & \qquad\qquad (P(a) \cdot Q(a)) \\ \hline KP(a)R(a) & \qquad\qquad (P(a) \cdot R(a)) \end{array}$$

You can easily show that this is invalid by giving $P(a)$ the value t, $R(a)$ the value f, and $Q(a)$ the value t. If you are going to test it for a universe of two, you must write it out differently, however. Since the first premise is universally quantified, it must be written out as a conjunction of two separate formulas that are about different subjects. So it comes out like this:

$$KCR(a)Q(a)CR(b)Q(b) \qquad \| \qquad ((R(a) \supset Q(a)) \cdot (R(b) \supset Q(b)))$$

Since the conclusion is also particularly quantified, it must be written out in as an alternation of two separate formulas that are about different subjects. So it comes out like this:

$$AKP(a)Q(a)KP(b)Q(b) \qquad \| \qquad ((P(a) \cdot Q(a)) \vee (P(b) \cdot Q(b)))$$

Since the conclusion is also particularly quantified, it must be written out in a similar way:

$$AKP(a)R(a)KP(b)R(b) \qquad \| \qquad ((P(a) \cdot R(a)) \lor (P(b) \cdot R(b)))$$

You can show that this is invalid by giving $P(a)$ and $R(b)$ the value f and everything else the value t. And now, if you want to test this argument for a universe of three, the first premise must be written as a conjunction of three separate formulas that are about different subjects, and the second premise and the conclusion must be written as alternations of three separate formulas that are about different subjects:

$$KKCR(a)Q(a)CR(b)Q(b) \qquad \| \qquad (((R(a) \supset Q(a)) \cdot (R(b) \supset Q(b))) \cdot$$
$$CR(c)Q(c) \qquad\qquad\qquad (R(c) \supset Q(c)))$$
$$AAKP(a)Q(a)KP(b)Q(b) \qquad \| \qquad (((P(a) \cdot Q(a)) \lor (P(b) \cdot Q(b))) \lor$$
$$KP(c)Q(c) \qquad\qquad\qquad (P(c) \cdot Q(c)))$$
$$AAKP(a)R(a)KP(b)R(b) \qquad \| \qquad (((P(a) \cdot R(a)) \lor (P(b) \cdot R(b))) \lor$$
$$KP(c)R(c) \qquad\qquad\qquad (P(c) \cdot R(c)))$$

This method of writing out argument-forms can be stretched to cover universes made up of any number of individuals.

25.10 An example of an argument-form that is valid in a universe of one but invalid in universes larger than one is this:

$$\Sigma x KR(x)Q(x) \qquad \| \qquad (\exists x)\,(R(x) \cdot Q(x))$$
$$\Sigma x KP(x)Q(x) \qquad\qquad (\exists x)\,(P(x) \cdot Q(x))$$
$$\overline{\Sigma x KP(x)R(x)} \qquad\qquad \overline{(\exists x)\,(P(x) \cdot R(x))}$$

25.10.1 Exercise

Show that the argument-form in subsection 25.10 is valid in a universe of one and invalid in a universe of two.

25.11 Because some arguments are valid in universes that have a certain number of individuals in them and invalid in universe with a greater number of individuals, you quite often have to decide on the size of the universe before you test an argument. This decision is easy to make for monadic predicate-logic, for it has been shown that an argument in monadic predicate-logic is valid if and only if it is valid in a universe of 2^n individuals, where n equals the number of different predicates in the argument. So to be sure that the argument-form in subsection 25.10 is invalid, you might test it in a universe of eight (since the argument-form contains three different predicates). But you do not always have to test an argument for a universe of 2^n individuals, for we also know that if an argument is invalid in a universe of a certain size, it is also invalid in any larger universe. So because we know that the argument form in subsection 25.10 is invalid in

155

a universe of two, we know that it is also invalid in a universe of eight. An argument in predicate-logic is universally valid if and only if it is valid in every non-empty universe, that is, in every universe that has members.

25.11.1 Exercise

By assigning truth-values to the parts of the following argument-forms, show that they are invalid.

(1) $\Pi x C Q(x) R(x)$ $(x)\,(Q(x) \supset R(x))$
$\Pi x C Q(x) P(x)$ $(x)\,(Q(x) \supset P(x))$
$\overline{\Pi x C P(x) R(x)}$ $\overline{(x)\,(P(x) \supset R(x))}$

(2) $\Pi x C R(x) Q(x)$ $(x)\,(R(x) \supset Q(x))$
$\Pi x C Q(x) N P(x)$ $(x)\,(Q(x) \supset\, \sim P(x))$
$\overline{\Sigma x K P(x) N R(x)}$ $\overline{(\exists x)\,(P(x) \cdot \sim R(x))}$

(3) $\Pi x C Q(x) N R(x)$ $(x)\,(Q(x) \supset\, \sim R(x))$
$\Sigma x K P(x) Q(x)$ $(\exists x)\,(P(x) \cdot Q(x))$
$\overline{\Sigma x K P(x) R(x)}$ $\overline{(\exists x)\,(P(x) \cdot R(x))}$

(4) $\Sigma x K R(x) Q(x)$ $(\exists x)\,(R(x) \cdot Q(x))$
$\Sigma x K P(x) N Q(x)$ $(\exists x)\,(P(x) \cdot \sim Q(x))$
$\overline{\Pi x C P(x) R(x)}$ $\overline{(x)\,(P(x) \supset R(x))}$

(5) $\Sigma x K Q(x) R(x)$ $(\exists x)\,(Q(x) \cdot R(x))$
$\Sigma x K Q(x) P(x)$ $(\exists x)\,(Q(x) \cdot P(x))$
$\overline{\Sigma x K P(x) R(x)}$ $\overline{(\exists x)\,(P(x) \cdot R(x))}$

(6) $\Sigma x K R(x) N Q(x)$ $(\exists x)\,(R(x) \cdot \sim Q(x))$
$\Pi x C Q(x) P(x)$ $(x)\,(Q(x) \supset P(x))$
$\overline{\Pi x C P(x) R(x)}$ $\overline{(x)\,(P(x) \supset R(x))}$

(7) $\Sigma x K Q(x) N R(x)$ $(\exists x)\,(Q(x) \cdot \sim R(x))$
$\Sigma x K P(x) Q(x)$ $(\exists x)\,(P(x) \cdot Q(x))$
$\overline{\Pi x C P(x) N R(x)}$ $\overline{(x)\,(P(x) \supset\, \sim R(x))}$

(8) $\Sigma x K R(x) N Q(x)$ $(\exists x)\,(R(x) \cdot \sim Q(x))$
$\Sigma x K P(x) N Q(x)$ $(\exists x)\,(P(x) \cdot \sim Q(x))$
$\overline{\Sigma x K P(x) N R(x)}$ $\overline{(\exists x)\,(P(x) \cdot \sim R(x))}$

(9) $\Pi x C P(x) A Q(x) R(x)$ $(x)\,(P(x) \supset (Q(x) \vee R(x)))$
$\Sigma x K P(x) N S(x)$ $(\exists x)\,(P(x) \cdot \sim S(x))$
$\overline{\Sigma x K Q(x) N S(x)}$ $\overline{(\exists x)\,(Q(x) \cdot \sim S(x))}$

(10) $\Pi x C A P(x) Q(x) A R(x) S(x)$ $(x)\,((P(x) \vee Q(x)) \supset (R(x) \vee S(x)))$
$\Sigma x K Q(x) N R(x)$ $(\exists x)\,(Q(x) \cdot \sim R(x))$
$\overline{\Sigma x K P(x) S(x)}$ $\overline{(\exists x)\,(P(x) \cdot S(x))}$

25.12 Another way of deciding whether arguments are valid is to build what logicians call tableaux. The basis of this method also comes from the truth-tables that define truth-functors. From those truth-tables we know the following eight things:

(1) If the negation of p has the value t, then p has the value f.

(2) If the negation of p has the value f, then p has the value t.

(3) If the conjunction of p and q has the value t, then both p and q have the value t.

(4) If the conjunction of p and q has the value f, then either p has the value f or q has the value f.

(5) If the alternation of p and q has the value t, then either p has the value t or q has the value t.

(6) If the alternation of p and q has the value f, then both p and q have the value f.

(7) If the material implication of p and q has the value t, then either p has the value f or q has the value t.

(8) If the material implication of p and q has the value f, then p has the value t and q has the value f.

By using these eight facts, we can build the following seven rules for the construction of tableaux: (Let the letters Φ and Ψ stand for any well-formed formulas.)

I	$NN\Phi$		$\sim\sim\Phi$
	Φ		Φ
II	$K\Phi\Psi$		$(\Phi \cdot \Psi)$
	Φ		Ψ
	Ψ		Ψ
III	$NK\Phi\Psi$		$\sim(\Phi \cdot \Psi)$
	$N\Phi \,/\, N\Psi$		$\sim\Phi \,/\sim\Psi$
IV	$A\Phi\Psi$		$(\Phi \vee \Psi)$
	$\Phi \,/\, \Psi$		$\Phi \,/\, \Psi$
V	$NA\Phi\Psi$		$\sim(\Phi \vee \Psi)$
	$N\Phi$		$\sim\Phi$
	$N\Psi$		$\sim\Psi$
VI	$C\Phi\Psi$		$(\Phi \supset \Psi)$
	$N\Phi \,/\, \Psi$		$\sim\Phi \,/\, \Psi$
VII	$NC\Phi\Psi$		$\sim(\Phi \supset \Psi)$
	Φ		Φ
	$N\Psi$		$\sim\Psi$

The formulas below horizontal lines are consequences of the formulas that are written above horizontal lines. For example

$$\Phi \qquad\qquad \| \qquad\qquad \Phi$$

is a consequence of

$$NN\Phi \qquad\qquad \| \qquad\qquad \sim\,\sim \Phi$$

and

$$N\Phi \;/\; \Psi \qquad\qquad \| \qquad\qquad \sim \Phi \;/\; \Psi$$

are alternative consequences of

$$C\Phi\Psi \qquad\qquad \| \qquad\qquad (\Phi \supset \Psi)$$

(A slash between two formulas merely means that the formulas are alternatives.)

25.13   To build a tableau for a formula, follow these steps:
(1) Negate the formula and write it as the first line of the tableau.
(2) By using the appropriate rule, write down the consequences of the formula that is written on the first line of the tableau.
(3) Then by using the appropriate rule or rules, write down the consequences of the formula or formulas that are written on the second line of the tableau.
(4) Next, by using the appropriate rule or rules, write down the consequences of the formula or formulas that are written on the third line of the tableau.
(5) Keep on doing this until all of the consequences of each line are written down. What you have when you are finished is a tableau.

25.14   For instance, look at the following formula and its tableau:

$$CKApqNpq \qquad \| \quad (((p \vee q) \cdot \sim p) \supset q)$$

Tableau

1. $NCKApqNpq$	$\sim(((p \vee q) \cdot \sim p) \supset q)$	the formula negated
2. $KApqNp$	$((p \vee q) \cdot \sim p)$	from 1 by rule VII
3. Nq	$\sim q$	
4. Apq	$(p \vee q)$	from 2 by rule II
5. Np	$\sim p$	
6. $p \quad /q$	$p \quad /q$	from 4 by rule IV

Lines 3, 5, and 6 have no consequences, so the tableau is complete. Because of the slash on line 6, this tableau is made up of two columns (or branches) of formulas. The branch on the left contains all the formulas on lines 1 through 5 and the formula p (on line 6). The branch on the right contains all the formulas on lines 1 through 5 and the formula q (on line 6.)

25.15 Let's look at another example:

Formula

$\quad$ KApqNCpq $\qquad \| \ ((p \lor q) \cdot {\sim}(p \supset q))$

Tableau

1. NKApqNCpq $\qquad \| \quad {\sim}((p \lor q) \cdot {\sim}(p \supset q)) \quad$ the formula negated
2. NApq $\quad$ /NNCpq $\qquad {\sim}(p \lor q) \qquad /{\sim}{\sim} \qquad$ from 1 by rule III
$\qquad\qquad\qquad\qquad\qquad\qquad (p \supset q)$
3. Np $\qquad$ Cpq $\qquad\quad {\sim}p \qquad\qquad (p \supset q) \quad$ from 2 by rule V, and
$\qquad\qquad\qquad\qquad\qquad\qquad\qquad\qquad\qquad$ from 2 by rule I
4. Nq $\qquad$ Np $\quad$ /q $\qquad {\sim}q \qquad\qquad {\sim}p \quad /q \quad$ from 2 by rule V, and
$\qquad\qquad\qquad\qquad\qquad\qquad\qquad\qquad\qquad$ from 3 by rule VI

The first formula on line 3 and the three formulas on line 4 have no consequences; so the tableau is complete. The tableau is made up of three branches (because of the slash on line 2 and the slash on line 4.) The first branch contains these formulas:

$\quad$ 1. NKApqNCpq $\quad \| \quad {\sim}((p \lor q) \cdot {\sim}(p \supset q))$
$\quad$ 2. NApq $\qquad\qquad {\sim}(p \lor q)$
$\quad$ 3. Np $\qquad\qquad\quad {\sim}p$
$\quad$ 4. Nq $\qquad\qquad\quad {\sim}q$

The second branch contains these formulas:

$\quad$ 1. NKApqNCpq $\quad \| \quad {\sim}((p \lor q) \cdot {\sim}(p \supset q))$
$\quad$ 2. NNCpq $\qquad\qquad {\sim}{\sim}(p \supset q)$
$\quad$ 3. Cpq $\qquad\qquad\quad (p \supset q)$
$\quad$ 4. Np $\qquad\qquad\quad {\sim}p$

And the third branch contains these formulas:

$\quad$ 1. NKApqNCpq $\quad \| \quad {\sim}((p \lor q) \cdot {\sim}(p \supset q))$
$\quad$ 2. NNCpq $\qquad\qquad {\sim}{\sim}(p \supset q)$
$\quad$ 3. Cpq $\qquad\qquad\quad (p \supset q)$
$\quad$ 4. q $\qquad\qquad\qquad q$

25.16 If a formula is tautological, each branch of its tableau will contain both a formula and its negation. For instance both p and its negation are in the left branch of the tableau presented in subsection 25.14, and q and its negation are in the right branch. If each branch of a formula's tableau does not contain both a formula and its negation, the formula is not tautological. For instance, no branch of the tableau presented in subsection 25.15 contains both a formula and its negation.

25.16.1 Exercise

Build a tableau that shows that the law of association for material equivalence

$$EEpEqrEEpqr \qquad \| \qquad ((p \equiv (q \equiv r)) \equiv ((p \equiv q) \equiv r))$$

is tautological.

25.17 Tableaux such as these can be used to show whether an argument is valid or invalid. What you do is write each premise down as a line of the tableau. Next negate the conclusion and write it down as the next line of the tableau. Then work out the consequences of these and all following lines. When the tableau is complete, check each branch to see if it contains both a formula and its negation. If each branch does, the argument is valid; if any branch does not, the argument is invalid.

25.17.1 Exercise

Build tableaux for the problems in 25.7.1

25.18 The tableau-method can be used to show the validity or invalidity of arguments written out in monadic predicate-logic also. But to do so, we need four more rules:

VIII	$\dfrac{\Pi x \phi(x)}{\phi(a)}$	$\|$	$\dfrac{(x)\phi(x)}{\phi(a)}$
IX	$\dfrac{N\Sigma x \phi(x)}{N\phi(a)}$		$\dfrac{\sim(\exists x)\phi(x)}{\sim\phi(a)}$
X	$\dfrac{\Sigma x \phi(x)}{\phi(a)}$		$\dfrac{(\exists x)\phi(x)}{\phi(a)}$

provided the subject a does not appear earlier in the tableau.

INVALIDITY AND UNSOUNDNESS

XI $\dfrac{N\Pi x\phi(x)}{N\phi(a)}$ ‖ $\dfrac{\sim(x)\phi(x)}{\sim\phi(a)}$

provided the subject a does not appear earlier in the tableau.

In using these rules on arguments, rather than on formulas, you must remember to work out the consequences of lines that must be done by using rules X and XI before you work out the consequences of lines that must be done by using rules VIII and IX. This requirement is related to the similar one that requires you to instantiate particular premises before you instantiate universal ones in doing ordinary demonstrations.

25.19 For example, look again at the argument-form we dealt with in subsection 25.10:

$\Sigma x KR(x)Q(x)$	‖	$(\exists x)\,(R(x)\cdot Q(x))$
$\Sigma x KP(x)Q(x)$	‖	$(\exists x)\,(P(x)\cdot Q(x))$
$\overline{\Sigma x KP(x)R(x)}$	‖	$\overline{(\exists x)\,(P(x)\cdot R(x))}$

First write down the two premises as the first two lines in the tableau and then write down the negation of the conclusion as the third line. Next, work out the tableau.

		‖		
1.	$\Sigma x KR(x)Q(x)$	‖	$(\exists x)\,(R(x)\cdot Q(x))$	1st premise
2.	$\Sigma x KP(x)Q(x)$	‖	$(\exists x)\,(P(x)\cdot Q(x))$	2nd premise
3.	$N\Sigma x KP(x)R(x)$	‖	$\sim(\exists x)\,(P(x)\cdot R(x))$	negated conc.
4.	$KR(a)Q(a)$	‖	$(R(a)\cdot Q(a))$	1, X.
5.	$KP(b)Q(b)$	‖	$(P(b)\cdot Q(b))$	2, X.
6.	$NKP(a)R(a)$	‖	$\sim(P(a)\cdot R(a))$	3, IX.
7.	$NKP(b)R(b)$	‖	$\sim(P(b)\cdot R(b))$	3, IX.
8.	$R(a)$	‖	$R(a)$	4, II.
9.	$Q(a)$	‖	$Q(a)$	4, II.
10.	$P(b)$	‖	$P(b)$	5, II.
11.	$Q(b)$	‖	$Q(b)$	5, II.
12.	$NP(a)$	‖	$\sim P(a)$	6, III.
	$/NR(a)$	‖	$/\sim R(a)$	
13.	$NP(b)/NR(b)$	‖	$\sim P(b)/\sim R(b)$	7, III.
	$NP(b)/NR(b)$	‖	$\sim P(b)/R(b)$	

This tableau has four branches: the first is made up of all the formulas on lines 1 through 11, the first formula on line 12, and the first formula on line 13; the second is made up of all the formulas on lines 1 through 11, the first formula on line 12, and the second formula on line 13; the third is made up of all the formulas on lines 1 through 11, the second formula on line 12, and the third formula on line 13; and finally, the fourth is made up of all the formulas on lines 1 through 11, the second formula on line 12, and the fourth formula on line 13. Notice that the consequences that are written on line 13 are written twice—once for each branch of line 12—and that lines 6 and 7 are each consequences of line 3—one for each of the two subjects of lines 4 through 7. Because the formulas on lines 1 and 2 require the use of rule X, while the formula on line 3 requires the use of rule IX, the consequences of the first two lines must be worked out before you work out the consequences of the third line. This argument-form is shown to be invalid by this tableau because the second and fourth branches do not contain both a formula and its negation.

25.20 Each branch of the tableau for a valid argument-form will contain both a formula and its negation. For instance, look at this one:

$\Pi xCQ(x)R(x)$ $(x)\,(Q(x) \supset R(x))$
$\Pi xCP(x)Q(x)$ $(x)\,(P(x) \supset Q(x))$
$\overline{\Pi xCP(x)R(x)}$ $\overline{(x)\,(P(x) \supset R(x))}$

The tableau for this argument-form looks like this:

1. $\Pi xCQ(x)R(x)$	$(x)\,(Q(x) \supset R(x))$	1st premise
2. $\Pi xCP(x)Q(x)$	$(x)\,(P(x) \supset Q(x))$	2nd premise
3. $N\Pi xCP(x)R(x)$	$\sim(x)\,(P(x) \supset R(x))$	negated conu.
4. $NCP(a)R(a)$	$\sim(P(a) \supset R(a))$	3, XI.
5. $CQ(a)R(a)$	$(Q(a) \supset R(a))$	1, VIII.
6. $CP(a)Q(a)$	$(P(a) \supset Q(a))$	2, VIII.
7. $P(a)$	$P(a)$	4, VII.
8. $NR(a)$	$\sim R(a)$	4, VII.
9. $NQ(a) \quad /R(a)$	$\sim Q(a) \quad /R(a)$	5, VI.
10. $NP(a)/Q(a)$	$\sim P(a)/Q(a)$	6, VI.
$NP(a)/Q(a)$	$\sim P(a)/Q(a)$	

This tableau also has four branches. However, since the formula on line 3 requires the use of rule XI while the formulas on lines 1 and 2 require the use of rule VIII, the consequences of line 3 must be worked out before you work out the consequences of lines 1 and 2. Notice that each branch of this tableau contains both a formula and its negation. The first branch contains $P(a)$ and its negation. The second branch contains $Q(a)$ and its negation. And the third and fourth branches contain $R(a)$ and its negation. Since each branch contains both a formula and its negation, the argument-form is valid.

25.20.1 Exercise

Build tableaux for the problems in 25.11.1.

25.20.2 Exercise

By either assigning truth-values or building tableaux, show each of the following argument-forms to be valid or invalid.

1. $CNCpqKrs$ $(\sim(p \supset q) \supset (r \cdot s))$
    Ns $\sim s$
    ___
    Np $\sim p$

2. $CpNANqNr$ $(p \supset \sim(\sim q \lor \sim r))$
    $CrKst$ $(r \supset (s \cdot t))$
    Ns $\sim s$
    ___
    Cpt $(p \supset t)$

3. $CpANqr$ $(p \supset (\sim q \lor r))$
    $CpCst$ $(p \supset (s \supset t))$
    $KNNpAqs$ $(\sim \sim p \cdot (q \lor s))$
    Nr $\sim r$
    ___
    t t

4. Cpq $(p \supset q)$
    Crs $(r \supset s)$
    Aqr $(q \lor r)$
    ___
    Aps $(p \lor s)$

5. $AApqKrs$ $((p \lor q) \lor (r \cdot s))$
    $KKNpsNKNpq$ $((\sim p \cdot s) \cdot \sim (\sim p \cdot q))$
    ___
    $KNpr$ $(\sim p \cdot r)$

6. $\Pi x CM(x) N P(x)$ $(x)(M(x) \supset \sim P(x))$
    $\Sigma x KM(x) S(x)$ $(\exists x)(M(x) \cdot S(x))$
    ___
    $\Sigma x KS(x) N P(x)$ $(\exists x)(S(x) \cdot \sim P(x))$

7. $\Pi x CP(x) M(x)$ $(x)(P(x) \supset M(x))$
    $\Pi x CM(x) S(x)$ $(x)(M(x) \supset S(x))$
    ___
    $\Pi x CS(x) N P(x)$ $(x)(S(x) \supset \sim P(x))$

8. $\Sigma x KM(x) P(x)$ $(\exists x)(M(x) \cdot P(x))$
    $\Sigma x KM(x) S(x)$ $(\exists x)(M(x) \cdot S(x))$
    ___
    $\Pi x CS(x) P(x)$ $(x)(S(x) \supset P(x))$

9. $\Pi x CP(x) N M(x)$ $(x)(P(x) \supset \sim M(x))$
    $\Sigma x KS(x) M(x)$ $(\exists x)(S(x) \cdot M(x))$
    ___
    $\Sigma x KS(x) N P(x)$ $(\exists x)(S(x) \cdot \sim P(x))$

10. $\Pi x C P(x) Q(x)$ $(x)(P(x) \supset Q(x))$
$\underline{\Sigma x K S(x) P(x)}$ $\underline{(\exists x)(S(x) \cdot P(x))}$
    $\Sigma x K S(x) Q(x)$ $(Ex)(S(x) \cdot Q(x))$

SECTION 26. Soundness and unsoundness

26.1 Although all invalid arguments are bad arguments, not all bad arguments are invalid. When dealing with an argument expressed in English, you may notice that one or more of its premises (and perhaps its conclusion) is false even though you can demonstrate the conclusion. This is possible because the definition of validity is written in terms of arguments that have true premises: an argument is valid, you remember, if whenever its premises are true, its conclusion must be true. So a valid argument can have false premises (and perhaps a false conclusion). Arguments with false premises are certainly not good arguments. Logicians call them unsound. A sound argument, then, is a valid argument whose premises are true. It is sound because its conclusion must be true, and it is the only kind of really good formal argument.

26.2 Some argument-forms are unsound, however. We call these formally unsound. Since an unsound, valid argument has at least one false premise, a formally unsound argument-form is a valid argument-form with logically false premises. Anything logically false is logically absurd. But how can an argument-form have logically absurd premises? The answer is this: an argument-form has logically absurd premises whenever a premise is logically absurd or whenever the premises contradict each other. Since the conjunction of the premises of a formally unsound argument-form is logically absurd, it is impossible to assign truth-values to the parts of the premises in order to give them the value t. If you cannot give the premises the value t, you cannot give them the value t when the conclusion has the value f. So any argument that is logically absurd must test out valid.

26.3 One of the basic ten laws of logic make the validity of such argument-forms certain. It is the positive law of absurdity. You may wonder why we use it then. The reason is that it is very useful in proving argument-forms to be valid that are not formally unsound. To see how, look at the demonstration of the rule called disjunctive syllogism:

1. Apq $(p \lor q)$
2. $\underline{Np}$ $\underline{\sim p}$
   q q

INVALIDITY AND UNSOUNDNESS

This rule is not formally unsound. Yet to prove that q follows from these premises, the rule of positive absurdity is very useful. Because the first premise is an alternation, we must use the rule of cases in the demonstration. To use cases, we must be able to get q from p and the negation of p. Without the rule of positive absurdity, this would be impossible. So the usefulness of the rule of positive absurdity completely overshadows the fact that it also makes certain that formally unsound argument-forms test out valid, for if you do not plan to get an absurdity when working with a demonstration (as you would if you were using positive or negative absurdity deliberately), and you get an absurdity anyhow, you should immediately know that the argument-form you are working with is formally unsound.

26.4   Of course, you can show that a formally unsound argument-form is unsound by making a truth-table for the conjunction of its premises. If you cannot assign values to the parts of the premises so that they each come out with the value t, the conjunction of the premises must have the value f. For instance, look at this argument-form:

1.	Cpq		$(p \supset q)$
2.	$KNqNr$		$(\sim q \cdot \sim r)$
3.	$CNrp$		$(\sim r \supset p)$
	p		p

This argument-form is formally unsound. To show it, try to give each of the premises the value t. To give the second premise the value t, q and r must each have the value f. If q has the value f, p must have the value f if the first premise is to have the value t. If p has the value f, however, r must have the value t if the third premise is to have the value t. But now r has two values at the same time—which is impossible! So you cannot give each of the premises the value t.

26.4.1 Exercise

Derive an absurdity from the premises of each of the following argument-forms. Then assign truth-values to the parts of the premises to show that each set of premises is absurd.

(1)	$CApqNr$		$((p \lor q) \supset \sim r)$
	$CNrNAst$		$(\sim r \supset \sim (s \lor t))$
	$KKNuqs$		$((\sim u \cdot q) \cdot s)$
	Ns		$\sim s$

(2)	$CKptCsu$		$((p \cdot t) \supset (s \supset u))$
	$ANqNu$		$(\sim q \lor \sim u)$
	Ktq		$(t \cdot q)$
	Kps		$(p \cdot s)$
	q		q
(3)	Cpq		$(p \supset q)$
	Cqr		$(q \supset r)$
	Crs		$(r \supset s)$
	Ns		$\sim s$
	$CKNrNsp$		$((\sim r \cdot \sim s) \supset p)$
	q		q
(4)	$\Pi x CS(x)P(x)$		$(x)(S(x) \supset P(x))$
	$\Sigma x KS(x)NP(x)$		$(\exists x)(S(x) \cdot \sim P(x))$
	$\Sigma x R(x)$		$(\exists x)R(x)$
(5)	$\Pi x CP(x)Q(x)$		$(x)(P(x) \supset Q(x))$
	$\Pi x CNP(x)R(x)$		$(x)(\sim P(x) \supset R(x))$
	$\Sigma x KNQ(x)NR(x)$		$(\exists x)(\sim Q(x) \cdot \sim R(x))$
	$\Sigma x P(x)$		$(\exists x)P(x)$

26.4.2 Exercise

Show that once you derive an absurdity from a set of premises, you can derive anything from them including any other absurdity. (Hint: Keep in mind the rule of addition.)

26.5 You can, of course, always use a truth-table to find out if an argument-form is valid or invalid. A truth-table can be built for every truth-functional argument. If the truth-table shows that the argument form tested is tautological, the argument is valid. If the truth-table shows that the argument-form being tested is not tautological, the argument is invalid. Because you can always build a truth-table for a truth-functional argument, you can always find out if an argument is valid even if you cannot work out a demonstration. Since you can always find out if an argument is valid by making a truth-table for its form, using truth-tables to find out if an argument is valid is an effective procedure—it always works! Students often like to count on effective procedures like truth-tables because they are effective. But if you count on effective procedures, you do not learn to think logically. For this reason, we have not introduced effective procedures until the very end of this book. Our goal has been to teach you to use the most basic laws of logic in your thinking rather than to teach you to test arguments.

26.5.1 Exercise

The following terms have been introduced in this chapter; you should know the meaning of each.

validity	tableaux
counterexample	invalidity
unsound argument	sound argument
effective procedure	formally unsound argument

SECTION 27. Abstract thinking and logistical systems

27.1 While you have been learning to think logically, you should also have learned two other things: (1) what abstract thinking is, and (2) what a logistical system is. This last section is a summary of this knowledge.

27.2 Abstract thinking is thinking that can be done without referring to any concrete things. This book is about abstract thinking because in it you have for the most part worked only with variables, connectives (that are defined abstractly), and argument-forms.

27.3 These variables, connectives, and argument-forms make up what is known as a logistical system. A logistical system consists of the following things: primitive symbols, formation-rules, transformation-rules and deductions, sometimes called theorems. In fact, in working through this book, you have worked with two logistical systems. The first of these is presented in chapters 1 and 2. The primitive symbols and formation-rules are in chapter 1, and the transformation-rules and theorems are in chapter 2. You can write out a description of this logistical system like this:
Primitive symbols; variables, connectives.
Formation-rules: the recursive definition in chapter 1.
Transformation-rules: the twelve basic rules.
Theorems: all the other rules plus many more that could be but have not been demonstrated.
The other logistical system you have worked with is presented in chapters 1, 2, and 3.

27.3.1 Exercise

Write out a description of the logistical system that is presented in chapters 1, 2, and 3.

27.4 When a logistical system has been worked out, certain questions can be asked about it. The branch of logic in which these questions are asked and answered is called metatheory. It is customary to ask three questions about any logical system:

(1) Is the system consistent?

(2) Are the elements of the system independent?

(3) Is the system complete?

A system is inconsistent if you can derive a logical absurdity as a theorem. The systems you have worked with are consistent. The elements of a system are dependent if they can be replaced by other elements of the system. The systems you have worked with are not independent: as you have probably noticed, some of the connectives can be defined in terms of the others (many of the logical equivalences show that this is true), and you do not really need all twelve of the basic rules (some of them can be derived from the others). Finally, a system is complete if either all true well-formed formulas can be demonstrated in the system, or the system becomes inconsistent when a well-formed formula that cannot be demonstrated in the system is added to it. The systems you have been working with are complete in both of these senses. In metatheory, proofs are given to show that statements like these about logistical systems are true.

SECTION 28. Comprehensive exercises

28.1   This section is made up only of exercises. Some of these exercises are valid, some are not. Some are sound, some are not. Some may even be formally unsound. Some of these exercises are propositional arguments. Others are predicate-arguments. Read each argument carefully. First decide whether it is a propositional or a predicate-argument, then symbolize it. Next analyze it. If you think it is valid, demonstrate its conclusion. If you think it is invalid, show this. If you think that any of these arguments are formally unsound, try to show that too. In short, completely evaluate the following arguments by using all the techniques that you know.

28.1.1 Exercise

(1) If Socrates didn't question the wisdom of others and had minded his own business, the Pythian Priestess would not have called him "Of all men living Socrates most wise," and he would have not earned the jealousy of his fellow Athenians. Of course, it is well known that Socrates did not mind his own business and the Pythian Priestess did call him the wisest of men; so Socrates questioned the wisdom of others.

(2) Those who embarrass people make enemies, while those who question the wisdom of others embarrass people. So all who question the wisdom of others make enemies.

INVALIDITY AND UNSOUNDNESS

(3) If Anytas and Lycon were embarrassed by Socrates, they were enemies of Socrates. Either Socrates was not accused by his enemies or Lycon was not an enemy of Socrates. But Lycon was embarrassed by Socrates and was his enemy, while Anytas was also embarrassed by Socrates and was also his enemy. So Socrates was accused by his enemies.

(4) No honest man is a rhetorician, but one of Socrates' accusers was a rhetorician. So some of Socrates' accusers were dishonest men.

(5) If Socrates had not been sentenced to death, he would have either been acquitted or proposed a reasonable fine. If he had been acquitted or proposed a reasonable fine, however, he would have had, in addition, to give up the practice and teaching of philosophy. But if he would have had to give up the practice and teaching of philosophy, he would have had to go against the voice within him that kept him from doing wrong. If he went against that voice, he would have had to deny what he thought was the voice of God. But if he would not have surrendered his philosophical ideals, he would not have denied what he thought was the voice of God. While if he had surrendered his philosophical ideals, he might just as well be dead. But if he might just as well be dead, it was natural for him to be sentenced to death. So Socrates was sentenced to death.

(6) A person can arrange an escape from prison if and only if the jailer can be bribed. Crito said he could arrange an escape; so someone could have bribed the jailer.

(7) A fugitive from justice is an unjust man, and all fugitives from justice are men who escape from prison by bribing a jailer. So anyone who escapes from prison by bribing a jailer is an unjust man.

(8) If Socrates was convicted at his trial, he was either a just man or a corrupter of the youth of Athens. But he was obviously not a corrupter of the youth of Athens. So if Socrates had not been a just man, he would not have been convicted.

(9) Of course, some who are not just are not honest, while many who are convicted are; so some who are convicted are just.

(10) If Socrates did not die to uphold the principle of justice, he misled himself, and if Socrates did not die to uphold the principle of justice and misled himself, he was nevertheless true to his principles. Yet, if he did not die to uphold the principle of justice, he was not true to his principles. We can only conclude then that Socrates died to uphold the principle of justice.

SECTION 28. Comprehensive exercises

Appendix ONE **GENERAL PREDICATE
LOGIC AND RELATIONS**

SECTION 29. The shortcomings of monadic predicate logic

29.1 Many valid inferences are made up of too many parts to be broken
down into the patterns of monadic predicate logic. So greater detail must
be built into the logical rules that were set down in chapter 3 if we are
going to be able to show the validity of more complicated inferences.
The logical system that has this greater detail is called *general predicate
logic*.

29.2 Some arguments that general predicate logic is needed for are plain
enough. Anyone can easily think of many arguments like the following
one:

Philosophers are men.
_____
Therefore philosophers' thoughts are the thoughts of men.

The premise of this argument can, of course, be written in monadic predicate logic. The conclusion, however, cannot without hiding the connection
between the premise and the conclusion.

29.3 For instance, the premise can be written

> For all x, if x is a philosopher, x is a man.

And, of course, the conclusion can be written similarly:

> For all x, if x is a philsopher's thought, x is the thought of a man.

But now the two predicates in the premise are different from the two in the conclusion. If this argument is written out symbolically, no connection between the premise and the conclusion is plain. For if we let the symbols $P(\ )$, $M(\ )$, $S(\ )$, and $T(\ )$ stand for the four respective predicates, the argument form comes out like this:

$$\frac{\Pi x C P(x) M(x)}{\Pi x C S(x) T(x)} \qquad \Big\| \qquad \frac{(x)(P(x) \supset M(x))}{(x)(S(x) \supset T(x))}$$

But the conclusion of this argument-form can never be gotten from its premise.

SECTION 30. Relations

30.1 What is needed obviously is a way of analyzing the conclusion into a greater number of parts. We have to be able to show that the thoughts mentioned are on the one hand the thoughts of philosophers and on the other, the thoughts of men. So we must find a way of putting into the conclusion the two predicates mentioned in the premise. To do this, a new kind of predicate must be introduced. This new kind of predicate is called a *relation* because it relates two or more subjects.

30.2 In order to correctly symbolize the sentence "Philosophers' thoughts are the thoughts of men," we need to be able to say that one thing (a thought) is the thought of another thing (a philosopher or a man). So we introduce a predicate that has two subjects: we can write $T(x, y)$ for "x is the thought of y." By using this predicate, we can write the sentence like this:

> If x is a philosopher and y is the thought of x, then x is a man and y is the thought of x.

Since we now have two subjects (x and y), we must have two quantifiers (one for x and one for y). Using these quantifiers, we can complete the sentence by writing

> For all x and for all y, if x is a philosopher and y is the thought of x, then x is a man and y is the thought of x.

Symbolically, it looks like this:

$\Pi x \Pi y C K P(x) T(y, x)$ ‖ $(x)(y)((P(x) \cdot T(y,x)) \supset (M(x) \cdot$
$\quad K M(x) T(y,x)$ $T(y,x)))$

This conclusion can easily be derived from the premise "Philosophers are men":

1.	$\Pi x C P(x) M(x)$	premise
2.	$C P(a) M(a)$	1, u.i.
3.	┌$K P(a) T(b, a)$	assumed
4.	│ $P(a)$	3, simp.
5.	│ $M(a)$	4, 2, m.p.
6.	│ $T(b, a)$	3, simp.
7.	└ $K M(a) T(b, a)$	5, 6, conj.
8.	$C K P(a) T(b, a) K M(a) T(b, a)$	3–7, assump.
9.	$\Pi y C K P(a) T(y, a) K M(a) T(y, a)$	8, u.g. on the subject b.
10.	$\Pi x \Pi y C K P(x) T(y, x) K M(x) T(y, x)$	9, u.g. on the subject a.

1.	$(x)(P(x) \supset M(x))$	premise
2.	$(P(a) \supset M(a))$	1, u.i.
3.	┌$(P(a) \cdot T(b, a))$	assumed
4.	│ $P(a)$	3, simp.
5.	│ $M(a)$	4, 2, m.p.
6.	│ $T(b, a)$	3, simp
7.	└ $(M(a) \cdot T(b, a))$	5, 6, conj.
8.	$((P(a) \cdot T(b, a)) \supset (M(a) \cdot T(b, a)))$	3–7, assump.
9.	$(y)((P(a) \cdot T(y, a)) \supset (M(a) \cdot T(y, a)))$	8, u.g. on the subject b.
10.	$(x)(y)((P(x) \cdot T(y, x)) \supset (M(x) \cdot T(y, x)))$	9, u.g. on the subject a.

30.3   Special attention must be paid to lines 9 and 10: only one subject can be generalized at a time, for you must be careful not to mistake one subject for another. In order to make sure that subjects are kept distinct, the four quantification rules must be rewritten with slightly more complicated restrictions. To rewrite these restrictions, we must have a way of distinguishing between quantified and unquantified variables. For example, in the statement form

$$\Pi x C P(x) M(x) \qquad ‖ \qquad (x)(P(x) \supset M(x))$$

x is the subject and it is called a *bound variable* because it is quantified. On the other hand, in the statement-form

$$C P(a) M(a) \qquad ‖ \qquad (P(a) \supset M(a))$$

a is the subject and it is called a *free variable* because it is not quantified. A statement form can have both bound and free variables; an example is line 9 of the above proof:

$\Pi y CKP(a)T(y,a)KM(a)T(y,a)$ $\qquad \| \ (y)\ ((P(a) \cdot T(y,a)) \supset (M(a) \cdot T(y,a)))$

In this expression, a is free and y is bound. Quantifiers, however, have limited *scope*. In the last expression, the scope of the quantifier is the whole sentence because there is a y in the very last predicate $T(y,a)$. But sometimes the scope of a quantifier is only a part of a sentence. For example:

$C\Pi x F(x)\Sigma x F(x)$ $\qquad \| \qquad ((x)F(x) \supset (\exists x)F(x))$

The scope of the universal quantifier is only the first $F(x)$, while the scope of the particular quantifier is only the second $F(x)$.

SECTION 31. Revised quantification-rules

31.1 Now look at a formula like the one on line 9 of the previous proof:

$\Pi y CKP(a)T(y,a)KM(a)T(y,a)$ $\qquad \| \ (y)((P(a) \cdot T(y,a)) \supset (M(a) \cdot T(y,a)))$

If we let the Greek letter ϕ stand for all of the formula within the scope of the quantifier, we can abbreviate the formula like this:

$\Pi y \phi$ $\qquad \| \qquad (y)\phi$

In order to show that ϕ has at least one predicate in it with the subject y, we will put y in parentheses after the ϕ. So the complete abbreviation is

$\Pi y \phi(y)$ $\qquad \| \qquad (y)\phi(y)$

This abbreviation will be used to stand for formulas like the one above and is to be thought of as having bound occurrences of the variable y and perhaps—but not necessarily—free occurrences of other variables. By using this abbreviation, we can write out the changes that are needed in the four quantifier-rules.

31.2 First let's look at the rule of universal instantiation. Its premise must always be a universally quantified formula; so we can use

$\Pi x \phi(x)$ $\qquad \| \qquad (x)\phi(x)$

to abbreviate it (where x rather than y is the bound variable). From this premise, we must be able to derive $\phi(a)$ which has the free variable a in it. That is, we must be able to replace every bound x in

$$\Pi x\phi(x) \qquad\qquad \| \quad (x)\phi(x)$$

by some other variable, say a, and drop the quantifier. So we must write the rule as follows:

$$\frac{\Pi x\phi(x)}{\phi(a)} \qquad\qquad \left\| \quad \frac{(x)\phi(x)}{\phi(a)} \right.$$

whenever $\phi(a)$ and $\phi(x)$ are identical except that $\phi(a)$ has free occurrences of a everywhere that $\phi(x)$ has free occurrences of x.

By using this rule, the following inference is possible:

$$\frac{\Pi y CKP(a)T(y,a)KM(a)T(y,a)}{CKP(a)T(b,a)KM(a)T(b,a)} \qquad \left\| \quad \frac{(y)((P(a) \cdot T(y,a)) \supset (M(a) \cdot T(y,a)))}{((P(a) \cdot T(b,a)) \supset (M(a) \cdot T(b,a)))} \right.$$

But so is this one:

$$\frac{\Pi y CKP(a)T(y,a)KM(a)T(y,a)}{CKP(a)T(a,a)KM(a)T(a,a)} \qquad \left\| \quad \frac{(y)((P(a) \cdot T(y,a)) \supset (M(a) \cdot T(y,a)))}{((P(a) \cdot T(a,a)) \supset (M(a) \cdot T(a,a)))} \right.$$

For

$$CKP(a)T(y,a)KM(a)T(y,a) \qquad \| \quad ((P(a) \cdot T(y,a)) \supset (M(a) \cdot T(y,a)))$$

and

$$CKP(a)T(a,a,)KM(a)T(a,a) \qquad \| \quad ((P(a) \cdot T(a,a)) \supset (M(a) \cdot T(a,a)))$$

are identical except that the latter has free occurrences of a everywhere the former has free occurrences of y. That the latter formula has other free occurrences of a does not matter just as long as it has free occurrences of a everywhere the former has free occurrences of y.

31.3   Next let's look at the rule of particular generalization. Its premise must always be a formula with a free variable; so we can use $\phi(a)$ to abbreviate it. From this premise, we must be able to conclude

$$\Sigma x\phi(x) \qquad\qquad \| \quad (\exists x)\phi(x)$$

GENERAL PREDICATE LOGIC AND RELATIONS

To do this without mixing up the variables, however, $\phi(x)$ and $\phi(a)$ must be identical except that $\phi(a)$ must have free occurrences of a everywhere that $\phi(x)$ has free occurrences of x. For if $\phi(x)$ has free occurrences of x in places that $\phi(a)$ does not have free occurrences of a, we would, by generalizing, bind up the extra x's, and we must be careful not to bind up anything except those x's which replace the a's. For example, this rule allows the following inference:

$$\frac{CKP(x)T(a,x)KM(x)T(a,x)}{\Sigma y CKP(x)T(y,x)KM(x)T(y,x)} \quad \Bigg\| \quad \frac{((P(x) \cdot T(a,x)) \supset (M(x) \cdot T(a,x)))}{(\exists y)\,((P(x) \cdot T(y,x)) \supset (M(x) \cdot T(y,x)))}$$

But it does not allow this one:

$$\frac{CKP(x)T(a,x)KM(x)T(a,x)}{\Sigma x CKP(x)T(x,x)KM(x)T(x,x)} \quad \Bigg\| \quad \frac{((P(x) \cdot T(a,x)) \supset (M(x) \cdot T(a,x)))}{(\exists x)\,((P(x) \cdot T(x,x)) \supset (M(x) \cdot T(x,x)))}$$

for

$$CKP(x)T(x,x)KM(x)T(x,x) \quad \Bigg\| \quad ((P(x) \cdot T(x,x)) \supset (M(x) \cdot T(x,x)))$$

has x free in places where

$$CKP(x)T(a,x)KM(x)T(a,x) \quad \Bigg\| \quad ((P(x) \cdot T(a,x)) \supset (M(x) \cdot T(a,x)))$$

does not have a free. So, we must write the rule as follows:

$$\frac{\phi(a)}{\Sigma x \phi(x)} \qquad\qquad \Bigg\| \qquad \frac{\phi(a)}{(\exists x)\phi(x)}$$

whenever $\phi(a)$ and $\phi(x)$ are identical except that $\phi(a)$ has free occurrences of a everywhere $\phi(x)$ has free occurences of x.

31.4   Now let's look at the rule of universal generalization. Its premise is always some line of a demonstration that is not inside the scope of some assumption and always is a formula in which some variable is free. We can, consequently, let $\phi(a)$ be the abbreviation for such a premise. From this premise, we must be able to derive

$$\Pi x \phi(x) \qquad\qquad \Bigg\| \qquad (x)\phi(x)$$

But we must write the rule so that only those variables that replace the a's in ϕ are bound up by the universal quantifier and also keep the restric-

175

tions we wrote into the rule's use in chapter 3. So the rule must be written like this:

whenever a is not free in any premise or undischarged assumption and $\phi(a)$ and $\phi(x)$ are identical except that $\phi(a)$ has free occurrences of a everywhere that $\phi(x)$ has free occurrences of x.

31.5 Finally, look at the rule of particular instantiation. Its premise must always be a particularly quantified formula; so we can use

$$\Sigma x\phi(x) \qquad\qquad \| \quad (\exists x)\phi(x)$$

to abbreviate it. First, you must remember the restrictions on the use of this rule that were set down in chapter 3. Remembering these, the rule can now be written like this:

$$\Sigma x\phi(x) \qquad\qquad \| \quad (\exists x)\phi(x)$$

where a does not occur free anywhere in the part of the demonstration that comes before the assumption (unless it's inside the scope of a discharged assumption) and where ψ stands for a formula in which a is not free and where $\phi(a)$ and $\phi(x)$ are identical except that $\phi(a)$ has free occurrences of a only everywhere that $\phi(x)$ has free occurrences of x.

31.6 By using these revised quantifier-rules in addition to the transformation-rules you learned in reading chapters 2 and 3, you should be able to demonstrate the following additional transformation-rules.

31.6.1 Exercise

Demonstrate the following additional rules of logic.

(1) $\dfrac{\Pi x \Pi y K(x,y)}{\Pi y \Pi x K(x,y)}$ and $\dfrac{\Pi y \Pi x K(x,y)}{\Pi x \Pi y K(x,y)}$ $\quad\Big\|\quad$ $\dfrac{(x)(y)K(x,y)}{(y)(x)K(x,y)}$ and $\dfrac{(y)(x)K(x,y)}{(x)(y)K(x,y)}$

(2) $\dfrac{\Sigma x \Sigma y K(x,y)}{\Sigma y \Sigma x K(x,y)}$ and $\dfrac{\Sigma y \Sigma x K(x,y)}{\Sigma x \Sigma y K(x,y)}$ $\quad\Big\|\quad$ $\dfrac{(\exists x)(\exists y)K(x,y)}{(\exists y)(\exists x)K(x,y)}$ and $\dfrac{(\exists y)(\exists x)K(x,y)}{(\exists x)(\exists y)K(x,y)}$

(3) $\dfrac{\Sigma x \Pi y K(x,y)}{\Pi y \Sigma x K(x,y)}$ $\quad\Big\|\quad$ $\dfrac{(\exists x)(y)K(x,y)}{(y)(\exists x)K(x,y)}$

31.7 These revised quantifier-rules are entirely general, and they are effective regardless of how many subjects and quantifiers are involved. Although we have only used monadic and dyadic predicates so far, predicates can have any number of subjects. The predicate *between,* for example, has three subjects. $B(x,y,z)$, for example, can be read as "x is between y and z." Predicates with three subjects are called triadic. There are also tetradic, quintadic, and other predicates of even larger sizes. Generically, such predicates are often called *n*-adic, where some word that designates the number of subjects is used in place of the *n*.

SECTION 32. Some properties of relations

32.1 A lot about dyadic relations can be accounted for in terms of specific properties and their relationships. This account is often called the logic of relations. It is made up of definitions of some properties and derivations of others from combinations of those that are defined. Ten such properties are usually defined, but they fall into only three groups.

32.2 The main relation in the first of these groups is *symmetry*: a relation is symmetrical if its subjects can be reversed. For instance, take the relation *is the spouse of*. Because we know that Socrates was the spouse of Xantippi, we can also say that Xantippi was the spouse of Socrates. If we let the capital letter R stand for any relation, symmetry can be defined as follows:

$$\Pi x \Pi y C R(x, y) R(y, x) \qquad\Big\|\qquad (x)\,(y)\,(R(x, y) \supset R(y, x))$$

The negation of this formula is a definition of *non-symmetry*. An example of non-symmetry is the relation *is the brother of*. For if Nicomachus is the brother of Pythias, Pythias may or may not be the brother of Nicomachus. Pythias, for example, may be his sister. Some relations, however, are merely *asymmetrical*. The relation *is older than* is a good example of one. This relation is asymmetrical because its subjects can never be reversed, for if

177

Socrates is older than Plato, Plato cannot be older than Socrates. Symbolically defined, asymmetry looks like this:

$$\Pi x \Pi y C R(x, y) N R(y, x) \qquad \| \qquad (x)\,(y)\,(R(x, y) \supset\, \sim R(y, x))$$

32.3 The second group is based on the property of *transitivity*. Look at the following argument: If Aristotle wrote more than Plato, and if Plato wrote more than Socrates, then it follows that Aristotle wrote more than Socrates. Because this argument is valid, the relation *wrote more than* is transitive. Symbolically, this property can be written like this:

$$\Pi x \Pi y \Pi z C K R(x, y) R(y, z) R(x, z) \quad \| \quad (x)(y)(z)((R(x,y) \cdot R(y,z)) \supset R(x,z))$$

A negation of this formula is a definition of the property of *non-transitivity*. *Being a friend of* is an example of a relation with this property, for although Hippothales was a friend of Lysis and Lysis was a friend of Menexenus, we cannot tell whether or not Hippothales was also a friend of Menexenus. He may or may not have been. On the other hand, some relations are *intransitive*. Since Nicomachus was the father of Aristotle, and Aristotle was the father of Pythias, it follows that Nicomachus was not the father of Pythias. Consequently, *being the father of* is a relation with the property of intransitivity. The following formula defines this property:

$$\Pi x \Pi y \Pi z C K R(x,y) R(y,z) N R(x,z) \quad \| (x)(y)(z)((R(x,y) \cdot R(y,z)) \supset\, \sim R(x,z))$$

32.4 The final group of properties is the reflexive group. It is somewhat more complicated than the others, although it may look less complicated at first. For instance, a relation is *reflexive* (sometimes called *totally reflexive*) if it always relates a subject to itself. We can say that Plato is identical to himself, for example; so the relation *being identical to* is reflexive. Such relations are defined by the following formula:

$$\Pi x R(x,x) \qquad \| \qquad (x)R(x,x)$$

Using this as the basic formula, we can define *irreflexive* relations as

$$\Pi x N R(x,x) \qquad \| \qquad (x)\sim R(x,x)$$

This is exemplified by the relation *being a descendant of*, for no one is a descendant of himself. Some relations, of course, are *non-reflexive*, i.e., neither reflexive nor irreflexive. (This property is sometimes called *meso-reflexive*.) Symbolically, non-reflexivity looks like this:

$$K \Sigma x F(x,x) \Sigma x N F(x,x) \qquad \| \qquad ((\exists x) F(x,x) \cdot (\exists x)\sim F(x,x))$$

Since some people love themselves and some do not, the relation "being in love with" exemplifies non-reflexivity.

32.5   Unfortunately, many relations that we would like to call reflexive are not reflexive by these definitions. For example, everything is identical to itself, but everything does not have the same color hair as itself, because many things have no hair. Relations like *having the same color hair as* are *reflexive in their fields* (sometimes merely called reflexive), for if something has hair, then it has the same color hair as itself. A definition of this notion of reflexivity must obviously be written as a conditional statement in which the antecedent indicates that the relation involved applies to its subject. Various ways (which are not always equivalent) have been used to do this. The following three are the most common:

1. $\Pi x C \Sigma y A R(x,y) R(y,x) R(x,x)$ $\|$ $(x)(((\exists y)(R(x,y) \lor R(y,x))) \supset R(x,x))$
2. $\Pi x \Pi y C R(x,y) K R(x,x) R(y,y)$ $\|$ $(x)(y)(R(x,y) \supset (R(x,x) \cdot R(y,y)))$
3. $\Pi x \Pi y C R(x,y) R(x,x)$ $\|$ $(x)(y)(R(x,y) \supset R(x,x))$

What each says is something like this:
   1. If either anything is related to a thing or that thing is related to anything, then anything is related to itself.
   2. If anything is related to any other things, then it is related to itself and the other thing is related to itself.
   3. If anything is related to any other thing, then it is related to itself. Although these expressions each describe the property differently, they all do the same thing, namely, stipulate that the property only holds when the relation actually relates some subjects.

32.5.1 Exercise

Show that the following are true:
(1) If a relation is irreflexive and transitive, then it is also asymmetrical.
(2) If a relation is symmetrical and transitive, then it is also reflexive.

32.5.2 Exercise

Which of the following statements are true?
   (1) Asymmetrical relations are also non-symmetrical.
   (2) Irreflexive, transitive relations are also non-symmetrical.
   (3) Irreflexive, transitive relations are also asymmetrical.
   (4) Intransitive relations are non-transitive.
   (5) Some non-transitive relations are not intransitive.
   (6) Symmetrical, transitive relations are also reflexive.
   (7) An asymmetrical relation can be non-transitive.

(8) A reflexive relation cannot be asymmetrical.

(9) A symmetrical relation can be non-transitive.

(10) A non-symmetrical relation cannot be intransitive.

32.6 The point in calling attention to these properties is that they are sometimes taken for granted in arguments. For instance, someone could easily argue that since Socrates was a compatriot of Plato's and Plato was a compatriot of Aristotle's, Socrates was a compatriot of Aristotle's. Symbolically, we would have something like this:

$$\frac{\begin{array}{c} C(s,p) \\ C(p,a) \end{array}}{C(s,a)}$$

There is no way to supply a demonstration of this argument unless you realize that the relation "being a compatriot of" is transitive. Then you can write this additional premise:

$$\Pi x \Pi y \Pi z CKC(x,y)C(y,z)C(x,z) \qquad \| \qquad (x)(y)(z)((C(x,y) \cdot C(y,z)) \supset C(x,z))$$

And now the proof is very simple.

32.6.1 Exercise

Show that the following arguments are valid:

(1) Gold is more valuable than silver, and silver is more valuable than brass; so gold is more valuable than brass.

(2) Plato was a follower of Socrates'; so Socrates was not a follower of Plato's.

(3) Speusippus succeeded Plato as head of the Academy, and Xenocrates succeeded Spseusippus at that post. So Xenocrates was certainly not Plato's successor.

SECTION 33. Identity and definite descriptions

33.1 Now let's take a look at sentences like "The man who wrote the *Republic* is the person who taught Aristotle." The expressions that form the subject and predicate of this sentence and which have the form "the so and so" are called definite descriptions. The sentence says that the man who wrote the *Republic* is identical to the person who taught Aristotle.

33.2 This relation of *being identical to* has three of the properties that were set out in the preceding section: symmetry, transitivity, and reflexivity.

In other words, identity can be characterized in the following ways:

$\Pi x \Pi y C I(x,y) I(y,x)$

$\Pi x \Pi y \Pi z C K I(x,y) I(y,z) I(x,z)$

$\Pi x I(x,x)$

$(x)(y)(I(x,y) \supset I(y,x))$

$(x)(y)(z)((I(x,y) \cdot I(y,z)) \supset I(x,z))$

$(x)I(x,x)$

33.3 From this relation, we can put together another transformation rule: the law of identity (id.):

$$\frac{I(x,y)}{\phi(x)} \over \phi(y)$$

where ϕ stands for any formula in which x occurs as a subject variable.

Examples of the use of this transformation-rule follow: Take, for instance, a look at this argument:

The Philosopher was Aristotle.
Aristotle's daughter was named Pythias.
The Philosopher's daughter was named Pythias.

Symbolically, it goes like this:

1. $I(p,a)$ — given
2. $D(s,a)$ — given
3. $D(s,p)$ — 1, 2; id.

Another example that gives us a different kind of conclusion is this:

Only philosophers are wise.
Plato is wise.
Alcibiades is not a philosopher.
Plato is not Alcibiades.

Symbolically, it goes like this:

1. $\Pi x C W(x) P(x)$ | $(x)(W(x) \supset P(x))$ | given
2. $W(p)$ | $W(p)$ | given
3. $NP(a)$ | $\sim P(a)$ | given
   $NI(p,a)$ | $\sim I(p,a)$ | to be proved
4. $CW(a)P(a)$ | $(W(a) \supset P(a))$ | 1; u.i.
5. $NW(a)$ | $\sim W(a)$ | 3, 4; m.t.

$$
\begin{array}{lll}
6. & \ulcorner I(p,a) \\
7. & \ \ NW(p) \\
8. & \ \ \underline{KW(p)NW(p)} \\
9. & NI(p,a)
\end{array}
\qquad
\begin{array}{l}
\ulcorner I(p,a) \\
\ \ \sim W(p) \\
\ \ \underline{(W(p) \cdot \sim W(p))} \\
\sim I(p,a)
\end{array}
\qquad
\begin{array}{l}
\text{assumed} \\
6, 5; \text{ id.} \\
2, 7; \text{ conj.} \\
6\text{-}8; \text{ neg. abs.}
\end{array}
$$

33.4 Now let's look at expressions like "The man who wrote the *Republic*" (which is sometimes written $(\imath x)(x$ wrote the *Republic*)). As we said, such expressions are called definite descriptions and they can replace subjects in relations. But such a use of definite descriptions is needlessly cumbersome. So we define an expression that is equivalent to a definite description and this new expression replaces definite descriptions in argument-forms. (The new expression is often called a *contextual definition* because it explains the meaning of a definite description in context rather than in isolation.) What we do is give a way of interpreting any sentence in which a definite description appears.

33.5 For example, look at the sentence, "The teacher of Aristotle was a great writer." It means three things:
(1) Some person taught Aristotle.
(2) At most one person (because of the definite article *the*) taught Aristotle.
(3) That person was a great writer.
Considered together, these three can be symbolized as follows:

$$
\begin{array}{ll}
(1) & \Sigma x \phi(x) \\
(2) & \Pi y C \phi(y) I(x,y) \\
(3) & \Sigma x \psi(x)
\end{array}
\qquad
\begin{array}{l}
(\exists x)\phi(x) \\
(y)(\phi(y) \supset I(x,y)) \\
(\exists x)\psi(x)
\end{array}
$$

Putting these three together, we get

$$
\Sigma x K K \phi(x) \Pi y C \phi(y) I(x,y) \psi(x) \qquad (\exists x)((\phi(x) \cdot (y)(\phi(y) \supset I(x,y))) \cdot \psi(x))
$$

Any definite description can be replaced by a similar formula.

33.5.1 Exercise

Show that the following arguments are valid:
(1) The person who founded the Academy was Socrates' most famous pupil. Since Socrates' most famous pupil wrote the *Republic,* the person who founded the Academy wrote the *Republic.*
(2) The inventor of the gnomon held that reality was unlimited. No one who believes that reality is unlimited also believes it to be mind. Anaxagoras held that reality was mind. So Anaxagoras was not the inventor of the gnomon.

SECTION 34. Additional properties of relations

34.1   Some properties that relations have can only be defined by making use of the relation of identity. Four of the most interesting follow:

34.2   A relation is *connected* if it in some way relates any two different subjects. This property can be defined symbolically as follows:

$$\Pi x \Pi y CNI(x,y) A R(x,y) R(y,x) \quad \| \quad (x)(y)(\sim I(x,y) \supset (R(x,y) \lor R(y,x)))$$

The relation of *being smaller than* is usually said to exemplify this property, for of any two different objects which have size but not the same size, either one is smaller than the other or *vice verse*.

34.3   Some relations relate only one thing to one thing. Such relations are said to be one-one. *Being a twin of* is such a relationship, for it relates one person to only one other person. Symbolically, this property is defined as follows:

$$\Pi x \Pi y CR(x,y) K \Pi z CR(x,z) I(z,y) \Pi w CR(w,y) I(w,x)$$
$$\overline{(x)(y)(R(x,y) \supset ((z)(R(x,z) \supset I(z,y)) \cdot (w)(R(w,y) \supset I(w,x))))}$$

34.4   Other relations relate one thing to many things. Such relations are said to be one-many. *Being the paternal grandmother of* is such a relation, for it may relate one person to many persons. The symbolic definition of such relations is

$$\Pi x \Pi y CR(x,y) \Pi z CR(z,y) I(z,x) \quad \| \quad (x)(y)(R(x,y) \supset (z)(R(z,y) \supset I(z,x)))$$

34.5   Finally, some relations relate many things to one thing. They are called many-one. An example of such a relation is *to be a day in some particular year*, for there are more than three hundreds days in any one year. This property is defined by the following expression:

$$\Pi x \Pi y CR(x,y) \Pi z CR(x,z) I(z,y) \quad \| \quad (x)(y)(R(x,y) \supset (z)(R(x,z) \supset I(z,y)))$$

SECTION 35. Relations of relations

35.1   Relations not only relate individual subjects, however; they also relate relations. As a matter of fact, all of the properties of relations that are set out in this chapter can be thought of as either predicates or relations of relations. In this section, five additional properties of relations will be set out and the idea of a predicate or relation of relations will be worked out.

35.2   Let's first look at the predicate of *being the converse of* a relation. Since this is a predicate of a relation, we can symbolize it as a predicate or as a relation. As a predicate, the usual way of symbolizing it is this: $Con(R)$. The symbol *Con* stands for *being the converse of* and, of course, the symbol R stands for the relation that $Con(R)$ is the converse of. As a relation, however, the usual way of symbolizing this predicate is $\breve{R}(\ ,\ )$. So if $R(x,y)$ means that x is related to y, then $\breve{R}(y,x)$ means the converse of the relation that relates x to y. Now what, however, is a converse relation? The following formula defines it:

$$\Pi x \Pi y E \breve{R}(y,x) R(x,y) \qquad \| \qquad (x)(y)(\breve{R}(y,x) \equiv R(x,y))$$

An example of such a pair of relations is the pair of relations *being a parent of* and *being a child of*. For if Aristotle is a parent of Pythias, then Pythias is a child of Aristotle's, and if Pythias is a child of Aristotle's, then Aristotle is a parent of Pythias. So using the symbol $P(\ ,\ )$ for *is a parent of* and the symbol $C(\ ,\ )$ for *is a child of*, we can write this:

$$\Pi x \Pi y E \breve{P}(x,y) P(y,x) \qquad \| \qquad (x)(y)(\breve{P}(x,y) \equiv P(y,x))$$

and

$$\Pi x \Pi y E C(x,y) \breve{C}(y,x) \qquad \| \qquad (x)(y)(C(x,y) \equiv \breve{C}(y,x))$$

35.3   A somewhat similar predicate is *being the complement of* a relation. This predicate can also be symbolized in two ways: as a predicate, the usual symbol is $Com\ (R)$; as a relation, the usual symbol is $\bar{R}(\ ,\ )$. A relation $\bar{R}(\ ,\ )$ is the complement of another relation $R(\ ,\ )$ if the following formula is true.

$$\Pi x \Pi y E \bar{R}(x,y) N R(x,y) \qquad \| \qquad (x)(y)(\bar{R}(x,y) \equiv \ \sim R(x,y))$$

Being a different color than and *being the same color as* are relations that satisfy this formula, for if the Parthenon is a different color than the Sphinx, then the Sphinx is not the same color as the Parthenon, and if the Sphinx is not the same color as the Parthenon, then the Parthenon is a different color than the Sphinx.

35.4   Now let us consider the relation of *being included in*. It will be symbolized as $Inc\ (R,S)$ and it is to be read like this: a relation R is included in a relation S. When is such a statement true, however? The answer is whenever the following formula is satisfied:

$$\Pi x \Pi y C R(x,y) S(x,y) \qquad \| \qquad (x)(y)(R(x,y) \supset S(x,y))$$

GENERAL PREDICATE LOGIC AND RELATIONS

To exemplify this relation, we need only consider such common relations as daughter and child, for if Pythias is the daughter of Aristotle, Pythias is the child of Aristotle.

35.5 Another relation that relates relations is *being equivalent to*. We will symbolize it as Equ(R,S), and this symbol means that a relation R is equivalent to a relation S. Such a statement is true when both Inc(R,S) and Inc(S,R) are true. *Being a son of* and *being a male child of* are relations that exemplify *being equivalent to*, for if Lamprocles is the son of Socrates, then Lamprocles is a male child of Socrates, and if Lamprocles is a male child of Socrates, Lamprocles is a son of Socrates.

35.6 Finally, look at the relation called *relative product*. It too can be symbolized in two ways: RelPro(R,S) and $R/S($, $)$. The symbol $R/S(x,y)$ means that x is an R of an S of y. An example of such a statement is this: Speusippus is a son of a brother of Plato. The relation is defined as follows: a relation $R/S($, $)$ is the relative product of the relations R and S if the following formula is true:

$$\Pi x \Pi y \Sigma z K R(x,z)S(z,y) \qquad \Big\| \qquad (x)(y)(\exists z)(R(x,z) \cdot S(z,y))$$

35.6.1 Exercise

Show that all of the following are true.

(1) if R is symmetrical, then Inc($R,\breve{R}$).
(2) if R is asymmetrical, then Inc($\breve{R},\bar{R}$).
(3) if Inc($\bar{R},\breve{R}$), then Con(R).
(4) Equiv($R,\breve{\breve{R}}$).
(5) Equiv($R,\bar{\bar{R}}$).
(6) Equiv($\breve{\bar{R}},\bar{\breve{R}}$).
(7) EInc(R,S)Inc($\breve{R},\breve{S}$). $\qquad$ (Inc(R,S) $\equiv$ Inc($\breve{R},\breve{S}$))
(8) EInc(R,S)Inc($\bar{R},\bar{S}$) $\qquad$ (Inc(R,S) $\equiv$ Inc($\bar{R},\bar{S}$))
(9) CInc(R,S)Inc($T/R,T/S$). $\qquad$ (Inc(R,S) $\supset$ Inc($T/R,T/S$))
(10) Equiv(($(R/S)/T$),($R/(S/T)$)).
(11) Eqiv($\breve{R}/\breve{S},\breve{S/R}$).

SECTION 36. General predicate logic

36.1 What we have done in the last section is merely expand our logical system. To work out the basis for propositional logic, remember, you needed two kinds of symbols:
1. Truth-functors, and
2. Statement-variables.

To work out the basis for predicate logic, you needed, in addition, symbols for

3. Monadic predicate variables,
4. Generic and specific subjects, and
5. Quantifiers.

In section 29, symbols for

6. Relations

were introduced, and in section 34, you came across

7. Symbols for relations of relations, and
8. Predicates and relations used as subject variables.

A natural question can now be asked: Can we quantify these predicates and relations that are used as subject variables? The answer is yes. To do this, however, you need to generalize the notion of a quantifier. So now you have

9. Generalized quantifiers where the relation or predicate being quantified is written after the quantifier symbols. To use these generalized quantifiers, the quantifier-rules described in this appendix must also be generalized. Such a generalization is easy to carry out. Logic extended to this point is called second-order predicate logic. Second-order predicate logic must, however, be put together very carefully in order to rule out the possibility of deducing absurd formulas (which have come to be known as paradoxes). Since there are various ways of putting second-order predicate logic together to avoid the possibility of deducing the paradoxical formulas, no further description of second-order predicate logic will be given in this book. There are many intermediate and advanced books that you can turn to to learn more about predicate logic if you have mastered the material in this appendix.

SECTION 37. English as a model of the system

37.1   Sentences that have relational predicates in them are often hard to symbolize. In this section, some techniques that are often useful in symbolizing such sentences are described.

37.2   Symbolizing some sentences should give you no trouble. You should be able, for instance, to symbolize all of the following sentences.

> Socrates was the teacher of Plato.
> Socrates taught Plato philosophy.
> Socrates taught Plato philosophy for free.

GENERAL PREDICATE LOGIC AND RELATIONS

Similarly, you should have no difficulty with these:

> *a* attracts everything.
> Everything is attracted by *a*.
> *a* attracts something.
> Something is attracted by *a*.
> Everything attracts *a*.
> *a* is attracted by everything.
> Something attracts *a*.
> *a* is attracted by something.

37.3   But the following sentences are more difficult to symbolize, because you need to use more than one quantifier:

> Everything is identical to everything.
> Everything is identical to something.
> Something is identical to everything.
> Something is identical to something.
> Something is not identical to something.
> Something is identical to nothing.
> Nothing is identical to everything.
> Nothing is identical to something.

These are to be symbolized as follows:

$\Pi x \Pi y I(x,y)$	$(x)(y)I(x,y)$
$\Pi x \Sigma y I(x,y)$	$(x)(\exists y)I(x,y)$
$\Sigma x \Pi y I(x,y)$	$(\exists x)(y)I(x,y)$
$\Sigma x \Sigma y I(x,y)$	$(\exists x)(\exists y)I(x,y)$
$\Sigma x \Sigma y NI(x,y)$	$(\exists x)(\exists y) \sim I(x,y)$
$\Sigma x \Pi y NI(x,y)$	$(\exists x)(y) \sim I(x,y)$
$\Pi x \Sigma y NI(x,y)$	$(x)(\exists y) \sim I(x,y)$
$\Pi x \Pi y NI(x,y)$	$(x)(y) \sim I(x,y)$

37.3.1 Exercise

Each of the following sentences is synonymous with at least one of the others. Which are synonymous with which and how are they to be symbolized?

(1) Everything is identical to everything.
(2) Everything is identical to anything.
(3) Everything is identical to something.

(4) Everything is identical to nothing.
(5) Anything is identical to everything.
(6) Anything is identical to anything.
(7) Anything is identical to something.
(8) Anything is identical to nothing.

(9) Something is identical to everything.
(10) Something is identical to anything.
(11) Something is identical to something.
(12) Something is identical to nothing.

(13) Nothing is identical to everything.
(14) Nothing is identical to anything.
(15) Nothing is identical to something.
(16) Nothing is identical to nothing.

(17) Everything is not identical to everything.
(18) Everything is not identical to anything.
(19) Everything is not identical to something.
(20) Everything is not identical to nothing.

(21) Anything is not identical to everything.
(22) Anything is not identical to anything.
(23) Anything is not identical to something.
(24) Anything is not identical to nothing.

(25) Something is not identical to everything.
(26) Something is not identical to anything.
(27) Something is not identical to something.
(28) Something is not identical to nothing.

(29) Nothing is not identical to everything.
(30) Nothing is not identical to anything.
(31) Nothing is not identical to something.
(32) Nothing is not identical to nothing.

37.4 A methodical way can often be used to symbolize complexly written sentences. It works by symbolizing a sentence in stages. For instance, look at the sentence

Anyone who believes everything everyone says is certain to be deluded sometime.

The first stage of symbolizing this sentence would be to do this:

For all x, if x is a person and x believes everything everyone says, then x is certain to be deluded sometime.

GENERAL PREDICATE LOGIC AND RELATIONS

In the second stage, take each of the parts separately:

(1) "x is a person" comes out as merely $P(x)$.

(2) "x believes everything everyone says" must be broken down into a number of parts: (a) First you can translate it into this:

For all y, if y is a person, then x believes everything y says.

(b) Now "y is a person" comes out $P(y)$, and (c) "x believes everything y says" must also be broken down into

For all z, if y says z, then x believes z.

What we get as the first part of the original sentence is this:

$$\Pi x KP(x)\Pi y CP(y)\Pi z CS(y,z)B(x,z) \quad \Big\| \quad (x)(P(x) \cdot (y)(P(y) \supset (z)(S(y,z) \supset B(x,z))))$$

Now for the third stage, you take the consequent of the first stage, namely, "x is certain to be deluded sometime." It comes out like this:

For some w, w is a time and x is deluded at w.

The final result, then, of the process is this:

$$\Pi x CKP(x)\Pi y CP(y)\Pi z CS(y,z)B(x,z)\Sigma w KT(w)D(x,w)$$
$$(x)((P(x) \cdot (y)(P(y) \supset (z)(S(y,z) \supset B(x,z)))) \supset (\exists w)(T(w) \cdot D(x,w)))$$

37.5   Finally, some exceptive and superlative sentences can be symbolized by using relations and multiple quantification. A list of sentences that illustrate the most common types follows:

37.6 Example 1.

Sentence

Plato was a member of the Academy and could outthink any other member.

Difficult word or phrase to be symbolized
    any other member

Translation of the sentence
    Plato is a member of the Academy, and for all x, if x is a member of the Academy and x is not identical to Plato, then Plato can outthink x.

Symbolization
$$KM(p)\Pi xCKM(x)NI(x,p)$$
$$O(p,x)))$$

$\parallel$

$$(M(p) \cdot (x)((M(x) \cdot$$
$$\sim I(x,p)) \supset O(p,x)))$$

37.7 Example 2.

Sentence

The Greeks could tolerate anyone but Socrates.

Difficult word or phrase to be symbolized

anyone but

Translation of the sentence

For all x, if x is Greek, then x cannot tolerate Socrates; and for all y, if y is a person and y is not identical to Socrates, then x can tolerate y.

Symbolization

$$K\Pi xCG(x)NT(x,s)\Pi yCKP(y)NI(y,s)T(x,y)$$
$$((x)(G(x) \supset \sim T(x,s)) \cdot (y)((P(y) \cdot \sim I(y,s)) \supset T(x,y)))$$

37.8 Example 3.

Sentence

Only Socrates loved Xantippi.

Difficult word or phrase to be symbolized

only

Translation of the sentence

Socrates loved Xantippi, and for all y, if y is not identical to Socrates, then y did not love Xantippi.

Symbolization

$$KL(s,x)\Pi yCNI(y,s)NL(y,x)$$

$\parallel$

$$(L(s,x) \cdot (y)(\sim I(y,s) \supset \sim L(y,x)))$$

37.9 Example 4.

Sentence

There is at most one Pallas Athene.

Difficult word or phrase to be symbolized

there is at most one

Translation of the sentence
　For all x and for all y, if x is a Pallas Athene and y is a Pallas Athene, then x and y are identical.

Symbolization
　$\Pi x \Pi y C K P(x) P(y) I(x,y)$　　　$\parallel$　　$(x)(y)((P(x) \cdot P(y)) \supset I(x,y))$

37.10 Example 5.

Sentence
　No more than two Aloeids were born to Iphimedia.

Difficult word or phrase to be symbolized
　no more than two

Translation of the sentence
　For all x, for all y, and for all z, if x was born to Iphimedia and y was born to Iphimedia and z was born to Iphimedia and x was an Aloeid and y was an Aloeid and z was an Aloeid, then x and y are identical or x and z are identical or y and z are identical.

Symbolization
$$\Pi x \Pi y \Pi z C K K K K K B(x) B(y) B(z) A(x) A(y) A(z) A A I(x,y) I(x,z) I(y,z)$$
$$(x)(y)(z)((((((B(x) \cdot B(y)) \cdot B(z)) \cdot A(x)) \cdot A(y)) \cdot A(z)) \supset$$
$$((I(x,y) \vee I(x,z)) \vee I(y,z)))$$

37.11 Example 6.

Sentence
　There are at least two Fates.

Difficult word or phrase to be symbolized
　there are at least two

Translation of the sentence
　For some x and some y, x and y are Fates and x and y are not identical.

Symbolization
　$\Sigma x \Sigma y K K F(x) F(y) N I(x,y)$　　$\parallel$　　$(\exists x)(\exists y)((F(x) \cdot F(y)) \cdot \sim I(x,y))$

37.12 Example 7.

Sentence
　There was one Greek called The Philosopher.

Difficult word or phrase to be symbolized

there was one (and only one)

Translation of the sentence

Some x was Greek and was called The Philosopher, and for all y, if y was Greek and was called The Philosopher, then x and y are identical.

Symbolization

$\Sigma x KKG(x)C(x)\Pi y CKG$
$(y)C(y)I(x,y)$ ‖ $(\exists x)((G(x) \cdot C(x)) \cdot (y)((G(y) \cdot C(y)) \supset I(x,y)))$

37.13 Example 8.

Sentence

Every person has two natural parents.

Difficult word or phrase to be symbolized

two (and only two)

Translation of the sentence

For all x, if x is a person, then for some y and some z, y is a parent of x and z is a parent of x and y and z are not identical, and for all w, if w is a parent of x, then either y and w are identical or z and w are identical.

Symbolization

$\Pi x CP(x)\Sigma y\Sigma z KKKT(y,x)T(z,x)NI(y,z)\Pi w CT(w,x)AI(y,w)I(z,w)$

$(x)(P(x) \supset (\exists y)(\exists z)(((T(y,x) \cdot T(z,x)) \cdot {\sim}I(y,z)) \cdot (w)(T(w,x) \supset$
$(I(y,w) \vee I(z,w)))))$

37.14 Example 9.

Sentence

Cerberus has three heads.

Difficult word or phrase to be symbolized

three (and only three)

Translation of the sentence

For some x, y, and z, x is a head of Cerberus and y is a head of Cerberus and z is a head of Cerberus, and for all w, if w is a head of Cerberus, then x and w are identical or y and w are identical or z and w are identical.

Symbolization

$\Sigma x \Sigma y \Sigma z KKKH(x,c)H(y,c)H(z,c)\Pi w CH(w,c)AAI(x,w)I(y,w)I(z,w)$

$(\exists x)(\exists y)(\exists z)(((H(x,c) \cdot H(y,c)) \cdot H(z,c)) \cdot (w)(H(w,c) \supset ((I(x,w) \vee I(y,w)) \vee I(z,w))))$

37.15 Example 10.

Sentence

The greatest philosopher was a Greek who lived from 427 to 347 B.C.

Difficult word or phrase to be symbolized

greatest

Translation of the sentence

For some x, x was a philosopher and x was Greek and x lived from 427 to 347 B.C., and for all y, if y was a philosopher and x and y are not identical, then x was greater than y.

Symbolization

$\Sigma x KKKP(x)G(x)L(x)\Pi y CKP(y)NI(x,y)G(x,y)$

$(\exists x)(((P(x) \cdot G(x)) \cdot L(x)) \cdot (y)((P(y) \cdot \sim I(x,y)) \supset G(x,y)))$

37.16 Example 11.

Sentence

A wise man is always honored.

Difficult word or phrase to be symbolized

always

Translation of the sentence

For all x, if x is a man and x is wise, then for all y, if y is a time then, for some z, z honors x at y.

Symbolization

$\Pi x CKM(x)W(x)\Pi y CT(y)\Sigma z H(z,x,y)$

$(x)((M(x) \cdot W(x)) \supset (y)(T(y) \supset (\exists z)H(z,x,y)))$

37.17 Example 12.

Sentence

An ignorant man is never honored.

Difficult word or phrase to be symbolized

never

Translation of the sentence

For all x, if x is a man and x is ignorant, then for all y, if y is a time, then, no z exists such that z honors x at y.

Symbolization

$\Pi x C K M(x) I(x) \Pi y C T(y) N \Sigma z H(z,x,y)$

$$(x)((M(x) \cdot I(x)) \supset (y)(T(y) \supset \sim (\exists z)H(z,x,y))$$

37.18 Example 13.

Sentence

A practical man is sometimes honored.

Difficult word or phrase to be symbolized

sometimes

Translation of the sentence

For all x, if x is a man and x is practical, then there exists a w such that w is a time and there exists a y such that y honors x at w.

Symbolization

$\Pi x C K M(x) P(x) K \Sigma w T(w) \Sigma y H(y,x,w)$

$$(x)((M(x) \cdot P(x)) \supset ((\exists w)T(w) \cdot (\exists y)H(y,x,w)))$$

37.19 Example 14.

Sentence

The Socratic Method has two parts.

Difficult word or phrase to be symbolized

two (and only two)

Translation of the sentence

For all x, if x is the Socratic Method, then for some y and for some z, y is a part of x and z is a part of x and y and z are not identical, and for all w, if w is a part of x, then either w and y are identical or w and z are identical.

Symbolization

$$\Pi xCS(x)\Sigma y\Sigma zKKKP(y,x)P(z,x)NI(y,z)\Pi wCP(w,x)AI(w,y)I(w,z)$$

$$(x)(S(x) \supset (\exists y) (\exists z)((P(y,x) \cdot P(z,x)) \cdot \sim I(y,z)) \cdot (w)(P(w,x) \supset (I(w,y) \lor I(w,z))))$$

37.19.1 Exercise

Symbolize the following sentences:

(1) Standing pools gather filth.
(2) Of idleness comes no goodness.
(3) Tis deeds must win the prize.
(4) Industry is the parent of virtue.
(5) Enjoyment stops where idleness begins.
(6) Honest men tell no lies.
(7) To err is human; to forgive, divine.
(8) Anyone who succeeds at anything is despised by someone.
(9) Every philosopher learns something but no philosopher learns everything.
(10) Everyone learns something from some teacher or other.
(11) There is a teacher from whom everyone learns something or other.
(12) Some people learn everything they know from a single teacher.
(13) No one learns everything any teacher has to teach.
(14) No one learns something from every teacher.
(15) No teacher teaches everyone anything.

37.19.2 Exercises

The following terms were introduced in this chapter. You should know the meaning of each.

general predicate logic
bound variable
scope of a quantifier
tetradic
n-adic
symmetry
asymmetry
non-transitivity
reflexive
irreflexive
mesoreflexive
definite description
contextual definition

relation
free variable
triadic
quintadic
logic of relations
non-symmetry
transitivity
intransitivity
totally reflexive
non-reflexive
reflexive in their fields
identity
connected relation

one-one relation
many-one relation
complement
equivalence (of relations)
paradox

one-many relation
converse relation
inclusion
relative product

37.20 Final Summary of Rules and Principles

Transformation-rules

1. Conjunction
2. Simplification
3. Assumption
4. Modus Ponens
5. Addition
6. Cases
7. Negative Absurdity
8. Positive Absurdity
9. Modus Tollens
10. Hypothetical Syllogism
11. Constructive Dilemma
12. Repetition
13. Assertion
14. Absorption
15. Simple Constructive Dilemma
16. Disjunctive Syllogism
17. Destructive Dilemma
18. Transitive Law of Material Equivalence
19. Revised Universal Instantiation
20. Revised Particular Generalization
21. Revised Universal Generalization
22. Revised Particular Instantiation
23. Identity

Replacement-rules

1. Material Equivalence (2)
2. Double Negation
3. Commutation (3)
4. Association (3)
5. Exportation-Importation
6. Transposition
7. Material Implication (2)
8. De Morgan's Laws (2)
9. Distribution (10)
10. Idempotency (2)
11. Tautology-Elimination
12. Absurdity-Purification
13. Contradiction-Elimination
14. Quantifier-Replacement (4)

Principles

1. Identity
2. Excluded Middle
3. Non-Contradiction

THE LANGUAGE OF TRADITIONAL LOGIC

SECTION 38. Traditional logic

38.1   Although you do not need any additional logical techniques to be able to handle what is known as traditional logic, the language of traditional logic is common enough to make understanding it worthwhile. This appendix is a brief description of this language.

SECTION 39. Categorical propositions

39.1   Traditional logic is logic as it was known from ancient times to the middle of the nineteenth century. It can be called the logic of categorical propositions. Such propositions predicate something of a subject directly and explicitly. This distinguishes them from conditional and disjunctive or alternative propositions. Categorical propositions have traditionally been classified into four distinct types: universal affirmative, universal negative, particular affirmative, and particular negative. Each of these names is made up of two words: the first indicates the quantity and the second, the quality of a proposition. So the quantity of a categorical proposition is either universal or particular and the quality is either affirmative or negative. Since each categorical proposition predicates something of a subject, categorical propositions can be analyzed into five parts: quantifier, subject, linking verb, qualifier, and predicate. The four kinds of categorical propositions analyzed in this way are

All *S* (for subject) is *P* (for predicate).
All *S* is not *P*.
Some *S* is *P*.
Some *S* is not *P*.

The second sentence in this list is usually written as

No *S* is *P*.

So the forms of the four traditional categorical propositions are these:

All *S* is *P*.
No *S* is *P*.
Some *S* is *P*.
Some *S* is not *P*.

These forms are usually designated by the four vowels *A, E, I,* and *O.* These vowels are taken from the two Latin words *affirmo* and *nego* which mean "I affirm" and "I negate," respectively.

39.2 The subject and predicate of a categorical proposition are called its *terms.* Some categorical propositions say something about all of the things named by a term and some do not. If a proposition says something about all of the things named by a term, the term is said to be distributed. If a proposition does not say something about all of the things named by a term, the term is said to be undistributed. Now if you examine the four types of categorical propositions, you will see that *A* propositions distribute their subjects but not their predicates, *E* propositions distribute their subjects and predicates, *I* propositions distribute no terms, and *O* propositions distribute their predicates.

39.3 Logicians have two different attitudes about whether categorical propositions imply the existence of the things named by the subject term in a categorical proposition. The traditional attitude is that categorical propositions imply the existence of the things named by the subject terms, that is, all categorical propositions are held to have *existential import.* Many

THE LANGUAGE OF TRADITIONAL LOGIC

modern logicians, however, think that only particular propositions have existential import, and that universal propositions do not. Plausible arguments can be given in support of both attitudes. In the end, the attitude a person adopts depends upon the assumptions he makes.

SECTION 40. Immediate inference

40.1 Some inferences can be drawn directly from the four basic categorical forms. Because these inferences can be drawn directly, they are called immediate inferences. There are three of them: conversion, obversion, and contraposition.

40.2 To form a proposition's converse, you merely interchange the subject and predicate. So the converse of "No S is P" is "No P is S." The techniques of monadic predicate logic can be used to show that E and I propositions can be logically converted. A and O propositions, however, cannot be logically converted. If you assume that categorical propositions have existential import, however, an A proposition can be logically *converted by limitation*, that is, in addition to converting it, you change its quantity.

40.3 To form a proposition's obverse you first change the proposition's quality and next negate the predicate term. In terms of monadic predicate logic, this operation introduces a double negation or leaves the original proposition unaltered; so, each categorical proposition can be obverted logically.

40.4 To contrapose a proposition, you replace its subject with the negation of its predicate and its predicate with the negation of its subject without changing the proposition's quality. The contrapositive of an A proposition is

All non-P is non-S,

and the contrapositive of an O proposition is

Some non-P is not non-S.

Again you can use the techniques of monadic predicate logic to show that A and O propositions can be logically contraposed. E and I propositions, however, cannot. The contrapositive of an A proposition can be justified by the law of transposition, while the contrapositive of an O proposition can be justified by the law of commutation. An *E* proposition cannot be contraposed logically, however, for what you get is equivalent to

Every non-*P* is *S*,

and this cannot be derived from

No *S* is *P*.

Similarly, an *I* proposition cannot be contraposed logically, for what you get is

Some non-*P* is non-*S*,

and this cannot be derived from

Some *S* is *P*.

If you assume, however, that categorical propositions have existential import, *E* propositions can be logically contraposed by limitation, that is, in addition to contraposing them, you change their quantity.

SECTION 41. The square of opposition

41.1 Traditionally, relationships between the four categorical propositions are set down in a diagram known as the *square of opposition*. Most of the relationships shown by this square hold only if you make the traditional assumption that categorical propositions have existential import.

41.2 The traditional square usually looks like this:

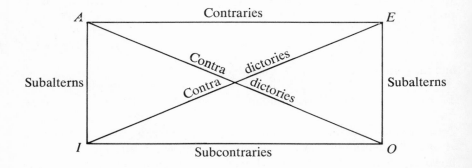

THE LANGUAGE OF TRADITIONAL LOGIC

A and *E* propositions are called *contraries* because they cannot both be true (but they can both be false). *I* and *O* are called *subcontraries* because they cannot both be false (but they can both be true). *A* and *O* propositions are called *contradictories*, and so are *E* and *I*, because when *A* is true, *O* is false and vice versa and when *E* is true, *I* is false and vice versa. *A* and *I*, as well as *E* and *O* are called *subalterns*, for *I* is true whenever *A* is true and *O* is true whenever *E* is true.

41.3   If you deny that categorical propositions have existential import, however, then the only relationship shown on the square that holds is contradiction. The others fail, that is, contraries can both be true at the same time, subcontraries can both be false at the same time, *I* propositions cannot be derived from *A* propositions, and *O* propositions cannot be derived from *E* propositions. The traditional square is then reduced to this:

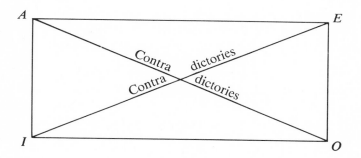

41.4   The four categorical propositions are usually symbolized in the simplest way:

A	$IIxCS(x)P(x)$		$(x)(S(x) \supset P(x))$
E	$IIxCS(x)NP(x)$		$(x)(S(x) \supset {\sim}P(x))$
I	$\Sigma xKS(x)P(x)$		$(\exists x)(S(x) \cdot P(x))$
O	$\Sigma xKS(x)NP(x)$		$(\exists x)(S(x) \cdot {\sim}P(x))$

This way of symbolizing them, however, does not account for existential import. In order to validate all of the relations on the square of opposition and all of the immediate inferences, a more complicated way of symbolizing these propositions—a way such as the following one—must be used:

A $KKIIxCS(x)P(x)\Sigma xS(x)\Sigma xNP(x)$

$$(((x)(S(x) \supset P(x)) \cdot (\exists x)S(x)) \cdot (\exists x){\sim}P(x))$$

$E \quad KK\Pi xCS(x)NP(x)\Sigma xS(x)\Sigma xP(x)$

$$(((x)(S(x) \supset \sim P(x)) \cdot (\exists x)S(x)) \cdot (\exists x)P(x))$$

$I \quad AA\Sigma xKS(x)P(x)\Pi xNS(x)\Pi xNP(x)$

$$(((\exists x)(S(x) \cdot P(x)) \vee (x)\sim S(x)) \vee (x) \sim P(x))$$

$O \quad AA\Sigma xKS(x)NP(x)\Pi xNS(x)\Pi xP(x)$

$$(((\exists x)(S(x) \cdot \sim P(x)) \vee (x)\sim S(x)) \vee (x)P(x))$$

These more complicated symbolic representations of the four traditional categorical propositions have little usefulness.

SECTION 42. The syllogism

42.1 Traditional logic is the logic of categorical syllogisms. A *syllogism* is any argument that has two premises and one conclusion. In a categorical syllogism, both premises and the conclusion are categorical propositions.

42.2 Because a categorical syllogism has only two premises, if it is reasonable, it must contain only three terms—viz., a subject, predicate, and middle term. The *subject term* is the conclusion's subject. The *predicate term* is the conclusion's predicate. Each of these appears as a term in a different premise. The middle term is the term that is to be found in both premises. Look at the following syllogism, for example.

All Greeks are men.
All men are mortal.
Therefore all Greeks are mortal.

The subject term is *Greeks*, the predicate term is *mortal*, and the middle term is *men*. The premise that contains the predicate term is called the *major premise*, while the premise that contains the subject term is called the *minor premise*. However, the subject term does not have to be the subject of a premise, nor does the predicate term have to be the predicate of a premise. These terms are called subject and predicate terms because of where they are to be found in the conclusion.

42.3 The consequence of this is that the various terms can be found in different places. If we use the letters S, M, and P for subject term, middle term, and predicate term, respectively, and if we always put the major premise first and the minor second, the following four patterns are possible:

M — P	P — M	M — P	P — M
S — M	S — M	M — S	M — S
1	2	3	4

These patterns are known as the *figures of the syllogism*.

42.4 The *mood of a syllogism* is determined by the quantity and quality of the propositions that serve as its major premise, minor premise, and conclusion. Since each categorical proposition is designated by a vowel, the mood of a syllogism can be designated by listing the vowels that designate the kind of proposition that serves as the major premise, minor premise, and conclusion, respectively. Thus combinations of these vowels such as AAA, EAE, EIO, etc. designate moods of syllogisms. The first vowel always designates the kind of categorical proposition that serves as the major premise, the second, the minor premise, and the third, the conclusion.

42.5 The form of any syllogism can be precisely designated by naming its mood and figure. Thus AAA-1 precisely designates a syllogistic form:

> All *M* is *P*.
> All *S* is *M*.
> Therefore All *S* is *P*.

Every possible syllogistic form can be designated in this way.

42.6 A syllogism is not always stated completely. Often one of its propositions is merely taken for granted. Any syllogism that has an unstated proposition is called an *enthymeme*. Since a syllogism only consists of three propositions, enthymemes are grouped into three classes: those that have unstated major premises, those that have unstated minor premises, and those that have unstated conclusions. They are called first order, second order, and third order enthymemes, respectively.

42.7 Syllogisms can be linked together in a chain by making the conclusion of the first a premise of the second, etc. Such a chain is a *sorites*. The intermediate conclusions in a sorites are usually left out, however, so the constituent syllogisms are usually enthymemes. There are only two traditional ways to put a sorites together. The first way is Aristotelian. In an Aristotelian sorites, the conclusion's subject is also the subject of the first premise, and the conclusion's predicate is also the predicate of the last premise. The middle terms turn up first as the predicate of one premise and then as the subject of the next one. The second way of putting a sorites together is Goclenian. In a Goclenian sorites, the conclusion's predicate is also the subject of the last premise. The middle term, then, must turn up first as the subject of one premise and then as the predicate of the next premise. In a sense, a Goclenian sorites is upside down, since the transformation-rule a sorites resembles most is hypothetical syllogism. If an Aristotelian sorites has a negative premise, it must be the last one, and if it has a particular premise, it must be the first one. In a Goclenian sorites, these rules are reversed: if a Goclenian sorites has a negative premise, it must be the first one, and if it has a particular premise, it must be the last one. At most, however, a sorites can have only one negative premise and one particular premise.

SECTION 43. A note on effective procedures

43.1 This summary of the language of traditional logic together with your knoweldge of monadic predicate logic is all that anyone needs to know to understand traditional logic. In most books, you will find that traditional logic is taught by the use of effective procedures. The effective procedures most often put to use are diagrams that are made up of intersecting circles. They are called Venn diagrams, because they were invented by the mathematician John Venn. Another way of evaluating syllogisms, however, is more traditional. It is made up of applying a list of rules. If a syllogism goes against any of the rules, it is invalid. Although these techniques are effective, they do not emphasize thinking; they emphasize testing. Since the thesis of this book emphasizes thinking, these effective techniques are not described. If you want to learn them, there are many books available that you can turn to.

43.1.1 Exercise

The following terms have been introduced in this chapter. You should know the meaning of each one.

categorical	existential import
immediate inference	conversion
obversion	contraposition
limitation	square of opposition
contrary	subcontrary
subaltern	contradictory

THE LANGUAGE OF TRADITIONAL LOGIC

syllogism

predicate term

distribution

minor premise

mood

first order enthymeme

third order enthymeme

Aristotelian sorites

subject term

middle term

major premise

figure

enthymeme

second order enthymeme

sorites

Goclenian sorites

Appendix THREE AN ESSAY ON INFORMAL REASONING

SECTION 44. What *informal* means

44.1   In the early parts of chapter 1, you learned that logic is the study of the methods and principles that distinguish good from bad arguments, that an argument is a sequence of statements the last of which is an affirmation and the rest of which are reasons given in support of the affirmation, that whether an argument is reasoned well depends upon how the premises are connected to the conclusion, and that for *a large class* of arguments, these connections can be seen best by studying the *forms* of arguments. Logic about this large class of arguments is formal logic, which the previous parts of this book are about.

44.2   But in addition to formal reasoning there are other kinds. One of these is called informal. *Informal* means not formal; so the form of an informal argument cannot be used to show how the premises are connected to the conclusion. Whether an informal argument is reasoned well depends not on its form but on its content. The conclusion in a good informal argument is connected to the premises by the information in the argument, not by its form. This appendix is about the most well-known kinds of informal reasoning.

SECTION 45. Fallacies

45.1 Poor reasoning of any kind is often called fallacious. Something is fallacious when it is an argument, and when the form is invalid (formal fallacy), a premise is false (material fallacy), or the evidence in the premises is true but not good enough and the form is irrelevant to the question of validity (informal fallacy). Thus arguments can be formally fallacious, materially fallacious, and informally fallacious. In chapter 4 you were introduced to formally fallacious (invalid) arguments; you also learned that valid arguments can have false premises and that a valid argument with a false premise is called unsound (materially fallacious). You are already familiar with these two ideas; only the idea of an informal fallacy is yet to be explained: informal reasoning is fallacious *when it can be shown that* the information in the premises is not good evidence for the conclusion. Unless this can be shown *convincingly*, informal reasoning cannot reasonably be call fallacious.

45.2 The most interesting informal fallacies, however, are often called paralogisms. These are faulty arguments whose fallacy the reasoner is not aware of. Thus they are not arguments that someone uses to trick someone else; they are arguments that a person tricks himself with. These arguments have an interesting quality that leads people to think of them as good arguments; so in this appendix, we will concentrate only on the most well-known paralogisms. The paralogisms will, on the one hand, be contrasted with similar arguments that are obviously valid, and on the other, with similar arguments whose validity is questionable. By means of these contrasts, you should learn to recognize the paralogisms, see why they can appear to be convincing, and learn to keep from being fooled by them. So to understand the nature of a paralogism, you should try to state why the information in the premises is not good evidence for the conclusion and why it nevertheless appears to be good evidence.

45.3 Generally speaking seven things give paralogisms the appearance of being good arguments. A paralogism may appear to be a good argument because (1) the information in the conclusion is taken for granted in the premises; (2) the premises prove something similar to but different from the conclusion; (3) the premises, although they do not prove the conclusion, do prove something; (4) the argument is ambiguous; (5) a generalization is based upon true but otherwise insufficient cases; (6) a statement which is generally true is misapplied; and (7) the information in the premises is related but irrelevant to the conclusion. The paralogisms set forth in this appendix will be organized in accordance with this outline.

SECTION 46. Paralogisms that assume their conclusions

46.1   The first group of paralogisms are those which in some way or another take their conclusions for granted. We will consider two such paralogisms: begging the question (which is sometimes referred to by its Latin name *petitio principii*) and complex question.

46.2

Type   A valid argument that begs the question.

Example   Since he never married, he is a bachelor.

Comment   In this argument, the premise "he never married" means the same thing as the conclusion; therefore, in a sense, the conclusion is being assumed in the premise. But the argument is not fallacious, for the argument functions as an explanation. The premise explains what the conclusion means.

46.3

Type   A fallacious argument that begs the question.

Example   Rural and urban peoples can never resolve the issues that separate them; therefore rural and urban peoples will always be at odds with each other.

Comment   This argument commits the fallacy of begging the question because the conclusion is doubtful; yet "can never resolve the issues that separate them" means "will always be at odds with each other." So the doubtful conclusion is being supported with the synonymous and thus equally doubtful premise. Something doubtful is not good evidence for anything; it is especially not good evidence for itself.

46.4

Type   An argument of questionable validity that begs the question.

Example   He is a good man, for he cares about others.

Comment   The reason this example is questionable is that men who care about others are generally good men, but this argument may be an attempt to define "good man" as one who cares about others. If so, the argument commits the fallacy of begging the question, for then the premise is synonymous with and as dubious as the conclusion. If the premise is not meant to be a definition but merely evidence for the goodness of the person, the argument does not commit the fallacy.

46.5

Type   A valid complex question.

Example   When are all persons going to enjoy the freedoms guaranteed by the Constitution of the United States of America?

Comment   The implied argument goes like this: A study of foreign governments reveals that the rights guaranteed by the Constitution to citizens of the United States are not guaranteed to citizens of other nations. So one can legitimately ask the question. However any answer to it— whether the answer be the word "never" or some specific date—commits the person answering it to the belief that all persons do not enjoy the freedoms guaranteed by the Constitution. But there is nothing wrong with that belief. The worst criticism of this argument one can give is that the premises of the conclusion are left unstated, but persons who argue often leave premises whose truth is obvious unstated.

46.6

Type   A fallacious complex question.

Example   Why isn't anyone wise?

Comment   If someone gives any reason in answer to this question, he commits himself to the dubious belief that no one is wise. But men, throughout the ages, have been known as wise men. So the implied conclusion is dubious at best and, more likely than not, downright false. If someone, however, in answering the question says something like "because men have limited intelligence," the argument commits the fallacy of begging the question, for it would then seem that "men with limited intelligence" is meant to mean "unwise men." But first of all, this definition is arbitrary and second of all, the statement that men have limited intelligence is not obviously true. It at least needs to be supported by evidence, and none appears in this "argument."

46.7

Type   A complex question of questionable validity.

Example   When are all persons going to be free?

Comment   If someone answers this question with the word "never" or with some date, he has committed himself to the belief that all persons are not free. The trouble is that what this means is uncertain. If it means that some people are still held in servitude, then it is false. If it means something else, however—like being able to exercise the freedoms guar-

SECTION 46. Paralogisms that assume their conclusions

anteed by the Constitution of the United States—then this argument is very much like the valid example.

46.8   Every question, of course, is not complex. A question is complex only if all possible answers to it commit you to the *same* belief. For instance the question, When will the world perish? is not complex. If you answer, "Never!" you are committed to the belief that the world *will not* perish. But if you answer, "On doomsday!," you are committed to the belief that the world *will* perish. These are not the same. When a question is complex, all possible answers commit you to the same belief. For instance, take the question, When will government not be corrupt? If you answer "Never!" you assume the government is corrupt. And if you answer by referring to some specific time, say for instance, "After the next election!" you are *still* assuming that government is corrupt.

46.9   Arguments that assume their conclusions have the logical form that we have named repetition. We know that repetition is a valid argument *form*. But arguments that merely assume their conclusions are fallacious, for if the conclusion is dubious, you cannot provide support for it by assuming it. Arguments such as the ones in this group illustrate why the paralogisms being set out in this appendix are called *informal* fallacies. The validity of the argument's form plays no role in the argument's evaluation.

SECTION 47. Paralogisms that prove something similar to but different from their conclusions

47.1   In the second group of paralogisms, the premises prove something different from but similar to the conclusion. It is the similarity, however, that gives the paralogisms their persuasiveness. In this group, there are seven different argument types: *ignoratio elenchi, ad populum, ad ignorantiam, ad baculum, ad misericordiam, ad hominem* circumstantial, and *ad hominem* abusive. The way to correct such arguments is to state their proper conclusions. (The Latin names mean *ignorance of the hookup, to the people, to ignorance, to force, to pity, to the man's circumstances,* and *abuse of the man*, respectively.)

47.2
Type   A fallacious *ignoratio elenchi.*
Example   A fundamental principle of American government is equality

210

for all under the law; therefore, there is no lawful discrimination in America.

Comment The proper conclusion of this argument is this: In America, no discriminatory law conforms to the principle. You should see that although the argument's conclusion is similar to the proper conclusion, the two conclusions by no means mean the same thing.

47.3

Type An *ignoratio elenchi* of questionable validity.

Example Because the bribery of judges was a widespread practice during the seventeenth century, when Francis Bacon accepted bribes, he was doing what most other judges of the period did.

Comment What makes this argument questionable is the uncertainty over whether "a widespread practice" implies that most did it. In other words, can a practice be widespread even though most people do not engage in it? If so, the conclusion does not follow; if not, it does.

47.4 Arguments that commit the fallacy of *ignoratio elenchi* have no valid examples. A valid example would have a proper conclusion rather than one similar to it and then the hookup would be all right. The other argument types in this section, however, are examples of various ways of proving something similar to but different from the stated conclusion. Whether they have valid examples depends upon what the argument is based on. Each type must be considered separately.

47.5

Type A valid *ad populum* argument (appeal to the people).

Example A Democrat should be president because a majority of people in states with a majority of electoral votes believed that he should and so voted.

Comment This is a valid argument because a president is chosen by appealing to the people.

47.6

Type A fallacious *ad populum* argument.

Example As time goes on, fewer and fewer Americans believe that capital punishment is morally acceptable; therefore, capital punishment is immoral.

Comment The proper conclusion is this: more and more Americans *believe* that capital punishment is immoral. For something to *be* immoral and for something to be merely *believed* to be immoral are not the same.

211

47.7

Type   An *ad populum* argument of questionable validity.

Example   Mark Antony, in his funeral oration, made many people believe that Caesar was wrongly assassinated; so his assassination was wrong.

Comment   The validity of this argument is questionable, because if the people believed that his assassination was wrong, it may very well have been wrong, for whether a ruler is fit to rule may very well depend on what people believe. This point can at least be argued.

47.8   The pattern that all *ad populum* arguments follow is this: because many or most people believe *A*, *A* must be true. Such arguments are only valid when the truth of *A* is the result of what most people believe. They are not valid in other cases.

47.9

Type   A valid *ad ignorantiam* argument (appeal to ignorance).

Example   The Pythagorean Theorem is true, because no one can prove it isn't.

Comment   Although this argument is trivial, it is nonetheless valid, for no one can prove that the Pythagorean Theorem is false, because the theorem has conclusively been proven to be true.

47.10

Type   A fallacious *ad ignorantiam* argument.

Example   There are other planets in other solar systems that support life much like human life, for no one can prove there aren't.

Comment   The proper conclusion is this: We don't know that there aren't other planets in other solar systems that support life much like human life. But not to know there aren't is not the same as to know there are.

47.11

Type   An *ad ignorantiam* argument of questionable validity.

Example   No one has been able to refute Einstein's theory of relativity, so the theory must be true.

Comment   This argument is questionable because reliable investigators have tried to think up and carry out crucial experiments. No experiment yet tried has refuted the theory, and this then is pretty good evidence for the theory. But no one has proven that no one can ever think of an experiment that will disprove the theory, so that slim possibility still exists. The fact that no reliable investigator has yet been able to refute the theory is, however, very strong evidence in the theory's favor.

47.12   The pattern for *ad ignorantiam* arguments is this: because no one can prove *A* to be false, *A* must be true. Such arguments are valid only when there are good reasons why *A* cannot be proven to be false. Otherwise these arguments are fallacious.

47.13

Type   A valid *ad baculum* argument (appeal to force).

Example   You ought to study hard; otherwise, I'll discontinue your allowance.

Comment   Although the threat to discontinue the allowance is an attempt to force the student to accept as true the statement that he ought to study hard, the argument is not fallacious, for "you ought" in the conclusion can only be taken to mean "it is to your advantage to," and it certainly is to a student's advantage to study hard and therefore receive an allowance.

47.14

Type   A fallacious *ad baculum* argument.

Example   Obeying the Ten Commandments is right; otherwise, you'll suffer eternal damnation.

Comment   The proper conclusion is not that obeying the commandments is right but rather that obeying them is necessary to avoid eternal damnation. But what is necessary to avoid damnation is not necessarily right. Its rightness must be proved (and, of course, theologians have tried to prove it) but it is not proved in *this* argument.

47.15

Type   An *ad baculum* argument of questionable validity.

Example   You ought to obey the Ten Commandments; otherwise, you'll suffer eternal damnation.

Comment   What makes the validity of this argument questionable is the ambiguity of "you ought." If it means "it is to your advantage," then the argument is all right. However, if "you ought" is meant to mean "it is morally right," then the argument is fallacious.

47.16   *Ad baculum* arguments follow the following pattern: because those who tell you to believe *A* are stronger than you, *A* must be true. The pattern yields valid arguments when the truth of *A* is the result of what those who tell you to believe *A* do. Otherwise the pattern yields fallacious arguments.

SECTION 47. Paralogisms that prove something similar to but different from their conclusions

47.17

Type   A valid *ad misericordiam* argument (appeal to pity).

Example   People deserve medical care, for illness brings suffering that no human should have to bear.

Comment   This argument is valid because medical care was created in order to alleviate human suffering.

47.18

Type   A fallacious *ad misericordiam* argument.

Example   You ought to play with your little brother, for the kids down the street just beat him up.

Comment   The proper conclusion is this: It would be kind for you to play with your brother.

47.19

Type   An *ad misericordiam* argument of questionable validity.

Example   People ought to support civil rights measures, for the plight of people denied their rights is unbearable.

Comment   This argument's validity is questionable because of the ambiguity of the word *ought*. It cannot be taken to mean "to be to the advantage of." Thus it either means "to be morally right" or "to be naturally right" (since civil rights may be thought of as natural rights). But there *may* be something morally or naturally unbearable in the denial of civil rights.

47.20   *Ad misericordiam* arguments fit the following pattern: Because *A* is pitiable, doing something to benefit *A* is right. Whether this pattern yields valid arguments depends on whether *A* is pitiable because he is denied the benefit.

47.21

Type   A fallacious *ad hominem* circumstantial argument (appeal to a man's circumstances).

Example   Schopenhauer had a well-known dislike for women, so his aphorisms about women are false.

Comment   The proper conclusion should be something like this: his aphorisms about women should be considered carefully before accepting them (for they may reflect a bias).

47.22

Type   A fallacious *ad hominem* abusive argument (abuse of the man).

Example Hegel, since he fathered an illegitimate child, is a worthless human being; therefore, his philosophical tenets are also worthless.

Comment The proper conclusion should go something like this: his philosophical tenets should be considered carefully (since they may have resulted from a tendency to be immoral).

47.23 Because there are two kinds of *ad hominem* arguments, such arguments follow either of two patterns. The first (circumstantial) goes like this: Because *A* is a person of a certain kind, what he says about things favorable to such persons is false. The second (abusive) is this: Because *A* has a bad character, what he says is false. What gives such arguments plausibility is that the persons mentioned are generally distrusted (because they exhibit bad character traits or because they are in distrustful circumstances). But that we should *distrust* what they say is different from *disbelieve* what they say. Since we should always perhaps distrust such persons, valid or questionable examples of such reasoning are not easily found. However, consider the following reasoning which involves an *ad hominem* appeal:

47.24

Type Valid *ad hominem* reasoning (appeal to a man).

Example Jeremy Bentham, one of the greatest thinkers of his time, originated the theory of utilitarianism and tutored John Stuart Mill, another great thinker. Mill, then, could have been expected to defend utilitarianism, and his defense deserves our close attention.

Comment Bentham and Mill are persons of a certain kind, that is, are of similar circumstances. However this argument does not fit the *ad hominem* paralogistic pattern, for the conclusion is not negative.

SECTION 48. A paralogism that proves something entirely different from its conclusion

48.1 One famous paralogism called *non sequitur* (it does not follow) occurs when the premises prove something which is entirely different from the stated conclusion. Obviously no valid examples of this can be invented, and the way to correct a *non sequitur* is to state the proper conclusion.

48.2

Type A *non sequitur*.

Example Episcopacy is of scriptural origin. The Church of England is the only episcopal church in England. Therefore the Church of England is the one that should be accepted.

Comment   The proper conclusion is this: The Church of England traces its origin to scripture.

48.3

Type   A questionable *non sequitur*.

Example   Every reasonable person generally wants to live a moral life. But we are all tempted to make exceptions in our own cases. To be fair, then, we ought to make allowances for the moral lapses of others.

Comment   Since the first premise is stated as general but not universal, the second sentence, if it means that everyone excuses himself for moral lapses, implies rightly that everyone is entitled to exceptions from the rule on the grounds of simple fairness. On the other hand, the second sentence says only that we are *tempted* to make exceptions for ourselves. So the conclusion perhaps is this: Although people generally want to be moral, everyone is sometimes tempted to be immoral—a conclusion not at all like the one above.

SECTION 49. Paralogisms that prove nothing because of ambiguities

49.1   As you have already seen, words are sometimes used ambiguously in arguments. When a word is used in two or more ways in an argument, and when these uses materially affect the argument's meaning, the argument is fallacious. Also the way sentences themselves are constructed sometimes makes them ambiguous. In this section, we will deal with arguments that prove nothing because of the ambiguities that exist in them. There are five such well-known paralogisms: equivocation, amphiboly, accent, composition, and division.

49.2

Type   A valid equivocal argument.

Example   In the general's speech to the National Security Council, he used technical terms typical of military speech; so the general's speech was about military affairs.

Comment   The word "speech" is used in two different senses, but this equivocation does not materially affect the sense of the argument. As a matter of fact, in this case, the equivocation contributes to the force of the argument.

49.3

Type A fallacious equivocal argument.

Example It doesn't make any difference whether you win or lose a war, for war is something everyone loses.

Comment Although the premise has the ring of truth, it certainly does make a difference whether one side or another wins a war. So the word "lose" has a different meaning in the premise than it has in the conclusion, and this ambiguity makes the argument meaningless.

49.4

Type An equivocal argument of questionable validity.

Example A person who does things properly is conscientious. Therefore it is proper to be guided by conscience.

Comment If the word "conscience" means "moral feeling," this argument is equivocal, for a conscientious person is not always one who is guided by moral feelings. But conscience need not be limited to *moral* feeling, for conscience also prods people to act courteously, do a good job, etc., and a person who does things like this is conscientious. So if a person who does things conscientiously does do things properly, and if conscience is taken in this broad sense, then it may very well be proper to be guided by conscience.

49.5

Type A valid amphibolous argument.

Example The president stated that he ordered troops into action at a meeting of the National Press Association on December 14. Therefore the president spoke to the National Press Association on December 14.

Comment The premise, because of the way in which it is written, can be taken to mean a number of different things; so it is amphibolous (ambiguous because of its grammatical construction). But the way the premise is taken by anyone who would argue in this way is perfectly reasonable.

49.6

Type A fallacious amphibolous argument.

Example The president stated that he ordered troops into action at a meeting of the National Press Association on December 14. Therefore, the meeting of the National Press Association must have degenerated into a riot.

Comment To construe the premise's meaning in a way that supports this conclusion is entirely unreasonable. Therefore the argument is fallacious.

Section 49. Paralogisms that prove nothing because of ambiguities

49.7

Type An amphibolous argument of questionable validity.

Example The president stated that he ordered troops into action at a meeting of the National Security Council on December 14. Therefore it was at a meeting of the National Security Council that the order was given.

Comment This argument is questionable, because the premise has two reasonable interpretations: that the order was given at the meeting of the National Security Council, or that the statement was made at the meeting of the National Security Council. Since the conclusion of the argument is one of these reasonable alternatives, the argument *may* be all right. Of course, it is always better to use statements that are not amphibolous in arguments, but common patterns of speech do give rise to such statements and it is only because of the context in which the statements are made that we are able to understand what the speaker means. The context in which an argument like the one in this example is made would probably clear up the ambiguity, and then you would know whether the conclusion is reasonable.

49.8

Type A valid argument that accents part of the premise.

Example Be kind to *dumb* animals is the aphorism; therefore, intelligent beings must earn our kindness.

Comment This conclusion is reasonable, because otherwise the reason for putting the adjective "dumb" into the premise would be lost. The argument does not commit the fallacy of accent.

49.9

Type A fallacious argument that accents part of the premise.

Example The commandment says do not covet thy *neighbor's* wife; so it is all right to covet a stranger's wife.

Comment This conclusion is wholly unreasonable. Surely the point of the maxim is to disapprove of *coveting*. So the argument commits the fallacy of accent.

49.10

Type An argument of questionable validity that accents part of the premise.

Example Jesus said, love thy *neighbor* as thyself; therefore I need not love strangers.

Comment This argument is questionable, because the commandment can

AN ESSAY ON INFORMAL REASONING

be read literally or metaphorically. One can reasonably wonder why Jesus said neighbor if he meant everyone.

49.11 Sentences which can be accented in order to produce fallacious reasoning are inherently ambiguous. So such sentences are in a sense amphibolous. To accent parts of unambiguous sentences to get fallacious conclusions usually results in trivial or silly arguments. But trivial or silly arguments rarely convince anyone, especially the person using them, so they would not be true examples of paralogisms.

49.12

Type   A valid argument that involves a composition (the putting together of parts into a whole).

Example   Because each leaf on the tree is alive, the tree is alive.

Comment   This argument is obviously valid. It does not commit the fallacy of composition.

49.13

Type   A fallacious argument that involves a composition.

Example   A tariff on wheat will benefit wheat farmers, a tariff on oil will benefit oilmen, so a tariff on all commodities will benefit everyone who produces any commodity.

Comment   This argument commits the fallacy of composition, for although a tariff on any commodity will benefit those who produce it, a tariff on every other commodity will harm them; so a tariff on *all* commodities will *not* benefit everyone.

49.14

Type   An argument of questionable validity that involves a composition.

Example   Since every human being needs love, we must learn to love mankind.

Comment   It may or may not be true that in order to love every individual person, we must love mankind. As a matter of fact, what "to love mankind" means is not very clear, for mankind is an abstraction. On the other hand, if someone is concerned for the welfare of mankind, meaning human beings collectively, then he probably also cares for the welfare of individual persons.

49.15 Arguments that involve compositions conform to a pattern that is very important to understand. The pattern is this: Because A is a property of each of the parts of B, A is also a property of B. Sometimes this pattern

Section 49. Paralogisms that prove nothing because of ambiguities yields valid arguments and sometimes it does not. Clear examples of both valid and fallacious arguments of this type are, however, apt to be trivial. The most interesting ones are always questionable, and they are always very difficult to deal with. One especially famous one was put forth by the great philosopher John Stuart Mill (who was a very good logician). His argument goes like this: Each person's happiness is a good to that person, so the general happiness is a good to the aggregate of all people. Philosophers have argued over the validity of this question since 1861. No one has been able to show that the premise is not good evidence for the conclusion.

49.16

Type   A valid argument that involves a division (dividing a whole into its parts).

Example   Because this tree is dead, each of its branches is dead.

Comment   The validity of this argument is also obvious. It does not commit the fallacy of division.

49.17

Type   A fallacious argument that involves a division.

Example   Mankind is adaptable; so anyone can adapt to life's changing conditions.

Comment   This argument commits the fallacy of division, because mankind collectively can be adaptable even though each and every individual person may not be. All that is required for mankind to be adaptable is that enough individuals be adaptable to propagate the species in the face of changing conditions. So from the fact that mankind is adaptable, it only follows that *enough* individual persons be also adaptable.

49.18

Type   An argument of questionable validity that involves a division.

Example   A liberal education fits one for life; therefore the study of Latin—a necessary part of a liberal education—fits one for life.

Comment   The study of a foreign language—especially one that has had a great deal of influence on one's own—may very well be a part of a liberal education that *is* necessary to properly fit one for life. For one's ability to utilize language well certainly fits one for life. The question is, however, what does the study of Latin do to fit one for life? That question is debatable.

49.19   So just as with compositional arguments, divisional arguments also follow a pattern. The pattern is this: Because A is a property of B, A is a property of each of B's parts. Valid and fallacious examples of arguments that fit this pattern are mostly obvious or trivial. The interesting ones are the debatable ones.

SECTION 50.   Paralogisms that prove nothing because of generalizations based on improper inductions

50.1   Some informal arguments prove nothing because they involve faulty generalizations. In this section, four paralogisms of this kind will be exemplified: hasty generalization, false cause, converse accident, and special pleading. For the most part, such arguments can only be corrected by carrying out carefully built inductive reasoning. Such reasoning differs from both formal reasoning and informal reasoning and is very complicated. The study of inductive reasoning involves techniques of sampling, probability, and methods of induction. Because it is so involved, inductive reasoning is not taken up in this book.

50.2

Type   A valid argument based on a small sample.

Example   Socrates, for instance, is mortal; so all men are mortal.

Comment   This generalization is trivial. Its validity rests upon the fact that Socrates is an arbitrarily chosen individual about whom there is nothing special in relation to his mortality. So what is true of him in this respect is true of everyone.

50.3

Type   A fallacious argument based on a small sample.

Example   Peel's remission of indirect taxes was beneficial to the economy; so the remission of indirect taxes always benefits an economy.

Comment   This argument commits the fallacy of hasty generalization, because the conclusion, a generalization, is based on a sample that is too small, namely, one case. Arguments that are fallacious because they are based on samples that are too small are called hasty generalizations.

50.4

Type   An argument of questionable validity that is based upon a small sample.

Example   Because rats fed the preservative sodium nitrite develop cancer, human beings should not eat foods preserved with sodium nitrite.

221
SECTION 50. Paralogisms that prove nothing because of generalizations
based on improper inductions

Comment If "human beings should not eat foods preserved with sodium nitrate" because it "may be dangerous to one's health," the argument is all right. If, however, "human beings should not eat foods preserved with sodium nitrate" because it "is dangerous to one's health," the argument commits the fallacy of hasty generalization, for what substances do to rats is not necessarily what those same substances do to human beings.

50.5

Type A valid causal argument based on mere temporal succession.

Example Because I took aspirin fifteen minutes before my headache went away, the aspirin caused my headache to go away.

Comment Although this causal reasoning is based on mere temporal succession, that is, the headache went away *after* the aspirin was taken, the reasoning is all right because it can be supported by numerous other cases. This argument does not commit the fallacy of false cause.

50.6

Type A fallacious causal argument based on mere temporal succession.

Example Before any commodity is ready for sale, a certain amount of labor is expended in either manufacturing or gathering it. Because this labor takes place before the commodity is ready for sale, labor is the cause of value.

Comment This argument is fallacious; it commits the fallacy of false cause, for people gather some commodities simply because these commodities already have value. So just because the labor is expended *before* the commodities are ready for sale is no proof that the value is caused by the labor.

50.7

Type A causal argument of questionable validity that is based on mere temporal succession.

Example Most people who develop lung cancer have a long history of cigarette smoking; so cigarette smoking is a cause of lung cancer.

Comment This argument is questionable because the correlation of lung cancer in many persons with a long history of cigarette smoking is strong evidence for some causal relation between the two. But whether the smoking is a cause or whether something coincidental with the smoking is a cause is another matter, for some people with long histories of smoking do not develop cancer and some non-smokers do.

50.8 Causal arguments based on mere temporal succession follow a pattern: Because *A* comes before *B, A* is the cause of *B*. This pattern, when fallacious, is sometimes referred to by a Latin phrase: *post hoc ergo propter hoc*. The fallacy of false cause, therefore, is sometimes referred to by this Latin phrase which means "after this, therefore on account of this."

50.9

Type A fallacious argument based on exceptional cases.

Example Logic as it was cultivated by the Schoolmen proved to be a fruitless study; so the study of logic is useless.

Comment This argument commits the fallacy of converse accident, because it is based on evidence that is exceptional. The Schoolmen were philosophers who lived in the Middle Ages. Not much was known about logic then. The greatest logical discoveries were made since the nineteenth century. So although many Schoolmen studied logic—so the generalization cannot be called hasty—the Schoolmen studied logic under conditions that are not now ordinary, that is, exceptional circumstances, and good inductions cannot be based on unordinary conditions.

50.10

Type An argument of questionable validity that is based on exceptional cases.

Example Since abuses and superstitions have crept into the invocation of the saints, the veneration of relics, and prayers for the dead, we ought to reject these practices.

Comment These practices are of such a nature that even though the exceptional evidence of abuses and superstitions is cited, it is hard to be sure that the evidence isn't nevertheless convincing.

50.11

Type A fallacious argument that ignores unfavorable evidence.

Example Prayer ought to be required in the public schools, for it serves to quiet the emotions of many students.

Comment This argument commits the fallacy of special pleading, that is, it ignores unfavorable evidence, such as, for instance, that prayer upsets some students.

50.12

Type An argument of questionable validity that ignores unfavorable evidence.

Example The states should legalize gambling; first because it would

SECTION 50. Paralogisms that prove nothing because of generalizations
based on improper inductions

provide a rich new source of revenue; second because it would encourage tourism; and third because it would cut off the main source of revenue to criminal syndicates.

Comment   Although the only evidence chosen is favorable, it is not clear that this evidence, in spite of unmentioned unfavorable evidence such as gambling's effect on public morals, isn't forceful, for in this case, the favorable evidence may simply overwhelm the unfavorable evidence.

50.13   It should be obvious why converse accident and special pleading have no valid examples. A valid example would have to involve a proper induction, but no proper induction can be based on exceptional or merely favorable cases. Such a generalization would violate the principles of sampling.

SECTION 51. A paralogism that proves nothing because a generalization is misapplied

51.1   There is one paralogism closely related to the fallacy of converse accident. Its name is the fallacy of accident, and it is committed when a statement that is generally true is applied to a situation that has special circumstances that render the generalization inapplicable. No valid arguments can result from such an application of a generalization.

51.2

Type   A fallacious argument that applies a generalization to a special case.

Example   Of idleness comes no goodness, so the unemployed will turn to crime.

Comment   The generalization that is stated in the premise as a maxim is based upon the generally true view that good things are the result of some kind of labor and not of laziness or self-imposed idleness. But unemployed persons rarely have chosen to go unemployed; rather, they are unable to find work. So they constitute a special group of people to whom the generalization cannot apply. (One might also wonder whether the words "no goodness" are meant to mean "crime," but you already know how to carry out analyses like that.)

51.3

Type   An argument of questionable validity that applies a generalization to a special case.

Example   The object of war is a durable peace; therefore soldiers are the best peacemakers.

Comment   Soldiers are, of course, a special class of persons to whom statements about persons in general may not apply. But after years and years of ineffective diplomacy, many people do wonder whether a preemptive war may be (or might not have been) the best solution. Since it is not obvious who the best peacemakers are, nor how to go about guaranteeing peace, soldiers may very well be the best peacemakers. But of course this argument does not prove that they are; it is merely an example of an argument to which the criticism that it commits the fallacy of accident cannot *obviously* be applied. So in respect to this fallacy, the argument is questionable.

SECTION 52. Paralogisms that prove nothing because the information in the premises is irrelevant to the conclusion

52.1   Finally there are two paralogisms that prove nothing because the premises are entirely irrelevant to the conclusion. These paralogisms are called appeal to authority and the genetic fallacy. Both argument types are patterned. The pattern for appeals to authority goes like this: Because *A* is an authority on *some* subject, what he says about *any* subject is true. This pattern yields valid arguments only when what the authority speaks about is the subject he is an authority on. Otherwise, it yields fallacious arguments. The pattern for genetic fallacies is this: Because the circumstances amid which *A* came to be believed are ridiculous, *A* itself is false. This pattern sometimes yields fallacious arguments because the circumstances amid which *A* came to be believed are sometimes irrelevant to whether *A* is true. Likewise, appeals to authority are irrelevant whenever the person making the statement is not an authority on the subject he is speaking about.

52.2

Type   A valid appeal to authority.

Example   Archimedes, a great scientist, mathematician, astronomer, and inventor stated the principle of specific gravity; so the principle is true.

Comment   Archimedes, being a scientist, is an authority on scientific subjects. As a matter of fact, his statement of the principle of specific gravity is known as Archimedes' principle.

52.3

Type   A fallacious appeal to authority.

Example   Thales, the Milesian, was reproached for his poverty, which was supposed to show that philosophy was of no use. By his knowledge of

225

astronomy, he predicted, while it was still winter, that there would be a good harvest of olives that year. So everyone who knew about the prediction should have expected a good harvest.

Comment   If Thales' prediction was based on his knowledge of astronomy, authoritative predictions should have been about stars, planets, etc., and not about the weather which cannot be predicted by studying astronomy. This argument commits the fallacy of illicit appeal to authority or, as it is known in Latin, *argumentum ad vericundiam.*

52.4

Type   An appeal to authority of questionable validity.

Example   Baudelaire, the great French poet, wrote much about the painting of his time. What he says about painting, therefore, must be true.

Comment   This argument is questionable because as a writer of poetry, his knowledge makes him an authority on that, but whether it makes him an authority on art in general—since poetry is one of the arts—is something to think about. It's not as though he were speaking about science either, for painting is more closely related to poetry than science is. In other words, since Baudelaire is an artist of one sort, he *may* therefore be an authority on art in general.

52.5

Type   A valid argument based on the circumstances amid which the conclusion came to be believed.

Example   Like all ancient peoples, the Babylonians felt that signs and omens lurked all around them. The unknown, the spirit world, was continually intruding and revealing itself in all events or phenomena, especially celestial phenomena. This belief was the origin of astrology. It is a ridiculous origin, and astrology is equally ridiculous.

Comment   The circumstances of the origin of astrology are relevant evidence because astrologers can cite no other confirming evidence that can be scientifically checked, so the argument is highly forceful.

52.6

Type   A fallacious argument based on the circumstances amid which the conclusion came to be believed.

Example   Archimedes ran through the streets stark naked yelling "eureka" (I have found it!) after having discovered the principle of specific gravity while in his bath. Anything discovered in such ridiculous circumstances is surely false.

Comment   The only valid conclusion from this premise is that Archimedes made a fool of himself by the manner in which he announced that he had found the principle. The argument in the example commits the genetic fallacy, for the information in the premise is absolutely irrelevant to the conclusion.

52.7

Type   An argument of questionable validity that is based on circumstances amid which the conclusion came to be believed.

Example   Anthropologists have learned that early man sought to control the course of nature by rite and spell, compelling wind and weather, animals and crops to obey his will. Finding this ability of limited effectiveness, he appealed to higher beings for help. In this ridiculous way religion came into being. So religious tenets are false.

Comment   This argument is questionable for religious tenets are not subject to proof and, when held, are held on the basis of faith, so the facts surrounding the origin of such tenets may very well be good evidence for this conclusion. Yet religious people do cite evidence for the truth of their beliefs. That evidence has to be evaluated separately.

SECTION 53. Exercises

53.1   Informal reasoning, because it cannot be broken down into patterns that are either always valid or always invalid, is more difficult to master than formal reasoning. Your knowledge of formal reasoning, however, should make it easier for you to understand the tricky nature of informal reasoning. After studying the examples presented in this appendix, you should be able to analyze the following arguments and say whether or not they are fallacious and what fallacies, if any, they commit.

53.1.1 Exercise

(1) Goodness and wisdom are rare and useful; so few men are truly wise.

(2) Mill's defense of utilitarianism is invalid because he could have been expected to defend it since its founder was his tutor, Jeremy Bentham.

(3) Each book in the library is exceptionally good; therefore the library is exceptionally good.

(4) Since he is a philosopher, he is a lover of wisdom.

(5) Since the existence of flying saucers cannot be verified by any available data, they must not exist.

(6) Each individual will further his own economic interest to the best

of his ability. The result is that society as a whole thereby achieves the maximum possible economic advancement.

(7) Because the city's revenues have fallen by 20 percent, the city will have to reduce its services by 20 percent.

(8) Because the union is corrupt, each of its members is corrupt.

(9) Idleness is the devil's booster, so only evil men are chronically unemployed.

(10) Since women will never understand men, women will never perceive the needs of men.

(11) Leibniz and Newton both claimed to have discovered the infinitesimal calculus. Since Newton was a natural philosopher while Leibniz was a metaphysician, Leibniz's claim must be false.

(12) Jesus said "In very truth I tell you, if anyone obeys my teaching he shall never know what it is to die," so good Christians live forever.

(13) Thales, the philosopher, was reproached for his poverty, which was supposed to show that philosophical knowledge is useless. One year, during the winter, he predicted a good olive crop that year, and having a little money, he rented all the oil presses in Chios and Miletus at low rates because no one bid against him. When the good crop was harvested, he sublet the presses at higher rates and made a small fortune. Thus philosophers can easily be rich if they should so wish.

(14) Because the bribery of judges was a widespread practice during the seventeenth century, it was all right for Francis Bacon to have accepted bribes.

(15) Because the leaves are green, the tree is green.

(16) The several species of brutes prey upon one another, so man was made to prey on them.

(17) You ought to devote your life to caring for your mother, for she suffers greatly from disease.

(18) Just fall in love with your job, and success will be yours.

(19) He is a good man, for he always does what is right.

(20) All religions are based on fables and superstitions, were founded by ignorant people, and are used by vested interests to oppose social reform and scientific progress. So all religions ought to be abolished.

(21) Since we cannot disprove the existence of telepathy, there must be something to it.

(22) When will the United States become a second-rate power?

(23) Fewer and fewer nations support an official church; so religious freedom is growing.

(24) You ought to obey the law; otherwise you'll be punished.

(25) Hippocrates, the father of medicine, wrote this: There are many

AN ESSAY ON INFORMAL REASONING

eunuchs among the Scythians, who perform female work, who speak like women, and who are called effeminates. The inhabitants of the country attribute the cause to a god. But to me such affections are no more divine than others, for each has its own nature and none arises without a natural cause. Therefore, effeminacy is as natural as normal behavior.

(26) No matter how you play the game, someone wins and someone loses. So how you play the game doesn't matter; it's winning that counts.

(27) A planned society is communistic; so social planning is communistic.

(28) It is foolish to try to abolish poverty, for no matter how much money people have, unless they all have the same amount, there will always be poor people.

(29) A *girl* unemployed is thinking of mischief; so *idle boys* need not be watched.

(30) Because you neglect your chores, you are neglectful.

53.1.2 The following terms are introduced in this chapter. You should know the meaning of each.

informal	equivocation
fallacy	amphiboly
paralogism	accent
begging the question	composition
complex question	division
ignoratio elenchi (ignorance of hookup)	hasty generalization
ad populum (to the people)	false cause (post hoc ergo propter hoc)
ad ignorantiam (to ignorance)	converse accident
ad baculum (to force)	special pleading
ad misericordiam (to pity)	accident
ad hominem (to the man)	ad vericundiam (to authority)
non sequitur (it does not follow)	genetic fallacy

INDEX

Entries are referenced by paragraph numbers

predicate term of, 42.2
subject term of, 42.2
terms of, 42.2f
Clauberg, Johannes, Intro.
Commutation (law of), 12.5f
proof of, 12.5f
Complement of a relation, 35.3
Complex question, 46.8
Composition (fallacy of), 49.1
examples of, 49.12ff
Compound statements, 5.1
Conclusion, 2.1
Conditional proof (rule of), 9.10
Conditional statement, 5.2, 5.12
(*see also*, Compound statements)
Conjunction, 5.2, 5.4, 17.6ff
kinds of, 17.7ff
law of, 9.2
truth-table for, 5.9
universal quantifier, 21.4
Conjunction-elimination rule, 9.10
Conjunction-introduction rule, 9.10
Connected relation, 34.2
Connectives, 5.1
Connector, 5.1
(*see also*, Alterants)
Consequent, 5.12
Constants, definition, 17.2
Constructive dilemma (rule of),
proof of, 12.4
Contextual definitions, 33.4
Contingencies, 7.4
Contraposition, 40.1
of a proposition, 40.4
Contraries, square of opposition, 41.3
Converse:
by limitation, 40.2
of a proposition, 40.2
Converse accident, 50.1, 50.13
examples of 50.9f
Converse implication, truth-table
for, 17.16
Converse law of double negation, 9.10
Converse non-implication, truth-
table for, 17.16
Converse of a relation, 35.2
Conversion, 40.1
by limitation, 40.2

Counterexample, 25.3ff
abstract, 25.5f

Declarative sentences, 4.1f
(*see also*, Statements)
Deduction, 10.7
and transformation-rules, 10.7
Definite descriptions, 23.10
and identity, 33.1
Definition:
contextual, 33.4
recursive, 6.1f
De Morgan's law, proof of, 15.8ff
Derivation, 11.1
Dilemma, constructive, 12.4
Disjunct, 5.11
Disjunction, exclusive, 17.16
Disjunctive statement, 38.1
Disjunctive syllogism (law of),
proof of, 15.2
Distributed terms of categorical
propositions, 39.2
Distribution (law of), proof of, 15.12ff
Division, 49.1
examples of, 49.16ff
Double Negation (law of), 9.2
converse law of, 9.10
Dyadic relations, 32.1
Dyadic truth-functors, 5.2, 5.10

Effective procedure, 26.5
Elimination-rules, 9.10
Enthymeme, 42.6
Equivalence:
logical, 7.4, 9.11
material, 5.2, 5.4
Equivalent relation, 35.5
Equivocation, 49.1
examples of, 49.2ff
Exceptive propositions, 23.15
Excluded middle (principle of), 14.1,
14.3, 14.5
Exclusive alternation, truth-table
for, 17.16
Exclusive disjunction, truth-table
for, 17.16
Exclusive propositions, 23.16
Existential import, 39.3

Obverse, of a proposition, 40.3
Obversion, 40.1
Ockham, William of, Intro.
One-many (relation of), 34.4
One-to-one (relation of), 34.3
Outlines of arguments, 3.1

Paradoxes, logical, 36.1
Paralogisms, 45.2ff, 46.1ff
Parameters, 23.18
Partial statement-forms, 19.2
Particular affirmative, categorical
    propositions, 39.1
Particular generalizations, 21.5, 21.9,
    21.14
    and universal generalizations,
        22.2, 22.5
    restriction of use of, 22.8
    revised quantificational rule, 31.3
Particular instantiation, 21.14
    revised quantificational rule, 31.5
Particular negative, categorical
    propositions, 39.1
Particular quantifier, 19.3
    symbol for, 20.1
    words to express, 23.8
Particular sentences, 23.4
Parts of categorical propositions, 39.1
Petitio principii (begging the
    question), 46.1ff
Polish notation, 5.3ff
    main truth-functor of, 7.3
Positive law of absurdity, 9.2, 26.3
    use of, 10.9
Predicate logic, 18.3
    general, 29.1f
    monadic, 29.1
    second-order, 36.1
    validity of arguments in, 25.11
Predicate term, 39.1
    n-adic, 31.7
Predicate term, in categorical
    syllogisms, 42.2
Premise, definition, Intro., 2.1
Principia notation, 5.3
Principle of excluded middle, 14.1,
    14.3, 14.5
Principle of identity, 14.1f, 14.5
Principle of non-contradiction, 14.1,
    14.4, 14.6

Proof, 10.7
Proposition, 17.2
    categorical, 39.1ff, 41.1
    contraposition of a, 40.4
    converse of a, 40.2
    exceptive, 23.15
    exclusive, 23.16
    obverse of a, 40.3
    (*see also*, Statements)
Propositional logic, 17.2, 18.3
    shortcomings of, 18.1ff
Propositional variables, 20.3

Qualifier, 39.1
Quality of categorical propositions, 39.1
Quantificational argument, 21.10
Quantifier:
    articles as, 23.10
    implied, 23.9
    negated, 23.11
    particular, 19.33, 20.1, 23.8
    parts of, 39.1
    replacement rules, 21.7, 21.19
    scope, 30.3
    universal, 19.2, 20.1, 21.2
Quantity of categorical propositions, 39.1

Ramus, Petrus, Intro.
Reason, 2.1
Reasoning, 1.1f, 3.2
    fallacious, 45.1
    inductive, 50.1
    informal, 53.1
Reflexive, in logic of relations 32.4f
Reimarus, Herman Samuel, xvii
Relations, 30.1, 35.1
    dyadic, 32.1
    logic of, 32.1
    predicates of, 35.1
Relative Product, predicate of, 35.6
Replacement-rules, 9.11, 10.11
Rule of conditional proof, 9.10
    of indirect proof, 9.10
    of particular generalizations, 31.3
    of particular instantiation, 31.5
    of universal generalization, 31.4
    of universal instantiation, 31.2
Rules of constructing a tableaux,
    25.12, 25.18
Russell, Bertrand, 5.3